THRESHOLDS OF INITIATION

THRESHOLDS

OF

INITIATION

BY

Joseph L. Henderson

Wesleyan University Press

MIDDLETOWN, CONNECTICUT

To Helena Darwin Henderson

Contents

Acknowledgments

IN ADDITION to the anthropologists and psychologists who are named in the body of this book, I should like to acknowledge the following analysts whose work has thrown light on the special subject of this study: M. Esther Harding, Erich Neumann, Bruno Bettelheim, Géza Róheim, Michael Fordham, John Layard, Edward Edinger, Gerhard Adler, and Erik Erikson. I am especially happy to acknowledge the many students in San Francisco and at the C. G. Jung Institute of Zürich for the correcting and fertilizing effect of their response to much of this material.

I should like to thank Dr. Elizabeth Osterman, Miss Maud Oakes, and Mrs. Mary Crile for their interest and encouragement in reading the original version of the manuscript. I am grateful to Mr. Alan Levensohn for his expert editorial work, and to Mrs. Virginia Detloff for her careful tending of the reference notes, the bibliography, and the index. Special thanks are extended to the Bollingen Foundation for a fellowship grant which helped bring the research to completion, and to Mr. John Barrett and Mrs. Vaun Gilmore personally for helping me find its publisher.

— J. L. H.

San Francisco
March 1967

THRESHOLDS OF INITIATION

Foreword

IN THE Foreword to the first edition of this book, published in 1967, I warned the reader that Jung's theory of archetypes, as a foundation for my study, was still subject to either stubborn skepticism or bland acceptance. This was indeed the case, as I found from most critical notices. Over the course of the next decade, however, I have observed a much more favorable and genuine response, not only to the theory of archetypes but to the definition of initiation as an archetype, than I would ever have imagined possible at that earlier time. This was partly due to the positive effect of the counterculture (when it was not purely rebellious) in awakening a sense of wonder and numinosity to counter the materialistic outlook of the modern Establishment, rendering it permeable to influences coming from the perennial philosophies, whether from the Far East or the ancient West or the eternal present of any age.

At about the same time, in the late 1960s, a new scientific verification of the inner reality of initiation (as different from outer forms) was emerging, in the field of anthropology. For the first time certain important anthropologists, from very different schools, seemed ready to acknowledge the psychological concept of the unconscious as a common basis for discussion of these matters. In studies of the African native cultures, such as *The Forest of Symbols: Aspects of Ndembu Ritual*, Victor Turner showed that initiation refers to a liminal state of mind occurring during an initiation rite wherein the neophyte is relieved of his social identity by making a transition from the natural man to the civilized man that the community expects him to become. This corresponds exactly to my view of the function of the puberty rites described in Chapter VII.

Turner also recognized the liminality inherent in those other rites or rituals that promote an individual discovery of the religious Mysteries:

> Liminality here breaks, as it were, the cake of custom and enfranchises speculation. That is why I earlier mentioned Plato's self-confessed debt to the Greek mysteries. Liminality is the realm of primitive hypothesis, where there is a certain freedom to juggle with the factors of existence. (P. 106)

In the puberty rites, as in our own countercultural movement,

> this liberty has fairly narrow limits. The neophytes return to secular society with more alert faculties perhaps and with enhanced knowledge of how things work, but they have to become once more subject to custom and law. (P. 106)

In a later application of the observations from his fieldwork, Turner found the same experience of liminality in larger societies where individual leadership instigates countercultural movements that may open permanent outlets for dissident or neglected groups. An excellent example is given in the description of the origin and development of the Franciscan Order, which can be taken as an analogy for our own counterculture. In *The Ritual Process: Structure and Anti-Structure*, therefore, Turner recognizes the liminality of the inherent initiation archetype in all cultures: "for a variable while, there was an uncommitted man, an individual rather than a social persona, in a sacred community of individuals" (p. 108). The word "sacred" here points to the essentially religious nature of initiation which I have found to be true of the individual subjects for my psychological study. This has been most interestingly elaborated by Professor I.M. Lewis in his *Ecstatic Religion: An Anthropological Study of Spirit Possession and Shamanism*.

In the field of structural anthropology Claude Lévi-Strauss, in *The Scope of Anthropology*, calls attention to the cultural ferment in tribal societies (and by inference in our own) whereby fixed patterns of behavior and myth are continually being modified to produce new patterns. He makes a statement that could have come straight from Jung: "If a conscious system exists, it can only result from a sort of dialectical average among a multiplicity of unconscious systems, each of which concerns one aspect or one level of social reality" (p. 29).

We have only to alter one word in this statement, changing "social" to "individual," to accommodate it to our psychological way of thinking. Both primitive societies and individuals have "hidden in them the character of a system, analyzable in terms of another system" (ibid., p. 19). By understanding even social structure as originally determined by the archetypes of the unconscious we are rescued from the depressing thought that society is only a haphazard arrangement that can be altered at will by anyone who cares to tamper with it. Lévi-Strauss concludes that social structure (and I continue to use this as analogous to individual psychic structure) is to be understood as:

> ruled by an internal cohesiveness; and this cohesiveness, inaccessible to observation in an isolated system, may be revealed in a study of transformations, through which similar properties in apparently different systems are brought to light. As Goethe wrote:
>
> > All forms are similar, and none are the same, so that their chorus points the way to a hidden law. (Ibid., p. 31)

I am here suggesting that the Jungian model for the understanding of mythology is essentially the same as this anthropological model, where the "forms" are the culture-patterns and the "hidden law" refers to the archetypal contents of the unconscious. If true, this goes a long way toward correcting the implicit assumption in some of the writings of Jung and his followers (including some of my own) that myth, ritual, and archetype are identical. The dream material I have collected for this study clearly shows that myth and ritual coexist but are separate from primordial, i.e., archetypal, images, but one cannot avoid the conclusion that some cultural forms or myths are themselves part of the unconscious system.

An example from dream material that indicates the existence of initiation as an archetype appears in Chapter IV (pp. 67–68). In the young man's dream, the transition from mother to father denotes the resolution of an original Oedipus complex. The dream, however, refers this back to a similar cultural transition found in ancient Greece. This is suggested by the "white marble house" as "a mausoleum and the stage of a Greek theater." The "golden disc bright as the sun, flooding the whole place with light," is an imperfectly formed symbol, being divided within itself between images of animal and man. It corresponds to no known artifact and, having no previous personal association for the dreamer, is what we may call an archetypal image. Still more important, because not expressed even by an image, is the anxious but pregnant time, during which there is an emotional suspension of ordinary consciousness, from the moment he experiences his "death" to the moment when he experiences his "rebirth." And this is the essence of initiation as an archetype.

Jung has often been accused, even by some of his own followers, of failing to *prove* the existence of the archetypes. In a letter written in 1960 he replied to a review of his book *Aion* by Dr. E.A. Bennett:

> Speaking of a hypothesis of archetypes you say there is no scientific proof of them yet. A scientific hypothesis is never proved absolutely insofar as improvement is always possible. The only proof is its applicability. You, yourself attest that the idea of archetypes explains more than any other theory, which proves its applicability. (*Letters: 1951–1961*, p. 558)

The fullest account of his hypothesis was presented in a paper Jung delivered under the title "On the Nature of the Psyche" and published in *The Structure and Dynamics of the Psyche.* Here he recapitulated and, for the first time, gave full value to the correspondence or complementarity existing between the archetypal image and the pattern of behavior. In this paper Jung used the visual image of the spectrum to illustrate how human consciousness, in any individual sense, mediates between the instinct, or the "psychoid" pole of experience, and the archetypal image at the opposite pole. Instinct is likened to the infrared area of the spectrum, the archetypal image to the ultraviolet area. The intermediate yellow area is then the meeting place, or place of blending, where the archetype is subjectively experienced as a whole. Instinct gives reality to the image; the image gives meaning to the instinct.

Although we do not know where the archetypal images come from, Jung continued, any more than we know where instinctual patterns of behavior come from, we do know that they both present predictable patterns of conditioning from within, not conditioning by some mechanism imposed from without. Man's capacity for bringing about certain basic changes in the archetypal patterns presented to his imagination, over and above the instinctually predetermined psychoid area of his being, becomes a challenge of unlimited ethical and spiritual consequence.

In the light of this paper, the need to prove the theory to everyone's satisfaction becomes irrelevant since it belongs to a type of research that is not an end but a beginning. It becomes an effective working hypothesis pointing toward a psychology of the future.

JOSEPH L. HENDERSON
San Francisco, 1979

REFERENCES

Jung, C.G. *Letters: 1951–1961*, vol. 2. Selected and edited by Gerhard Adler in collaboration with Aniela Jaffé. Bollingen Series. Princeton: Princeton University Press, 1976.

———. "On the Nature of the Psyche," in *The Structure and Dynamics of the Psyche*. Vol. 8 of *The Collected Works of C.G. Jung*, 2d ed. Bollingen Series XX. Princeton: Princeton University Press, 1969.

Lewis, I.M. *Ecstatic Religion: An Anthropological Study of Spirit Possession and Shamanism*. London: Penguin Books, 1971.

Lévi-Strauss, Claude. *The Scope of Anthropology*. Translated by Sherry Ortner Paul and Robert A. Paul. London: Jonathan Cape, 1967.

Turner, Victor. *The Forest of Symbols: Aspects of Ndembu Ritual*. Ithaca: Cornell University Press, 1967.

———. *The Ritual Process: Structure and Anti-Structure*. Chicago: Aldine, 1969.

CHAPTER I

The Rediscovery of Initiation

INITIATION, more than any other body of knowledge, has suffered throughout history from the fate of continually being forgotten and having to be rediscovered. Many records of what has been lost and found again in ancient times will be noted in the course of this study, but for a beginning I should like to present a brief account of the psychological rediscovery of initiation in the twentieth century.

The first decisive event in this rediscovery was the publication in 1909 of Arnold van Gennep's book, *Les Rites de Passage*.[1] Until then, the study of initiation had been a mere recording of the brutal devices invented, supposedly, to frighten boys into becoming men. Van Gennep recognized them as educational processes for accelerating growth, the various rites in each series making possible a passage from one stage to the next. He saw that initiation was not merely a man's rite for admission to the Man's House;[2] women also needed to be made women by means of appropriate rites, beginning with early menstrual rites and culminating in the marriage ritual.

Van Gennep belonged to the École Sociologique in Paris, among whose members was Émile Durkheim, who (with van Gennep, Lucien Lévy-Bruhl, and Emile Doutté) showed that religion and philosophy are essential parts of man's social life. This social life, however, had not come into being by the whim of some all-powerful chieftain, nor was it merely the result of economic necessity. Much less was it due to an act of God. Social life in this sense was seen to have its roots in certain quite simple "collective representations" gathered from mankind's innate experience of group identity. The collective representations were believed to be manifest in civilized behavior as well as in the behavior of primitive people.[3] Durkheim thus gave the first impetus to a psychology of social custom, which contributed enormously to both psychology and anthropology in subsequent years. Meanwhile, in England a group of scholars of Greek religion and philosophy were independently uncovering evidence for the social origin of religion, leading F. M. Cornford to conclude that "the power of society is in fact the only known moral power in the universe."[4] Behind the Olympian gods he perceived the shadowy outline of an older image of godlikeness, Moira, a goddess of personal destiny represented in society by the partition or allotment of original familial moieties. He also found that cosmogony has its roots in ritual and, being no act of God, is also a collective representation.

Jane Harrison, archaeologist and historian of Greek religion, was driven to acquire the elements of psychology and sociology to understand the religion of primitive peoples. Working from Durkheim's concept that God is a projection of the will and emotions of his worshipers, and applying her own intuition and scholarship, she discovered the meaning of an obscure inscription from Crete, the "Hymn of the Kouretes." This turned out to be the record of a ritual dance of initiation performed by a group of young men in arms for the protection of a holy child born of the earth goddess, Rhea. The goddess (representative of a matriarchal order) gave way to the child, Zeus (representing the new patriarchal principle). She was replaced by the group of initiated young men — the Kouretes, the "shielded nurturers" — who through the "noise of beating feet" subjected the god as an infant to the rite of the new birth.[5] In another version of the hymn, the rite was expressed as a "mystery" in which the Kouros, as leader of the band, was reborn from the thigh of his father, Zeus — a veiled but unambiguous reflection of a typical *rite de passage* from a religion of the Mother to a religion of the Father and thence to Society, represented by Themis.[6]

Just as Cornford had shown that Moira, a sanctity older than the gods, was identical with the origin of social order, so Miss Harrison pointed to the ensuing process of social evolution, where Themis represents the behavior dictated by social conscience:

"What must be done, what society compels."[7] Above all, Themis was "Justice in the realm of Zeus," which checked the primitive law of sacrifice and atonement, symbolized in a Mother Goddess who suffered a yearly death and rebirth through her son. The yearly cycle of change still took place, reminding mankind of the cosmic order presided over by Moira, but human government had changed and was conducted by reason, not by magic. The Eumenides as favorable goddesses supplanted the Furies as daimons in accordance with social change, in the sense that a judicial trial for criminal behavior supplanted the primitive law of vengeance.

Following this early work of the religious historians and anthropologists, still in the first part of this century, psychology began to explore the subject of initiation. Freud and Jung dealt with initiation at first tangentially, Freud in his *Totem and Taboo,* Jung in his *Symbols of Transformation.* A more direct approach was made by Herbert Silberer in *Problems of Symbolism and Mysticism,* which provided an interpretation of a Rosicrucian parable that revealed a basic initiation pattern. The book was soon to appear prophetic, for Silberer defined the divergent modes on which Freud and Jung parted, Freud limiting his psychoanalytic interpretation to a retrospective study of origins (the titanic mode), while Jung pursued a constructive or synthetic interpretation of the same material (the anagogic mode). This divergence became so acute in subsequent years that Freud and Jung went their separate ways, Freud remaining the founder of psychoanalysis and Jung going on to found his own school of analytical psychology.

Traumatic as this split has so often seemed in the development of modern depth psychology, we may now be in a position at last to see it as a fortunate, or at least inevitable, occurrence. It forced Jung out of the purely psychoanalytic approach and brought him into the same unprejudiced style of research represented by the new breed of anthropologists and religious historians. Both *Totem and Taboo* and *Symbols of Transformation* were published in the same year (1912). Both show in significant detail a correspondence between the myths and ritual observances of ancient societies and the fantasy material of modern individuals. Both arrive at the same conclusion to be drawn from this fact: that in the unconscious there exists an archaic heritage (Freud) or a collective unconscious (Jung) which is intimately bound up with the symptomatic behavior of all people, irrespective of their personal idiosyncrasies and cultural conditioning. Freud continued to regard this kind of behavior as pathological,* whereas Jung began to see it as a fragment, however distorted, of a valid archetypal pattern from which cultural patterns are formed.

At a somewhat later date, Jung asserted the existence of an archetypal pattern of initiation:

> The fact is that the whole symbolism of initiation rises up, clear and unmistakable, in the unconscious contents. . . . The point is not — I cannot be too emphatic about this — whether the initiation symbols are objective truths, but whether these unconscious contents are or are not the equivalent of initiation practices, and whether they do or do not influence the human psyche. Nor is it a question of whether they are desirable or not. It is enough that they exist and that they work.[8]

This discovery gave a new psychological meaning to the contemporary studies in comparative religion; and it has frequently been suggested that Jane Harrison, had she lived longer, would undoubtedly have found in Jung's archetypes a much better theoretical basis for her work than was provided by Durkheim's "collective representations," whose weakness lay in the assumption that social conscience can supplant the idea of God. Cornford's description of Moira as embodying the partition of primitive tribal social groups can be understood better by applying to it Jung's concept, which then shows that the power he ascribed to Society (so closely akin to moral power) is only one of many archetypes of the collective unconscious and need not therefore be identified with its origin. In this light it can be seen to re-create itself forever

---

* "In *Totem and Taboo* he [Freud] first drew attention to the correspondence existing between certain neurotic (Obsesssional) rituals, and the totemic observances followed by primitive tribes. From that time onward he maintained that religious phenomena were to be understood only on the model of neurotic symptoms as a return of long-forgotten important happenings in the primeval history of the human family." (Edward Glover, *Freud or Jung?* [New York: Meridian, 1956], p. 39.)

anew out of the mysterious underworld of history, changing, as it does so, the prevailing fashion of conscious belief. The strength of Jung's concept in binding together the opposite poles of this early research may be seen from his recognition of a "collective conscious" region of psychic activity which, like Themis, is concerned with the conscious elaboration of archetypal forms or images.

Jung himself did not describe the full range of possibilities by which archetypal symbols of the unconscious may be transmuted into cultural forms. One of his followers, Erich Neumann, has occupied himself with this problem on the level of mythology; the social scientist Ira Progoff has given an account of the modern social meaning of Jung's psychology; and I myself have postulated the existence of a "culture-complex" which is a mediating force between the primordial unconscious and the cultural forms.[9]

According to this postulate, the new cultural forms are not merely religious or social, but both; and they contain in their totality something more, which I have described as aesthetic and philosophic. Whether the cultural forms originally took a religious or social or aesthetic or philosophical direction seems to have depended upon the psychological differences among native types of men in response to the exigencies of history, climate, and geography. At one end of the scale, emerging from the undifferentiated matrix of the archetypal world of prehistory, is the fresh and timeless phenomenon of a ritual dance, drama, or painting which serves the function of providing religious, aesthetic, social, and philosophic experience all at once. Structurally it contains the four-fold pattern of Moira. At the other end of the scale, but in a continuous line of development from Moira, is Themis, representing the final socio-religious, artistic, or philosophic cultural form of any given community, varying in its character from nomadic hunting cultures and the herdsmen to settled agricultural groups and larger organizations of hieratic city states.[10] As these simpler groups merge into still larger groups of nations with extensive satellites and colonies, the archetypal content is spread out and becomes much thinner than it was at its primordial source. Finally Moira and Themis are separated and may be in conflict with each other.

From this conflict there is born a need for reconciliation such as is mirrored in the unconscious of modern people, especially in the reappearance of the archetypal forms of initiation—a need which seems to mediate in a special way between the archetypal images and the social customs. Since modern man cannot return to his origins in any collective sense, he apparently is tempted and even forced to return to them in an individual way at certain critical times in his personal development. And in this resides the relevance today of reinforming ourselves of the nature of primitive forms of initiation.

TODAY WE ARE ALL in our varying ways social scientists, psychoanalysts, cultural anthropologists, analytical psychologists; the ideas arising from these disciplines are in the air we breathe, in the language we speak. But it took some time for this to happen. Education, in the decade following these important discoveries, did not profit from their revelations about the inner meaning of archetypes and about initiation. Instead, we went on teaching students according to the eighteenth- and nineteenth-century ideals of intellectual rationalism — what the mind knows is all we need to learn, with ever higher and more specialized standards of scholarship — or else it struck out blindly into the labyrinth of "progressive education," which all too often resulted in a lowering of the standard of education to the level of a trade school. Perhaps this is why writers used to speak of a "lost generation" in the 1920's. In one sense, those of us who were educated at that time were certainly lost: we were confused or torn by conflict between the highly self-conscious nineteenth-century goal of intellectual enlightenment and the intoxicating twentieth-century temptation to venture into the unconscious unprepared.

Knowledge of the initiation pattern could have provided a sobering corrective to these excesses, and in the fullness of time it did begin to find its way beyond the works of specialists and into literature, and hence to the general public. T. S. Eliot's *The Waste Land* was a poem about initiation, admittedly influenced by Jessie L. Weston's scholarly work, *From Ritual to Romance*. Less obviously but nonetheless certainly influenced by the work of Freud and the early work of Jung was Thomas Mann's *The Magic Moun-*

tain, a novel whose hero experiences the full effect of the conflict between the way of the intellect and the way of the unconscious. Because of the pattern of initiation in these works, the central speaker of Eliot's poem and the hero of Mann's novel willingly gave themselves up to the spirit of the time, embracing the principle of death and rebirth at the heart of initiation into manhood, whether it should lead to life or death. Eliot, in *The Waste Land,* speaks of:

> The awful daring of a moment's surrender
> Which an age of prudence can never retract. . . .

Leaving his safe Alpine retreat, Hans Castorp, the hero of Mann's novel, responds to the urgency of participating in the First World War as an act of coming of age:

> He saw himself released, freed from enchantment. . . . Though his tiny destiny fainted to nothing in the face of the general, was there not some hint of a personal mercy and grace for him? . . . Would life receive again her erring and "delicate" child — not by some cheap and easy slipping back to her arms, but sternly, solemnly, penitentially — perhaps not even among the living . . . ?

Along with these fine and honest writers who attempted to express the new knowledge, there were many who cheapened it by sentimentalizing it. There were others who longed ecstatically to return to the actual sources from which these experiences were thought to arise — among African, Indian, or Polynesian natives; among Tibetan Buddhists; and among domesticated cult practices à la Gurjieff in Fontainebleau. Our nostalgia for the simplicity and unity of primitive ways of life began to be seen everywhere — in music, in dance, in art, and even in the way people began to walk and talk and exhibit their feelings. The main thing was to avoid that cardinal Freudian sin, inhibition. But the age of cubism, psychoanalysis, early Communism, and American technology was the antithesis of all that was natural, "primitive," and unified. Even those writers who influenced the taste of their time, though they talked about the importance of making deep basic commitments and showed the disastrous results of failing to do so, were essentially uprooted and drifting away from the fixed points of their culture.

Be that as it may, in the 1920's the first serious and entirely inevitable appearance in this century of a healthy new movement took place in the arts, in anthropology, in psychology, in philosophy, and above all in education, which insisted upon looking at life without nineteenth-century illusions. Thanks to this movement, twentieth-century man could correct the hubris of Nietzsche's time; accepting his weakness in humility, he could puncture the inflation of that period which had allowed itself to believe in the possibility of creating supermen. Alas! Looking back, we see the precarious life the new insight was to have when it encountered the inertia of collective man in that period. We had still to live through those worst of all reprisals for the hubris of our grandfathers, the Fascist and Nazi uprisings in Italy and Germany.

At first these movements appeared to offer on the political level precisely the healing elements needed to cure the sickness of the times. Law and Order, Discipline, and Enthusiasm, led by groups of young men in arms — was this not like the Kouretes of old, the "shielded nurturers" who "with noise of beating feet" guarded the holy child who should become the leader of the band, the Kouros as Führer, the weak who had become strong? The archetype of initiation seemed convincing to many educated and responsible people at the time of the early Hitlerism in Germany, and they therefore did nothing to alter the development of the events which eventually led to the catastrophe. "The young people will know what to do," they said. Then, much later, these highly cultivated people, along with all the sentimentalists who had longed for a revival of the primitive forms of life, asked, "What went wrong?"

Has anything changed since the Second World War? After the First World War we had a "lost" generation; and after the last we had a "beat" generation, and our fears were multiplied a hundred-fold. Having lived through this postwar period, we seem now to be at the bottom of that cycle which began on the heights of nineteenth-century optimism. Yet, in spite of much that is still regressive or degenerate in our cultural life, we see everywhere a wholesome willingness of twentieth-century man to dispense with unrealizable ideals. Starting from the zenith of a culture which had become enamoured of its rosy hope for enlightened self-fulfillment, then passing through a half-way stage of painful doubt and disillusionment, we have finally touched the nadir of resigned acceptance of the imperfectibility of human nature. Those whose education dates from that earlier time (and who are still trying to apply the old humanistic principles to modern life) are bound to doubt the very capacity of civilization now to survive.

But it is perfectly possible that the younger generation, those who have come to maturity and completed their education since the Second World War, are in the process of hatching out a cultural attitude as appropriate and distinguished as that of any other century at its best. There are even signs that humanism will not die but will be transformed so that there may be in reality a meeting between the culture of Art and the culture of Science, long kept apart but now beginning to influence each other in a way that has not been possible since the Renaissance.[11] If these potentials can be realized, it means nothing less than a revival of interest in the power of the human spirit to transcend purely social and material goals and to re-create a culture with religious content.

I began my own study of initiation many years ago; and only now, after the most careful sifting of what can be told from what is essentially inexpressible in language, can I record some modern initiatory experiences which show how certain essential transitions in psychological development are made. These experiences are revealed in dream material, which in turn is derived from the living experience of the individuals who produced the material — and who delivered it to me because I was humanly interested above all in *them*, rather than in scientific theories about them. I have chosen to let this dream material speak partly for itself. My interpretations of it are made possible by a combination of methods derived partly from psychoanalysis and partly from analytical psychology. To each dream or fragment of fantasy I have added the most relevant free associations of the patient — that is, what he or she associated immediately and spontaneously to the imagery of the dream. To this I have added the data of amplification of symbolic material in the Jungian sense, the result of a process wherein the analyst (out of his knowledge of comparative mythology) and the patient (from his innate subjective sense of the significance of archetypal imagery) collaborate in producing a background or context from which the individual meaning of the archetypes may emerge.

These methods are partial, never final. No symbol can ever be completely analyzed, for, as all our experience verifies, any material is capable of endless reinterpretation in the light of new experience or new dreams. Amplification, however, gives the widest context for interpretation because it opens the way for a confrontation between the historical remnants (the archaic heritage) and the immediate needs of the personal psyche. The archetypal symbols can then be accepted or rejected by the individual's own choice; this is of the greatest importance in depth psychology, for no one can experience the archetypal images without being temporarily fascinated, terrified, or possessed by them. The free associations and the amplifications, when properly handled by analyst and patient, gradually reduce the undesirable power of these images and render them accessible to consciousness as organs of healing. What can be integrated remains; what is dangerous or unacceptable falls back into the unconscious, whence it may reappear later, when ego-consciousness is ready to receive and integrate it.

In such a process and with such a background, the pattern of initiation can be clearly seen. Not only is the process itself undertaken in response to a need for initiatory change; the art of depth analysis inevitably simulates the art of the initiatory ritual during at least a part of the analytical period. At first this ritual tends to recapitulate in significant ways the initiation of youth, with its so-called puberty rites. The sense of such rites always has been expressed as the need to outgrow old, regressive childhood patterns and to become adapted to the social group. Later on, especially for people who have already made a satisfactory social adaptation, initiation appears as a wish to withdraw in order to discover some secret knowledge, perhaps to participate in a mystery. At still another stage a re-entry into the social group seems to provide initiation with a goal, not (like the first adaptation) an undifferentiated, blind participation, but a conscious process of relating to the group while maintaining individual identity. The completion of this process, again through the mediation of the archetype of initiation, appears to be synonymous with the psychological concept of individuation.

But is there not a danger that in the use of this special material with such a specialized method as psychotherapy, initiation might become unnaturally systematized and therefore become the vehicle for a philosophical error? I can only answer that the artificiality of the analytical situation is one we analysts and our patients continually recognize, discuss, and even analyze whenever it gets in the way of our explorations. Thus the cure itself requires a cure — and here we find one of the deepest secrets of the meaning of initiation. Just because the situation is strange, difficult, and beset by certain ritual obstacles, the psyche deepens its experience of itself and finds a way to the sickness needing to be healed. Like Parsifal's seeking the Grail Castle, the modern initiate partially loses his way and only with difficulty comes into the presence of his own Fisher King, whose wound can never heal until he asks a true symbolic question.

Thus the fact that some of the people whose material is represented in these pages were literally patients — that is, sick or severely disturbed — does not disqualify their material for examination, any more than the relative normality of the other analysands qualifies their material for it. What is important for our study is to seek to discover in all these materials specific thresholds of initiation, the rites of passage which make possible the transition from childhood to adolescence, from adolescence to early maturity, and from maturity to the experience of individuation.

CHAPTER II

The Uninitiated

THE MORE HOPEFULLY one wishes to say something definitive about initiation, the more paradoxically indefinite it becomes. For this reason we had better approach it cautiously and start by defining what it is not.

The psychiatrist, the teacher, the social worker, the parent, and the responsible citizen are all painfully aware of a recurrent problem in our society — the problem of arrested development in children, in adolescents, and even in the whole groups of supposedly mature people who live delinquent, dissocial, or frankly criminal lives. Somehow these individuals have escaped the meaningful disciplines which could have carried them safely though the phases of childhood development into adolescence and then into maturity.

What do psychologists already understand of this failure? The several differing theories about the origin of arrested development are well-known, and the partial validity of each is clearly demonstrable. There may occur a fixation at any of the levels of psychosexual development described by Freud and his followers, especially Abraham and Erikson.[1] There may be a psycho-biological inferiority arising in early childhood, which later is overcompensated by an attitude of superiority or lust for power, as described by Adler. In recent years the followers of both Freud and Adler have tended to explain the problem of arrested development as arising from a failure to achieve a stable identity through the normal development of ego-structure. Jung originally referred to the ego as a special form of *complex* which has the characteristic of maintaining a sense of the continuity of identity throughout life. Being a complex, it would be subject to the same shocks, surprises, and distortions of consciousness as are found in other complexes.

In all theories of arrested development the emphasis was laid originally upon environmental factors (traumata) as seeming to cause the fixation to take place with only a minimal reaction on the part of the ego. This view has tended greatly to diminish, if not actually to disappear. What is now considered psychologically important is not what happened to the developing ego from without, but how it reacted to this event within. This endo-psychic viewpoint has increasingly favored Jung's "complex theory," since it places the emphasis much more firmly upon the ego as mediator between inner and outer worlds. Thus the differing views of the founders of modern psychology have met in large areas of agreement.

When we turn away from psychogenesis, however, and concentrate upon the actual symptoms of any severe case of arrested development, there is still a bewildering psychological picture. In addition to psychoneurotic behavior, we may speak of infantile behavior, delinquent behavior, antisocial behavior or criminal behavior (psychopathy), and so on. Even if these could all be explained by a common origin, it does not follow that they present a single front in action or can be treated by the same methods. Hence our eternal dilemma: in one case the proper treatment is psychiatric, in another psychoanalytic, in another educational, in another legal — and in many cases we try them all, hoping that by some happy combination of coercion and persuasion we can effect a favorable change. And occasionally we do. More often we do not; and even when we have achieved a good result, we may be unable to say why and unable to repeat this success even in an apparently similar case.

Historically, Jung was the first to try seriously to correct the one-sidedness of genetic theories of psychopathology by implying that the developing ego is arrested, not only by what has previously happened, but also by its fear of taking the next step in its normal development. It therefore suffers a quite normal reaction of psychic recoil. If this recoil becomes fixed into a habit pattern which more or less dominates the personality and against which ego-consciousness is helpless to contend without strenuous efforts from all sides, we can speak of arrested development. It has been described as a "renegade tendency"[2] which tends to isolate the individual from his normal relationship with others. Axiomatically, in terms of Jungian theory, this would present itself on the extraverted plane as dissocial behavior and on the introverted plane as a more or less megalomaniac self-centeredness.

In recent years the renegade tendency has been somewhat more specifically described by another of Jung's followers, Marie-Louise von Franz,[3] as arising from a special archetype which impresses its image upon the personality in such a way as to dominate it — to the point where the personality is, as it were, possessed. The renegade pattern becomes, in this view, merely the inevitable complex of signs and symptoms which proceed from the image, embodying a self-renewing youthfulness as an end in itself, never reaching and by its very nature never intending to reach maturity. Jung originally had described it as follows:

> Iacchus was one of the chief gods in the Eleusinian cult; he was a *puer aeternus,* the eternal boy, whom Ovid apostrophizes as follows:
>
>> For thine is unending youth,
>> eternal boyhood:
>> thou art the most lovely
>> in the lofty sky;
>> thy face is virgin-seeming,
>> if without horns
>> thou stand before us.[4]

Having started with a psychopathic behavior pattern, we come, by this type of research, to the postulate of a clear-cut image which seems to be the cause of it all.

But just as we had to mistrust the word *origin,* we must also mistrust the word *cause.* Jung's theories have frequently been discredited on the ground that they seem to assume that an image alone can bring about all the essential changes we observe in personality and behavior. The belief that an image can bring about such changes has a very respectable history, stretching from William James's psychological theories back to the empirical schools of philosophy in England and Scotland, on the one hand, and to the metaphysical tradition of Germany, on the other. However, it is wrong to think of archetypes as *causing* anything, Jung

himself being one of our greatest modern liberators from the
tyranny of causal thinking. Archetypes are unknown and unknow-
able, and we can infer they exist only by observing the specific
changes that are generated mysteriously between the environment
and the inborn psychic disposition of each individual. Out of this
interaction, at certain times and under certain conditions, there
appears a synchronous pair of related events — the image and its
corresponding behavior pattern — together forming a totality
which we may describe either as archetypally imagined or as
archetypally expressed.

Knowing what we do of the image of the *puer aeternus,* what
is its corresponding behavior pattern? So far we have seen it as
purely negative, a mere renegade tendency, whereas the image
described by the quotation from Ovid is of a boy who is "the most
lovely/ in the lofty sky." But if we read the next sentence very
carefully, we may find our negative component. His face may be
"virgin-seeming" — that is, innocent and good — but only if he
appears "without horns." This we know refers to the Thracian
Dionysus-Zagreus, who characteristically underwent a transformation from the image of a seductively beautiful youth into a bull.
In the former guise he seduced the women of Thebes (shown in
the *Bacchae* of Euripides) and had them dancing through the
countryside like maenads, bringing calamity to the city and in-
flicting on the king a death by dismemberment. This represented
a triumph of the matriarchal orgiastic principle, as the Way of
Nature, over the patriarchal principle of Law and Order in the
Realm of Zeus. But a terrible fate periodically overtook Zagreus.

> Hera, we are told, had stirred up the Titans against Zagreus, who
> tried to escape them by changing into various shapes. In the end
> they caught him when he had taken on the form of a bull. They
> then killed him, cut him in pieces, and threw the pieces into a caul-
> dron; but Zeus slew the Titans with a thunderbolt and swallowed
> the still-throbbing heart of Zagreus. In this manner he was regen-
> erated, and Zagreus stepped forth as Iacchus.[5]

None of this violence, however, is apparent in the famous bas-
relief in which we see this figure as the Greeks in the most splendid
period of their culture saw him — as Triptolemus, standing as a

manly boy between the two goddesses, Demeter and Persephone, from whom he receives the ears of corn he has earned from his labor of plowing and seeding. Harrison observes:

> The relation of these early matriarchal, husbandless goddesses, whether Mother or Maid, to the male figures that accompany them is one altogether noble and womanly, though perhaps not what the modern mind holds to be feminine. It seems to halt somewhere half-way between Mother and Lover, with a touch of the patron saint. Aloof from achievement themselves, they choose a local hero for their own to inspire and protect. They ask of him, not that he should love or adore, but that he should do great deeds . . . As their glory is in the hero's high deeds, so their grace is his guerdon. With the coming of patriarchal conditions this high companionship ends. The women goddesses are sequestered to a servile domesticity, they become abject and amorous.[6]

From this account we may conjecture that when things go wrong with the archetype of the *puer aeternus,* it is because the mother is too demanding or too rejecting, thus frustrating the youth in his normal orientation to the feminine principle as anima-function,[7] or because the youth for some other reason falls into a passive-dependent attitude upon the mother or her substitute. Overcompensating his underdeveloped masculinity, he may fall into a rage, either against the mother or against his own dependent mood, which is destructive in the way of a wild animal.

We must remember that we are studying the abnormality of this pattern and that there is a perfectly wholesome form of behavior in which the mother, instead of retarding her children's development during childhood and adolescence by keeping them in bondage to her, frees them and encourages them to develop, as far as possible, both initiative and the identity appropriate for their age. The result of this healthy behavior may be recognized in any youthful person who is living up to the fullness of his power before meeting the challenge of society to become independent. We see in him a stage of initiation which is already beginning to be unconsciously accepted. The full content of this stage of initiation, to which older people may need to return for reinitiation, forms the subject of the next chapter. Our present inquiry leads us to the supposition that when the normal relation to the mother in its initiatory phase is frustrated, we get a pathological behavior pattern, characterized by abnormally passive femininity alternating with overaggressive masculinity, which is essentially autoerotic and dissocial.

A case of this kind reported by Aichhorn is instructive. An eighteen-year-old delinquent boy was examined and found to have a passive-dependent, feminine behavior pattern alternating with acts of brutal aggression toward one of his sisters.

> The boy made a feminine impression; he seemed shy and ill at ease. . . . It was hard to believe that this boy was capable of the aggressive acts ascribed to him, and I realized at once that they must be momentary outbursts of affect rather than the expression of a brutal nature. . . .
>
> The mother was a widow; the father . . . had died many years before. . . . There were three more children: girls, aged fifteen, thirteen and ten years. . . . [The boy] seemed especially to hate the oldest sister. I learned that his fits of anger were chiefly directed against her. He felt insulted because his sisters belittled him and laughed at him. The oldest sister was the leader in this, and his mother, instead of standing up for him, took the side of the girls. . . . He liked his mother best, and the sisters in the order of their age, the youngest first. He could not bear his oldest sister because she was always disagreeable and wanted to boss everything.

This delinquent boy had been in love with a girl who was very unlike his oldest sister. When asked if he had ever kissed her, he replied, "A boy doesn't do that." The mother had had an unsatisfactory relationship with her husband, who "was a cheerful person but took life lightly." She withdrew more and more into herself because her "religious upbringing was very strict"; the mother and sisters were very pious and associated only with other Catholics. The boy "had liberal socialistic views" but "did not dare tell his mother of the conflict about the difference of their ideas."

The mother spoke of her son in a deprecating way as though he no longer meant anything to her:

He is not a man, just a stupid, stubborn boy who thinks he knows
it all. He tries to lord it over his sisters, and naturally they won't
stand for it. He carries on so and talks so foolishly that the girls
laugh at him; this makes him furious and *he attacks them like a
wild animal,** especially the oldest. If I don't get him out of the
house something terrible is bound to happen. . . . He acts like
a child. After he has been up to something, he is very obedient
and cleans up everything around the house nicely. . . . He has
no initiative; housework and reading books are no work for a
grown boy; he ought to have a steady job.

This was just what the boy could not do because his mother's
choice of a job did not encourage him to develop his own initiative. We learn also that the father, when alive, had slighted the
boy and shown favoritism for the older girl. Aichhorn concludes:
"The constellation in this family is one we frequently encounter.
The father prefers the daughters to the son, the mother has no
special need for affection, and the son is cheated. . . ."[8]

Aichhorn's interpretation from the psychoanalytic viewpoint
is correct when he say that the boy "has been only partially successful" in freeing himself from infantile fixations to his mother and
sisters, especially the oldest sister, with whom at one time in childhood he used to play father and mother. But this derivation of an
antisocial pattern solely from repressed incest wishes is less convincing, I think, than the fact that the boy's behavior has been
inevitably conditioned by his being the only male in an unsympa-
thetic female society. This situation would have been bearable
and could have led to the development of healthy manly qualities
if his mother had encouraged him in the process of emotional
development by which he could find his identity as a man. Instead,
she and the sisters seem to have expected him instantly to become
a man in the narrow terms of our society — that is, a responsible
adult who works diligently to support himself and his family. He
could not do this, and his masculinity, finding no appropriate
outlet, broke out in irrational behavior, fighting the mother. Since
he could not get the better of his mother, who still had the power
to force him to obey, his wrath was directed chiefly against his
elder sister as a mother surrogate.

---

* The italics are mine.

The boy's conflict between matriarchy and his own one-sided conception of patriarchy created an insoluble problem in which the negative features of the *puer aeternus* archetype tended to become fixed into a definite personality. The mother characteristically complains that he is still a "boy," not a man, stubbornly refusing to grow up. Yet we are bound to ask how she could expect him to grow up without the educational attitude on her part necessary to make a man of him. The therapeutic role of Aichhorn introduced the needed outer stimulus by providing him with an initiatory father figure, a father who could also explain the nature of his abnormal reaction to his mother. We can imagine what a lifesaving operation it must have been when his therapist offered support for his religious protest so that his mother and sister had to respect his religious orientation as different from theirs, a progressive outlook in contrast to their (to him) reactionary one. Behind this brief account one may discern the broad outline of a new kind of psycho-social attitude in which a youth such as this can learn for the first time the difference between the originating or inventive powers of patriarchal man and the world of traditional values represented by effective matriarchy.

This was the case of a proletarian or, at least, lower-middle-class youth who, because of his economic importance to the family, was treated early for his irresponsible tendencies. Thanks to the discoveries of Freud, made available to such educationists as Aichhorn, he did not have to become a social outcast or a legal problem, but could be treated for a psycho-social illness. In privileged families where there is no economic strain, this sort of illness may be neglected until it is almost too chronic to treat. Instead of psychological insight, the young person is offered more and more opportunities in the hope that he will eventually find what interests him and settle down or, in the case of a girl, that she will make an advantageous marriage. But this is not a cure; on the contrary, it usually encourages the young person to postpone growing up and may lead to a wholly provisional way of life socially sanctioned by parents and well-meaning friends. In a paper entitled *The Provisional Life,* H. G. Baynes refers to this as "a descriptive epithet borrowed from Jung. . . . It denotes an attitude that is innocent of responsibility towards the circumstantial facts of reality as though these facts were being provided for either by the parents or the State, or at least, by Providence."9

The most extreme case of this kind I have seen was that of a mother who so magnificently subsidized a psychopathic boy that he achieved an academic success he did not want and did everything to destroy. Everyone except the mother and son saw the true state of affairs from the beginning, but was powerless to do anything except watch the inevitable unfolding of the tragedy. It ended with his suicide, after a court trial in which the mother tried to prove him insane.

Most cases are not so obvious. Typically, the son is perhaps gifted, and his parents have given him what seems like a deserved advantage of education and the opportunities to "make good." When he fails, everyone blames him: "How disgraceful, after all your parents have done for you!" But he was doomed from the start because he could not go on forever being a good boy only and never showing his horns. Instead he turns against himself and them by achieving failure.

It would be quite wrong, however, to suggest that the abnormal features of the *puer aeternus* derive solely from children being spoilt by their parents. Some of the most exaggerated examples come from exceedingly responsible, hard-working families. In these cases it seems to be the liberalism of our culture itself that has somehow aided and abetted a tendency innocently begun at home. Frequently it begins with one or both parents' recognition that one of the children is brighter, quicker, or cleverer than the rest. Into him they pour an unconscious expectation of heroism. He seizes the first opportunity to go away to school or college, where he distinguishes himself, and from there on society furthers his cause because of the utter sincerity of that "virgin-seeming face." His idealism prevents even him from knowing that he has any horns to show. I have occasionally seen him in our American society as personifying an ego-ideal of the nonconformist type; everyone around him is charmed because, of course, he has chosen friends who also have this ideal.

But gradually doubt begins to appear either in him or in his friends. Why does he never finish his education, marry, and settle into a consistent way of life? Approaching the age of thirty, he has become a perpetual student, living on scholarships and changing his residence whenever the spirit moves him. Surprising how spiritually plausible he can make those changes appear when they are really so self-centered, how bold when really they are evasive! He has the talent to convince others of his divine right to live a provisional and experimental life. "Divine" is not even a figure of speech in his case. I remember the dream of a young man of twenty-seven, still seeking a vocation, unmarried and subsidized by his family's money and endless patience. He dreamt he was floating in a vast cave among cloudy shapes, which on closer inspection were the huge bodies of the Olympian gods as they drifted about in the atmosphere of their eternal divinity. I was relieved to hear him say that in the dream on recognizing these figures as the gods, he also recognized the inappropriateness of his position among them; in a state of panic he escaped by a stone ramp, which led him down to safety and the association of mere mortals.

Sometimes the danger of this kind of inflated isolation is clearly registered in a dream, and one has the task of trying to puncture the balloon upon which the patient is riding high. This may be dangerous, as it would be in reality if one took away such a support, no matter how flimsy. For this reason von Franz points out how important it is for the therapist to fly along with the airborne hero and persuade him to come down of his own accord by gradual stages.

A young man of this type once came to me professing great enthusiasm to receive treatment and asked how soon he could begin and how long it would take. When I told him that I could not take him immediately, that analysis would take its own time, which I could not predict, and that he must count on six months as an initial trial period, his face fell and all enthusiasm evaporated. I asked him why his mood had changed so quickly. "Because," he replied, "I find it extremely depressing to think I shall be in this city as long as two months and be unable to travel east to visit my friends." He had managed for three years after graduation from college to find temporary jobs which took him from place to place, and this perfectly agreed with his intuitive pattern of enjoying each fresh possibility without having to give himself wholeheartedly to any one vocation or circle of friends. Why, then, did he ask for analysis? Because he was beginning to feel dissatisfied with his provisional life and the isolation it brought, in spite of the many exhilarating opportunities for experiment. After a considerable struggle he settled down to work at this problem and began the difficult descent from his stratospheric ego-ideal.

A later dream by the same patient shows the dangers attendant upon thus coming down to earth. Here he was one of a group of young men bringing first aid to a large company of airmen reaching the earth in parachutes; as they landed, these men sustained minor injuries such as sprained ankles. Besides showing the recognition of an Icarus-like danger to his psyche, the dream told me that his natural instinct for saving himself from fatality had begun to collaborate in his therapy with me. It marked the successful completion of his trial analysis, and I could assure him that his psyche could be grounded (his analysis could be terminated, at least temporarily) without suffering anything worse than a temporary shock. This period of analysis enabled him to accept the experience of initiation, at least in principle, and brought him to the choice of a career which would engage his full attention and would therefore postpone further analysis until much later. It is a common experience of young men — and of some young women, though not so dramatically — that a brief period of analysis may be enough to begin with. It apparently takes a considerable time for these young people to establish the initiation pattern which allows them ultimately to find their rites of passage. In the meantime they need to live as closely as possible to whatever reality seems most immediately available, so as to avoid the danger of rocketing off into space again.

Another such intuitively oriented patient, a woman in her early thirties, came to consult me at a time when my office was in a twenty-six-story medical building. One of her initial dreams showed her on the ninety-fifth story, or some such impossibly lofty height, starting to come down in the elevator so rapidly that she was in danger of crashing through the basement, but somehow she was able to stop it at the thirty-fifth floor. This dream told me that while her initial reaction to analysis was strongly positive in promising to lower her degree of psychic isolation, she was still a long way from getting down even to the level upon which she could effectively work at her analysis, the twenty-first floor where I worked, much less all the way down to the reality of ground level. Accordingly I went slowly with her and did not expect any great change for a long time. She was an intelligent woman in whom the *puer aeternus* pattern was functioning positively by rescuing her from a dominating mother and giving her the initial impulse to develop her individual capacities. But in her rebellion she had soared too high. Analysis brought her down from a pinnacle of rational pre-eminence through may layers of self-confrontation to a rediscovery of her essential womanhood.

The levitational image so commonly associated with the *puer aeternus* pattern is mainly true of intuitive-function people and is not necessarily found in those in whom other functions predominate. In sensation-function people the boy may be not a superhuman but a subhuman type, the archetypal image of which is not an Icarus but a dwarf-like creature, earthbound in an unconscious creative-destructive manner suggested by the Greek Kabeiroi, which I shall describe in a later chapter in association with a typical man's initiation dream. Also, I should not like to convey the impression that this pattern in women is true only for the type of woman who successfully competes with men.

We all know or know about that fabulous woman (usually blonde) whose strongest function is feeling but who uses it in a never-ending campaign to find the right man. She will give up everything in her love for him, but he in turn is supposed to give up everything in his love for her. As one man after another goes down in defeat before this impossible demand, she reveals, in a horrifying kind of psychological strip tease, the full image of her goddess-like autonomy — a picture as terrible and astonishing to behold as the one Racine gives us of Phaedra, who in her love for Hippolytus was like an animal clutching its prey (*"Venus toute entière à sa proie attachée"*). In the woman it is not horns but claws (sometimes tusks) which we perceive as an alternative to the "virgin-seeming face." Harding has given us a fine study of this "anima woman," who, by impersonating a man's inferior image of what a woman is, seduces him through his own self-love. Naturally, when he at last rejects his own boyish tendency to see only his own projections of the feminine image instead of real women, he rejects the anima woman, recognizing in her the undesirable features of *puella aeterna*.[10]

There is also in this boyish type of man a tendency frequently to play the inferior masculine role for women, and as an impersonator of the animus he becomes a kind of "animus man." Although this occurs upon a boyish, even childishly erotic level, we should not underestimate his power. He may be what the French laughingly call the village rooster, but on another level he becomes the embodiment of a universal trickster because of his extraordinary talent for causing trouble and disrupting the social order in which he lives. Ordinarily one does not see the worst specimens of tricksterism in psychotherapeutic practice because they do not suffer from their own evil; they merely provide the evil from which others suffer and accordingly comprise a part of the sickness from which society suffers.

I have had only two extreme cases of this type, one so close to the edge of criminal behavior that the police were beginning to show interest. But they never could catch him because of his tricksterish capacity to find a way out of all difficulties in the nick of time. He found his way out of completing his analysis, too.

Another patient of this type was sensitive and did suffer from his condition. In fact, he had that rare blend of intellect and feeling which makes the best kind of social reformer, and the trickster became in him a force for good in its influence upon certain tradition-borne evils of society. But like all tricksters he was divided within himself. This division he described as consisting of two separate personalities, the dreamer and the man of action. In relation to women this was especially apparent: the dreamer had a remarkable gift for planning the romantic voyage of discovery he would take with each new woman, but when it came time to give more tangible assurance of the good faith of his intentions, the man of action proceeded to scuttle the ship.

This patient was married, yet he lived alternately with two other women as if he were free to marry them; indeed, he promised, or seemed to promise, them that he would do so. Like Don Giovanni in Mozart's opera, he was completely unable to act as if he felt there was a moral problem in such behavior. Because I was unable to show him how to resolve this immediate problem and because my own moral sense was too severely disturbed by what I had to appear to condone, I told him I would have to discontinue seeing him until he had made clear to the various women exactly where they stood. With his expectations for achieving a cure for his condition, this temporary termination was just the kind of challenge I least wished to deliver, and I was not surprised when a year or so later he returned to express his anger. I had taken, it seems, a terrible risk in what I had done because it could have driven him to insanity. But he wanted me to know that he had withstood the shock and was all right, no thanks to me. In spite of his overt hostility we parted friends, and I felt a better, more real sense of rapport with him than before.

Since that time I have learned more about the nature of the dissociation occurring in the ego-complex of men identified with the *puer aeternus* image. I am chiefly indebted to one such man, who, in his emergence from its unconscious power over him, described how his personality seemed at times to be taken over and his feelings conditioned by identification with what he described as the Boy, the Woman, and the Animal. His dreams and his fantasy activity both corroborated that this unholy trinity constitutes an essentially irresponsible, power-driven, pleasure-loving attitude toward life. Clearly this is much more complex than that combination of youthful appeal and obvious delinquency to be found in the boy-animal combination. The presence of the woman, denoting a maternal derivative, gives the finishing touch to its dehumanization and marks it as a state of anima possession, arbitrary and moody in a false-feminine way. In the case of women the same factors are present, except that the state of possession takes place through the animus and therefore has a false-masculine quality. Archetypally we get a paradoxical figure which does justice to the full complexity of this type of person and has been a special subject of research by Jung and numerous analytical psychologists in recent years as the trickster-figure.[11]

There is nothing new in this figure. History is full of the catastrophes of men who overreached themselves in their quest for power or pleasure; and the Greek law has been endlessly repeated, that hubris is always punished by nemesis. For this we have always had and, as far as anyone can tell, always will have need of a penal system and a standing army. Infinitely more effective than either of these for the control of tricksterism, however, is maintaining a continuity of humanistic cultural tradition, in response to which symptoms such as the fear of insanity or neurotic suffering may act as psychic brakes to hold back the overweening ambitions of youth to attain the impossible. But none of these is a final safeguard with which to be smugly confident, and every generation has to meet this emergency as if for the first time. The Greek law that hubris is always punished by nemesis has its exceptions or is experienced by those who need it least, and Don Juan goes unpunished even into Hell.

From this point of view there is a precious piece of psychological wisdom in a Navaho myth telling how Coyote, as trickster, escapes punishment for his delinquencies and even proves his immortality. Primitive man appears to have a much better developed sense of the reality of evil than we supposedly civilized people, which enables him to recognize the deep, malevolent, intractable, and immortal propensity for wrongdoing at the root of every trickster's dissocial acts. From this point of view we psychologists have discovered to our chagrin that we may be dealing not with an unruly boy but with the devil himself.

But this kind of devil is not all bad. We never know how the trickster is going to act, even when we think we know, and he is always upsetting our best-laid plans whenever we forget his power. This is perhaps why the Indians are careful never to lose sight of Coyote, obeying the warning of Baudelaire that the "devil's cleverest wile is to convince us that he does not exist." The Navahos even place him among the gods, where they can, so to speak, keep an eye on him. Whether upon the "yellow trail of evil" or the "white trail of virtue," Coyote "just keeps traveling along — by which the myth seems to be telling us that the trickster archetype has the capacity to help man mediate between the powers of good and evil. Hence we are dealing not with mere diabolism but with a creative experimentalism such as Goethe found in Mephistopheles, as being "part of the Power, not understood, which always wills the Bad, and always works the Good."[12]

Such observations inevitably lead us to postulate the existence of an archetype of initiation which can provide the psychological transition in modern youth, corresponding to the rites of passage found in tribal societies, whereby a trickster cycle is converted into a hero cycle.[13] This conversion is indicated in Paul Radin's description of the Winnebago hero cycles. He tells us that the trickster-figure is "completely controlled and dominated by his appetites" and "is cruel, cynical, and unfeeling," but that "as he passes from one exploit to another . . . the diffuseness of his behavior gradually disappears and . . . he emerges with the physical outlines of a man." He sees the trickster cycle as a "rogue's progress, a picaresque novelette," and the hare cycle as a "prose epic in which Hare is the typical hero." "The Hare cycle symbolizes the first correction of instinctual man as we saw him portrayed in the Trickster cycle," so that he "must, first and foremost, become a socialized being."[14]

In comparing modern dream material with mythical hero cycles, it becomes increasingly probable that we are studying the development of ego-consciousness[15] from infancy to the later stages of childhood and that only in late childhood does a real transition become possible from trickster to hero in the archetypal sense. At this point we are in a position to study that particular emergence of the ego which might be likened to Radin's description of the Winnebago's Red Horn cycle, in which the problem of passing tests or meeting successfully certain trials of strength first appears. Like the youthful ego, Red Horn needs some strength which his small human ego necessarily lacks. This needed strength materializes in the myth as a kind of hero-maker. Accordingly, Red Horn was accompanied by a powerful companion, "a thunderbird, Storms-As-He-Walks."[16]

The most highly developed hero cycle in Radin's schema is represented by the Twins, who are essentially human and together constitute one person. On the mythological level, Radin tells us, they represent the static and dynamic sides of man's nature. One is "rooted" and the other "unattached." On the psychological level they appear to represent a form of ego-ideal combining in one process of development the introverted power of reflection and the extraverted capacity for effective action. Identity at this stage is no

Trickster –
Hare
Red Horn
Twins

longer purely egoistic but is capable of developing personality, and the foundation is laid for a later development of character as this personalized ego becomes integrated with a consistent cultural attitude and style of life.

But so long as the youthful ego needs to go on testing its power in accordance with the hero myth, there need be placed no bounds to the ambition engendered by it. Eventually, like the Warrior Gods of Navaho mythology, this form of ego-consciousness grows sick from the exercise of its power because, finally, there are no monsters left to overcome. In the Winnebago cycle the Twins are at last "completely unattached and unanchored. Nothing is safe from them. . . . When they slay one of the four animals that uphold the earth, they have overstepped all limits and their activities must be brought to a halt. . . . Their punishment should be death" as a necessary penalty for the power that overreaches itself. In European mythology, we meet the theme of sacrifice or betrayal of the hero as a ritual punishment for hubris. This happens inevitably and tragically, even when the hero is represented as innocent of any conscious intention to overreach himself. The Winnebagos, like the Navahos, imagine that the erring heroes are not killed but become so frightened of their lawless deeds that they "are permitted to live forever but in a state of permanent rest" or learn to sing songs that will cure them of their quest for power.[17]

Here is the point at which a will-to-power normally gives way to a willingness to submit, forced inevitably upon the developing ego by inner laws of change or by outer necessity to conform to reality (cf. Freud's "reality principle"). It seems clear from the comparison to be drawn between ego formation and the evolution of the hero myth that this submission does not take place automatically with the normal process of growth. It takes place only against the full force of a basic resistance to change inherent in the hero-image from its origin in the trickster-figure, he who knows no difference between right and wrong and accepts no discipline other than his own experimental attitude toward life. Hence for young people the trickster impulse provides the strongest resistance to initiation and is one of the hardest problems education has to solve because it seems a kind of divinely sanctioned lawlessness that promises to become heroic.

SUMMARY

ON THE BASIS of previous studies, we may make a preliminary postulate that the earliest development of ego-consciousness proceeds in accordance with an archetypal trickster cycle. At the lower level of this cycle we find a state of infantile dependence; at the upper level we find a *puer aeternus* figure combining infantile power or pleasure-loving traits with an attitude of nobility or heroism. In normal development the trickster cycle is superseded by a hero cycle in which an archetypal father-figure seems to replace the original mother-figure or world of matriarchal consciousness. Both trickster cycle and hero cycle are in turn superseded or transformed by the appearance of the initiation archetype, which appears to put an end to the self-perpetuating tendency of these two cycles. There remains, however, an internal connection or overlapping between the trickster cycle and the hero cycle which the experience of initiation has to bridge so that elements of the two cycles may be transformed either into a psycho-social modality or into a quest for individual identity. Some of our material for this study derives from the experiences of modern people and some from a comparative study of initiation ceremonies in history or among alien cultures. We approach the subject of initiation with the belief that analytic therapy today can illuminate many puzzling aspects of initiation in other cultures and times, and in turn be illuminated by the knowledge derived from them.

CHAPTER III

Return to the Mother

THE UNIVERSAL AIM of initiation in tribal societies is to ensure that the novice will renounce all allegiance, even all feeling, toward his mother and be willing to be taken from her to the man's house, where he will meet the trial of strength, set by the tribal fathers, in which he will either achieve manhood or die. What is true in the simpler societies is also true, though less drastically enforced, in a more complex society. In our own culture, initiation into manhood is not accompanied by a physical ordeal, but it is felt as a no less powerful demand for the boy or girl to put away childish things and deny his mother's solicitude for his welfare, thus re-enacting in his own way those scenes from the New Testament in which we are told Jesus said to his mother, "Woman, what have I to do with thee? mine hour is not yet come." (John 2:4) and "Wist ye not that I must be about my Father's business?" (Luke 2:49).

It comes, therefore, as something of a surprise to find how many of our patients during the course of analysis needing, even begging for, this stern discipline (because they have remained too long in their mother's world) instead of being ready to go about their father's business fly like homing pigeons back to the maternal dovecote. At some point, re-education in a psychological sense seems to require a recapitulation of the whole life history, a reactivation of the mother's image together with the childhood pattern of behavior all the way back to infancy. From there it may stretch back into the depths of the collective unconscious, where the return is to the archetypal rather than to the personal mother. This is already well known from the literature of analytical psychology. "Essentially, this return to the mother is the return to the primordial psyche, where the potential of complete human capacity is to be found, though still in the impersonal balance of nature."[1] The present chapter is concerned with the relationship between such a return to the mother and the archetype of initiation.

In this connection, three kinds of return to the mother may be identified: (1) *passive-regressive and restorative,* with little or no appearance of the initiation archetype; (2) *transitional* between passive-regressive and active-purposive, with partial appearance of the initiation archetype; and (3) *active-purposive and transforming,* with full cooperation of the initiation archetype.

A case of the first type is represented by a young man who used to draw pictures of a snake coiling about the trunk of a tree, straining to reach upward into its branches. This would be followed by pictures in which the snake returned to the earth, where in greatly diminished size it would form a circle with its head and tail meeting. The snake, as a connection with unconscious powers, would normally seek to encompass the principle of psychic growth as suggested by the trunk of the tree, from which it could then reach into the discriminating and productive levels of consciousness suggested by the branches. In this case, however, because of a persistently negative attitude toward his father and father substitutes, the patient fell into a movement of regression back to the state of unconsciousness described by Erich Neumann as *uroboric,* expressing the inactivity and isolation of the infantile state.[2]

But the symbol of the *uroborus,* or tail-biting snake, is not only regressive. It is also a simple form of mandala which represents integration and in this case provided a suitable compensation for the danger of creating a complete split between the conscious and unconscious worlds. This patient's drawings illustrated this danger very well. Sometimes the snake was cut in two, and sometimes the danger of a split was represented by the snake at the foot of the tree and a red bird perched in its topmost branches, seeming to represent a division in the sum of psychic life, with the unconscious (snake) utterly detached from the conscious (bird). The return to the *uroboros* thus marked a reaffirmation of the patient's ability to restore the integrity of the ego-structure and regain a feeling of wholeness, albeit on a regressive level.

An expression of the second type of return to the mother —

transitional between the passive, largely autonomous cycle of regression to the primordial psyche and an active return — is seen in
an *uroborus* symbol drawn by a woman patient at the onset of an
involutional depression which required hospitalization for four
months. This representation showed the snake surrounded by stars
and with the caption *Per Aspera ad Astra*. It was impossible for
me or for her to find any significance in this symbol at the time.
It merely seemed to mark the beginning of a catastrophic return to
the terrors of preconscious life. The symbol nonetheless carried on
the work of integration in its mysterious way. The patient, while
confined in the hospital, thought she was going to die and lived in
a perpetual state of anxiety, waiting for the end. Then one day she
felt she could let herself die, and she described this as a feeling of
plunging into water with no thought of survival. But instead of
drowning, she seemed to hit bottom and then rise to the surface,
where life began again for her.

She made a gradual but steady recovery during the following
year, but this did not mean a simple return to her former way of
life. Her regressive longings and her dependency, together with
the fierce self-absorption of one who is determined to reach the
stars, had fallen away, leaving her in a state of dignified human
submission to life's realistic demands. Her *uroborus* symbol then
came into another focus: instead of a regressive longing for the
mother, it meant the achievement of a healthy attitude toward her
mother problem. She was liberated from a lifelong bondage to a
negative mother image, and the symbols appearing to her in her
psychotic experience became in the end vehicles of initiation. This
she saw as a paradoxical experience of death and rebirth, which at
her time of life (age 48) represented liberation from her bondage
to her purely natural impulses and provided that necessary step
into the world of those who are ready to accept consciously the
process of aging.

Starting with a negative mother complex, this woman had become at an early age a father's daughter. Her belated experience of
the initiation archetype thus led her back to the mother as an
archetypal image and away from the father, through whom she had
become, as it were, fixed into the attitude of a *puella aeterna*.

The problem of the young man, in contrast, lay in his maintaining only a regressive relation to the primordial level of the unconscious and being unable to risk himself consciously in an heroic effort to achieve his autonomy. Thus his psychic energy remained in an early identification with the trickster cycle, without the necessary detachment which would allow him to become even a good example of a *puer aeternus* with its creative spark.

It appears from these two cases that the *puer aeternus* (or *puella aeterna*) is found in the common ground shared by the trickster cycle and the hero cycle. The young man was still purely an infantile trickster; the woman had become an inflated heroine. The symbol of the snake in the man's case was limited to playing safe within the trickster cycle, whereas for the woman it was oriented to the highest spiritual aspiration. In her case, therefore, it was bound to overreach itself and lead to psychic destruction in accordance with the myth of the death of the hero.

The phenomenology of the third type of return to the mother — i.e., active-purposive and transforming, associated with the initiation archetype — is shown in the following examples.

Case I (Female, age 45)

This was an unmarried career woman who had consciously undergone certain initiatory changes before coming to analysis. By recording her own dreams she had acquired a good deal of insight and had achieved a real increase in consciousness over her youthful state of unconscious impulsiveness. This awareness was associated with the beneficent influence of a strong father and other men who helped her set up significant standards for vocational achievement. Her actual achievement in the world was satisfactory to herself and approved by others. What she had never been able to accomplish by herself was to find release from a deep-seated fear of her mother. The first clue to this solution finally came to her in a dream, and this dream brought her to analysis, since she realized that she could not interpret it without help.

DREAM 1: I knew that my mother had died, that her viscera had been removed and her liver given to me to be buried. I held it in my left hand; it was large and flabby, but there was no blood. I decided to make it into a neat package and, to do this, cut it into smaller pieces. Then I seemed to be on a flat plain with many people at a great distance that I did not know. I searched for white paper or white material to wrap it in. I rejected many pieces till I found pure white ones. The next step was to get it through customs without the customs official making difficulties. To do this I impersonated a soldier in khaki and passed through. Then I repeated the act of wrapping the liver, but this time I put some of my mother's jewelry and some of mine in it.

ASSOCIATIONS: At the time of the dream the patient's mother had been dead several years. Toward the end they had been on good terms, but in childhood the patient had felt antagonistic or disapproving of her mother's handling of her. She had had a warmer feeling toward her childhood nurse than toward her mother. She had begun to establish rapport with her mother during adolescence.

INTERPRETATION: The unpleasant task of burying her mother's liver probably represents a duty that the patient has to perform in relation to the maternal function in herself which is flabby, large, and lifeless. First she must dispose of this dead thing, associated with her early failure to identify with her mother in the normal manner of daughters, especially her inability to express feeling towards her mother in accordance with her mother's expectations and those of her family or friends. The dream shows her concern with performing this duty — disposing of the maternal function — in such a way as to give this dark act a deceptively bright appearance and to minimize its importance (the small pieces of liver wrapped in pure white paper). This wrapping presumably refers to her conscious notion that she had found peace by comforting her mother in her last years and then by doing everything a dutiful daughter should do in settling her mother's estate. But she had no real feeling for this role; and in spite of an immaculate persona, the dream remembers her early, abiding sense of guilt, which still needs to find a decent burial. In order to accomplish this she must get past the barrier of collective opinion, which she had introjected in order to keep her true feelings repressed.

The customs official as representative of collective opinion is in himself neither good nor bad. He is the guardian of a threshold, here a threshold between two different attitudes toward femininity. Mythological guardians of thresholds are represented as both friendly and fierce, showing that what is aroused from the unconscious by the approach to a new threshold of consciousness is a feeling of ambivalence, a mixture of attraction and repulsion. Frequently expressed as an animal or bird, the guardian of the threshold is demonic; and this impression, combined with the sense of its ambivalence, most accurately embodies the kind of projection of psychic contents met with at the point where we have to overcome a resistance to further development. To overcome this resistance the patient repeats in her dream the habitual pattern of masculine identification, thus appropriating, so to speak, the courage of a soldier. Having passed this patriarchal barrier, she can permit herself an appropriate expression of feminine feeling by rewrapping the liver and giving to it some of her own feminine values as jewels to be combined with similar maternal values surviving her actual mother's death. Only by becoming a softer kind of woman can she, in this symbolic act, express the feeling necessary to bury her guilt at long last.

This interpretation was borne out by a secondary association to this dream in which the patient recalled with considerable affect a situation during her childhood when she had failed to express feeling for her mother when her mother particularly needed it. This marked the culmination of many small failures to give herself freely, an inhibition which is verified and elaborated in a second dream from the period before she decided to seek help through analysis.

DREAM 2: I met a man and woman analyst at a party and decided to go to the woman. She put me through a series of mysterious tests, and each time it was a dreadful experience. It was dark, and there were snakes I had to take in my hands and they bit me. There was water and I became sicker and sicker. I fainted and vomited and never passed the test she expected of me. I felt she was a hard, unfeeling woman. Finally in desperation I gave something to her and everything cleared. I seemed to have passed the test and I saw she was not hard or unfeeling.

ASSOCIATIONS: The analysts referred to were unknown to her;

the dream merely represents her conscious dread of having to submit to a woman's power. She was surprised to find that it cleared the situation to give something to the woman. The dream convinced her that she did in fact need analysis.

INTERPRETATION: It is most probable that the woman therapist is a surrogate mother, though the patient knows that mothers are not really so unfeeling. All around her are snakes and water, denoting something which she cannot clearly grasp with her mind and of which she is accordingly fearful. The suggestion of witchcraft looms threateningly: this means that if the mother image were to be activated too powerfully, she would be overwhelmed by an inability to respond to her therapist's expectations, just as she had failed with her mother in childhood. But if she were to give something of herself (cf. the act of giving some of her jewels in the previous dream), she would redeem her guilt and feel accepted through accepting. Presumably she can now effect this change to recover her sealed-off feeling and discover the new womanly qualities. Although I, as a man did not convey this threat to her, it still took an act of high courage for her to undertake analysis in view of her premonition that it would lead her back to the world of the Terrible Mother, where she would have to lose herself in order to find herself anew.

How the initiation archetype appeared and enabled her to accomplish her return to the mother will be described later. For the present we shall turn to another example of this theme.

Case II (Male, age 26)

It might be considered natural that a woman who had lived too exclusively in the world of approved masculine standards should return to re-establish her connection with the feminine world of the mother, but that this could happen to a young man would seem most inappropriate. Yet I find the same theme even more positively expressed in the dream of such a young man.

DREAM 1: I see my mother dressed in veils, her face beautiful and shining. I go forward to embrace her, but my way is blocked by a wooden beam placed horizontally on the ground between us.

ASSOCIATION: I would like to show more feeling for my mother. In her presence I feel painfully reserved. She has always shown more feeling for me than I wished.

INTERPRETATION: A psychoanalytic interpretation fits this case very well to begin with. The dream clearly expressed an incest wish which is blocked by an incest prohibition. But why is the incest prohibition represented this way? Wilhelm Stekel reports a dream almost identical to this one in which the beam is interpreted as a symbol for homosexuality, the beam being equivalent to the phallus.[3] Why should this be a barrier to a return to the mother? Homosexuality in men is a symptom-complex which combines hatred and denial of the mother's supposed desire to keep the son's love in her possession (i.e., not to let it go out to another woman), together with a longing to reach manhood through intimate sexual contact with another man or boy. This frequently has the meaning of an initiation into manhood via sexuality, but it usually ends in a failure of initiation because the sexual relation activates the feminine component in one or another of the two men involved so strongly that the manly relationship is devoured by the feminine, just as the boy's love was originally devoured over and over again by the mother. This reversal of the original goal of liberation from the mother sets up a strong resistance to the mother and/or women in general; at the same time, it prevents progress to the truly masculine image of the father, who now, as always, appears threatening.

All this we know from the Freudian description of the Oedipus complex, which is seen in intensified form in male homosexuals. What the psychoanalytic interpretation does not perceive is the purposive, necessary task of removing the incest barrier and returning to take possession of the mother symbolically, this being the only way in which the man can win back from the unconscious his masculine feeling.

After this dream and his assimilation of its content, the patient allowed himself to express for the first time the love which he had felt for his mother but could never show for fear of being devoured by it. Yet he had as a boy received with pleasure and indulged himself in the selfless love which his mother had lavished upon him, as upon her other children and her closest friends. It was the passivity born of his own self-indulgence which had really crippled him and turned his wish for love into a false-feminine need to be loved, not to give love. His dream points to the positive reversal of this tendency and suggests a wish to show his feeling actively, put limits to its expression, and overcome his fear.

When, following the insight gained from this dream, he acted upon impulse to express feeling for his mother, she responded with great circumspection. Far from feeling caught in any incestuous involvement, he felt liberated, as though his feeling were for the first time ready to detach itself from his mother and find its way in a mature response to other women.

This case is instructive for the management of therapy. It is frequently efficacious for a man with this type of mother-complex to be treated by a woman analyst capable of playing the mother role temporarily. One might assume that such a youth would need to work with a sympathetic older man with whom he might establish a positive homosexual transference and thereby win freedom from the regressive tendency to return to the mother for support. Yet this very good idea is frequently untenable because the feeling which could invest such a transference with the power of an initiation experience is still too bound in the original mother fixation. Only she or her surrogate can free him by his own claim.

But is there not a danger that this return will further imprison him? Jung has voiced this danger very clearly in describing the case of a homosexual youth in which a most positive dream of symbolic marriage with a mother substitute resulted, not in freedom, but in many regressive returns to the inertia of the mother-complex.[4] Yet the initiatory threshold indicated in the present dream seems ultimately to have been crossed, for the patient made a healthy transition to heterosexuality.

Case III (Male, age 25)

Another young man, whose mother-complex had initially been treated by a woman analyst and who had won from his experience of the transference some gift of feeling for her as mother, had a still more revealing dream structured according to the initiation archetype. The dream came soon after he had changed from the woman therapist to work with a man in accordance with his readiness to give up being a mother's son and to develop his masculine identity as a son also of the father.

DREAM 1: I was marching in a slowly moving procession of young men. Suddenly I left the procession and ran swiftly to the head of the line, where I was handed a staff surmounted by a carved bust of the Queen Mother. I then led the procession forward, carrying this standard.

ASSOCIATIONS: The carrying of the Queen Mother reminded me of an impressive porcelain figure of the Chinese goddess Kuan Yin (the Goddess of Mercy) which I had seen at the house of an older woman who had taken an interest in me and had encouraged me in the artistic interests which led to my career as a writer. Hence she had played something of the role of a spiritual mother, though she was not nearly as important to me as the woman analyst, with whom I had experienced a truly emotional response.

INTERPRETATION: In contrast to the previous dream expressing the incest wish, this dream presents the mother as a supra-personal figure. She appears not even as a woman but as a symbol. This Queen Mother can therefore be taken as an archetypal image of the mother. That the dream is a collective, not a personal, dream is further emphasized by the procession of young men. We know nothing about the symbol except the dreamer's cryptic comment that it is "strange, ancient, and venerable." His failure to produce further associations indicates that the movement thus begun comes from an unexpected and hitherto untouched region of the unconscious. We are therefore obliged to amplify the dream by means of mythological or ritual parallels.

A suitable comparison to the dream ritual procession is the ritual of ancient Crete involving the group of men called Kouretes (which means literally "initiated young men"), as reported by Harrison:

> The Kouretes are the young men just come to maturity, just initiated into the fertility dance of their tribe; they invoke their leader

as lord of moisture and life, or as they say, "Lord of all that is wet and gleaming." The band of initiated youths are the prototypes of all the Satyrs and Seilenoi the Salii and Maruts of Europe and Asia. . . . The cult of the Kouretes was at home in Crete and the great central worship of the Mother Goddess. In the bridal chamber of Crete the young men . . . were initiated to the Mountain Mother and became symbolically her consorts or husbands.[5]

By analogy, the procession of young men in the patient's dream — and the dreamer himself, as a member of the group — are initiated to the mother and become symbolically her husbands or consorts.

In addition to their function as "Seers and worshipers" of the Mother, the Kouretes "are armed and orgiastic dancers" who guard a holy child. This child is as yet in no way distinguished, he is simply the son of his mother. In the *Hymn of the Kouretes,* a ritual hymn containing very early material, the Kouretes tend a holy child.

The Child grows up into the young initiated man and the young initiated man becomes the consort of the perennial mother. . . . Then . . . they project from their own body a leader, a Greatest Kouros, to whom they hand over the functions they themselves performed. . . . The religious rites of the Satyrs centre round the Mother Semele, the Phrygo-Thracian Earth goddess, and in like fashion the Satyrs project from their band the arch-satyr Dionysos; the *thiasos* [band of revelers] is before the god.[6]

By analogy, the dreamer begins his initiation as a member of the band devoted to worship of the mother symbol; he is then, so to speak, one of the Kouretes. We can also suspect that until then he had, like the babe, remained in an infantile state of solitary dependence upon the mother archetype, as well as upon the personal mother. Finally, in the dream, he is separated from the group, becoming like the Greatest Kouros, the leader chosen to take over the function hitherto performed by the group as a whole. Unlike the dream of Case II, where the young man merely *longed* to possess the mother who was shielded from him by a beam, the present subject actually does possess the mother in the guise of her symbol. This designates a more fundamental, and at the same time a transcendent (for the staff is equivalent to the principle of transcendence), solution of the original fixation.

The analogy with the Cretan tradition is so exact that we can accept this case as an example of how a personal complex may be replaced and superseded by a cultural pattern of an archaic nature. For another example of this phenomenon we return to Case I.

Case I (continued)

The motif of coming to possess the symbol of the mother was represented in a later dream by this patient, after the dream of burying her mother's liver. Several of her initial dreams, after beginning analysis, were characterized by initiatory threshold experiences: (1) a dream of crossing a border between two countries by passing a special test; (2) a dream of a serpent coiled into a complicated knot suggestive of a labyrinth, representing the apparently insoluble nature of her mother problem; and (3) a dream of getting into a special container, representing a return to the mother for the sake of self-incubation. Then she had a more specific initiation dream as follows:

DREAM 3: I was to go through an initiation ceremony in a rectangular room. Up each nostril I had birds' feathers, soft and gay, hooked into each nostril, in a pattern resembling a trout fly. I could breathe but it was uncomfortable. I had to put up with it as it was a necessary part of the ceremony. A woman was to initiate me in another rectangular room. I dreaded this but knew I must go through with it.

The scene changed back to the period of coming of age. There was a party and the people were mother's age or my age at that period. The room was disorderly and I was burning things in a fire. Near the fire, almost in the middle of the room, was a large black safe in which I had left something for safekeeping. It was as important as a key that would unlock anything, but it was not a key. It was the shape of a beehive and it was extremely important to get it out of the safe.

(In another dream the same night, the patient was about to pass over a border into a strange country where the shape of one's head is changed.)

ASSOCIATIONS: Insignificant.

INTERPRETATION: The first part of the dream expresses in the strangely original manner of the unconscious a totally unexpected and spontaneous version of an initiatory ordeal. The ordeal is, as Eliade points out, an expression of "initiatory death."[7] The soft, gay birds' feathers penetrating the patient's nostrils suggest both the elation of a transcendent experience and the painful feeling of being caught in a process which cannot be reversed, as a fish is caught by the fisher.* Being caught and submitting to a process over which she has no control would be a new experience for her, in contrast to the more familiar, active trials of strength.

A further ordeal awaits her. She says, "A woman was to initiate me in another rectangular room. I dreaded this. . . ." We know from Dream 2 that she feared submitting to a woman therapist, during which experience she might be bitten by snakes. To be bitten by snakes can be a symbolic representation of a regressive return to the Terrible Mother. Psychologically this would denote falling into helpless infantility, or paralyzing inertia, or a sudden, overwhelming psychotic invasion (catatonia). But there the stage is

---

* The delicate symbolism of being caught like a fish as an expression of initiatory death, leading to the promise of rebirth on a more highly evolved level — that is, a transition from boyhood to manhood — is expressed in a poem which a young man spontaneously produced at a similar point in his analysis:

Caught

I am the fish who's drawn from the sea
By a man on shore who's me.
He who plotted with the bait
And drew the line is me.
I want to go back and down and deep
But the man on the land won't wait.
My boyhood's dying on the sand.
It's lying in the larger hand
That drew the line and removes the hook
And takes me to his wife to cook.

set for the initiatory change, and she can presumably submit to this ordeal, which inevitably follows.

The scene of the dream then shifts to a significant period in her personal history. It is the period of "coming of age," and the gathering includes her friends and some of her mother's friends. The suggestion is that this was the time when she normally would have married and left home, as her friends did. Instead she had determined to resist the conventional pattern, espouse a career, and live as an independent woman. In so doing she adopted a pseudo-masculine style of life which caused her to neglect those excellent feminine qualities to which she had been exposed by her mother and her friends. The dream tells us that the room was disorderly, and as she was normally a very orderly person, we can guess that what was disorderly is the neglected feminine principle left behind. Burning things in a fire suggests a need to get rid of old, useless parts of her earlier adaptation — that is, the burning-her-bridges-behind-her attitude with which she had left home and which still has meaning for her in order to preserve that spirit of independence she had won from her mother in not having to obey exclusively conventional standards. But there is one important thing which she must retrieve, and the dream makes clear that it is in an absolutely safe place from which to be retrieved.

A key that will unlock anything yet is not a key but is shaped like a beehive — what kind of object is this? The symbolism of initiation is full of such riddles in accordance with that curious instinct that forever seeks to veil the meaning and keep the rite a secret. But an acquaintance with the natural language of symbolism allows us to conjecture that the key is a representation of the masculine mind, creative or inventive, and thus a symbol of effective patriarchal consciousness. This key, by some magical device, is transformed into a beehive, which is a symbol for the autonomous matriarchal principle in nature, a social order presided over by a specifically feminine being, the queen bee.

That the bee was in ancient times associated with the rites of the Great Mother and of Dionysos is confirmed by Harrison:

> The Thriae are nurses like the Maenads [who] rave in holy madness . . . but their inspiration is not from Bacchos, the wine-god,

not even from Bromios or Sabazios or Braites, the beer-gods; it is
from a source, from an intoxicant yet more primitive, from honey.
They are in a word 'Melissae,' honey-priestesses."

The honey service of ancient ritual was carried out in service to
the Mother of Wild Things and the Corn Goddess and is therefore
basic to the Great Mother symbol as a universal mythologem. Not
only were the "priestesses of Artemis at Ephesus 'Bees,' but also
those of Demeter, and, still more significant, the Delphic priestess
herself was a Bee . . . She was figured by art as a goddess and half
human with high curled wings and a bee body from the waist
downwards."[8]

Translating this symbolism into the specific psychology of our
patient, we can say she had, so to speak, used the masculine side
of her personality as her key to unlock her door to the world and
especially to her chosen career. But in so doing she had left behind
the key to the natural forms of life to be lived for their own sake,
a paradoxically feminine key in form of a beehive reposing in the
safekeeping of the maternal traditions of her family, a tradition
which might impart those qualities of womanly sweetness and
passion which she had feared and therefore scorned. Having discharged her duty to the personal mother in Dream 1, she now
finds herself in a position to return to the cultural and familial
group in order to claim her heritage as a woman belonging to the
community of women. In the beehive (as in the bust of the Queen
Mother in the young man's dream) we have a collective representation which replaces a personal mother-complex by a universal
symbol of social organization in nature and in primitive culture.

Thus in both Case I and Case II we have seen the appearance
of two prime symbols of the Great Mother revealed by means of
the archetype of initiation. That initiation in this sense represents
a true psychological change of consciousness and not just a release
from the original fixation is indicated in the last dream of this
woman patient, in which she came to another initiatory threshold
beyond which, she said, "the shape of one's head is changed."

Case IV (Female, age 38)

The emergence of archetypal imagery in Cases I and III is
characteristic of the response of a large number of people to anal-

ysis by the Jungian method, especially after the full expectation of a symbolic return to the mother, configured in the unconscious, begins to be realized consciously through the mediation of the analyst. Presumably this emergence is made possible by an openness on the part of the analyst. If the therapist — whether intentionally, or through lack of interest, or merely through ignorance — responds unintelligently or unsympathetically to such archetypal imagery, the symbolism of initiation will probably not develop or, if it does, only in a distorted manner. A patient of mine who had two years of Freudian-oriented analysis later came to me out of curiosity to know what a Jungian would say about a certain dream, which her analyst had interpreted on a purely personal level.

DREAM 1: I went to a strange place in the mountains. In a cave-like opening I observed a deep cleft in the rock which filled me with awe.

ASSOCIATIONS: No significant association. The analyst had interpreted the dream as sexual curiosity associated with early childhood frustration at not receiving adequate information as to where babies come from.

INTERPRETATION: From what we have learned in the previous case, it is not difficult to sense that the patient is approaching in this dream a significant threshold between the conscious and the unconscious which calls for some initiatory expectation. Initiation in this sense fits the archetype of return to the mother, even in the meaning of the word itself, which in one sense means "going-into (in itia)."⁹ The cleft in the rock has many mythological associations: as a place where underworld powers lurk, a place where the ancestral spirits live, a place where the hero might encounter the dragon, and a place where an oracle may be heard. The practical meaning in this case was clear to me from the patient's attitude of religious expectancy, and that she needed to enter into the region of the collective unconscious without denying thereby the validity of her personal analysis. Finding in me an attitude favorable to entering the dark region of this psychological underworld, she began an analysis which gradually prepared her to descend into that cleft (or to hear the message of its oracle), which then led to an initiation.

About a year later, the patient had the following dream:

DREAM 2. Into my family house, as I remember it from girlhood, came a huge bear dressed in a woman's dress. It came in abruptly and began to dance about the room. It was very important for me to stand quietly and witness this dance without showing fear or trying to get away.

ASSOCIATIONS: These were mainly feelings of inhibition concerning family gatherings, where the patient felt criticized or unable to express her own feelings or opinions because of traditional or conventional attitudes.

INTERPRETATION: The familiar old home becomes the dancing ground of an impersonal and therefore archetypal personification (a bear in feminine guise), presenting her with an initiatory test of endurance. This room, with its humdrum associations of family life, fades as there comes into focus the patient's need to withstand something of superhuman force. Her further associations led to thoughts of how her relationship to her mother had been interfered with by all her aunts, cousins, and grandmothers, whom she felt standing invisibly behind her with an unspoken exhortation to obey the rules of the conventional family pattern. She had broken many of these rules, in spirit if not in fact, and she had her conscience to reckon with. One almost believes in cases of this kind that a questioning, critical ancestor comes forth on purpose to test such a person for her fitness to carry her cultural responsibilities from past to future and, if she fails, to rob her of all pride of identity and reduce her to a quivering jelly of neurotic guilt. But the ancestor who has the power to make such a test really impressive may come from no known personal or family tradition, not even from any historically familiar culture pattern.

In this case the dream shows a bear-woman who invades the domain of the known mothers to test the patient's strength more powerfully than any of the others had done. This particular animal is perhaps the oldest known example of what we may call the animal master of initiation, forming an archetypal image which can be traced back through and beyond history to paleolithic man. Joseph Campbell tells us of recent discoveries of a bear ceremonial "dating from the period (it is almost incredible!) of Neanderthal Man" in the period between 250,000 and 75,000 B.C., towards the close of the Glacial Age.[10] As the patient had no personal association with bears and was herself thoroughly surprised by the dream content, we may conjecture that the bear in her dreams represents this ancient lost tradition, as an elementary and original archetypal image untouched by cultural concretions. (For a discussion of the bear as an archetypal image, see Appendix.)

The patient's family home and the nature of the inhibitions she acquired there are illustrated by the following typical episode: being unable to express a differing opinion from her elders', this woman would either lose her temper and leave the room or else burst into tears. Most embarrassing in this display of emotion was her feeling of weakness, which denoted an incapacity to state her differing point of view in a humanly differentiated or tactful way. In other words, she behaved childishly. But she knew it was not all her own weakness; there was also something in the family pattern which brought forth an inappropriate emotional response which she could never resolve, either objectively or subjectively. It is this family-complex which in analysis undergoes a significant change, making way for the animal master of initiation to play the role of the animal mother, like the Dea Artio of Gallo-Roman times or the bear maiden of the Navaho Indians. An immeasurably primitive form of matriarch comes to life in this image, perhaps because only a fundamental solution to her problem could have the power to change her from the child, who would run away from or feel defeated by danger, into the woman, who can feel its invigorating challenge. These qualities of the bear defined in the Appendix — courage, independence, and the capacity for self-renewal — are made available to the dreamer in the mimetic rite of the bear dance.

Why a dance? Because the dance is considered necessary and productive work in the life of any tribal community: it arouses enthusiasm and enables primitive man to pursue the absorbing tasks of hunting, planting, fighting, healing, and so on. Psychologically this represents the work done in mobilizing psychic energy in general, and it applies to individuals no less than to tribal groups. Instead of a tribal meal or ritual dance in which a large number of people participate, we find in the case of an individual a single shamanic experience of either a visionary or a mimetic character. The single animal dancer is probably a shaman, who is a more pointed and more dramatic representation of the archetype. What, then, is the archetype thus represented, besides being the archetypal mother in bear form?

It is the rite of initiation in that moment when the initiate is poised between the basic wildness of her animal nature and the civilizing force of an instinct for domestication, represented by the woman's dress which the bear is wearing. The ordered movement of the dance is the transforming symbol itself. What this woman has needed from her analysis is an invigorating shock from her own deeper nature, causing her to integrate her untamed and her overtamed natures.

The ordeal as a shock of surprise[11] is a frequent device of the initiation scenarios, which probably have as their purpose an awakening of the child, youth, or maiden from a certain complacency, from a clinging to the past or to the self-indulgence of childhood. Also, and above all, it frees them from the night terrors which inevitably compensate a falsely benevolent attitude of the parents. Certain sicknesses are treated in this way. A healing ceremony of the Navaho Indians consists in placing the patient in a semicircular enclosure of spruce boughs. At a certain moment the medicine man, dressed as a bear, leaps into this enclosure in a frightening, unexpected confrontation with the patient. Even little children are sometimes terrorized by a hideous old witch (Zuñi) who brings into the dancing ground of the central plaza the Terrible Mother's presence, so that the personal mother can at the same time protect, mediate, and comfort the child. In this way the child is enabled to integrate fear instead of repressing it.[12] Our society provides very little of this healthy prophylaxis which is adequate to cure the sickness resulting from repression of fear. But the imagery of the dream, ever ready to express the patient's needs, seems to go even further and at times delivers part of the shock necessary to awaken people to their essential needs.

The present dream accomplished this function extremely effectively. The dreamer took its message seriously and, by lifting its meaning from the unconscious into the conscious, experienced an archetypal moment of initiation which enabled her to make certain important decisions about her life, decisions which she had never been able to envisage making before because of her timidity. Though she later fell back many times into regressive ways and needed a great deal more psychological help during the next three years, she closed at this time, once and for all, the door which led back to the world of childhood with all its artificial comforts and unknown terrors. To that extent she had experienced a return to the mother in an act of submission instead of rebellion. Thence she had passed through a deeply primitive test of endurance and had symbolically achieved the *rite d'entrée* of the adolescent girl in becoming a woman on both a personal and an archetypal level, as dramatized in the ritual dance-drama of her dream.

THE FOUR CASES I have described all returned to the mother as if to retrieve a valuable part of themselves which had been left behind or which had never developed. Their dream adventures, after unpromising beginnings, appear to end victoriously, and we may be inclined to forget the theme of death so commonly emphasized in all initiations (e.g., Case I, Dream 1).

Furthermore in the dream of the Queen Mother symbol and the triumphant procession led by the dreamer (Case III, Dream 1), we have a strong compensation for the young man's conscious feeling of failure and utter incompetence to express, in any but the feeblest way, a basic passion for life. He was ostensibly depressed and without hope of finding a solution for his mother problem. His dream, as in dreams of the other cases, was far ahead of his achievement. At the time of recounting his dream the feeling of death was full upon him but did not appear in a dream until very much later, when he was ready to emerge from his world of the mother into the world of the father. In fact, that whole dream takes place symbolically in the underworld of matriarchal prehistory uninfluenced by effective patriarchy. One could say that this young man had not returned to the mother, for in a sense he had never left her.

In contrast to this case — and to demonstrate how this return to the mother can also happen to a young man who is consciously a son of the father, fully functioning within the hero cycle — I present the final case of this series:

Case V (Male, age 27)

A young man in his late twenties had been a pilot in the Army Air Corps during the Second World War. He completed sixty-five missions over Germany from an air base in England; finished his period of service as aide to a general stationed in a château in Belgium, where he enjoyed a privileged position; and, when his period of service ended, was discharged back into civilian life, covered with the honors of his achievement. It might be supposed that he would have returned content to take up one of the fruitful careers for which he was well fitted by education and family background. But he was not at all content with this prospect. Like many ex-servicemen he was still riding high in an expectation that life had an even more exciting adventure in store for him. He looked upon civilian life as a humiliating descent into mediocrity from the high, even heroic, position sustained by adulation, which he had learned to enjoy.

In a tribal society the treatment for such a young man would be the *rite de sortie,* or ritual of withdrawal, in which the passions aroused in warlike combat would be carefully and systematically reduced to normal limits. In a society such as that of the Navaho Indians, the myth of the Warrior Gods might be recounted to the youth in question, especially that part in which Talking God, the embodiment of civilized protocol and humanistic behavior, enjoins the Twin Heroes to take care lest the arrows of their aggression, given them by the Sun Father, should harm the earth and the peaceful ways of settled folk.

The lack of any such wise counsel made this patient more depressed, more and more helpless to heal his wounded feelings of rejection, deflation, and war fatigue. This modern war hero discovered, as so many others did, that he was suffering from pathological inflation, and a friend persuaded him to wend his way to a psychiatrist. I was by no means as skilled as the Indian medicine man to initiate a *rite de sortie.* In fact, I might never have known that this was his trouble had he not presented me with an initial dream which gave the whole picture in great detail. The dream left no doubt that I was dealing with a case of post-war depression following a period of ego-inflation artificially induced by the enthusiasm of battle and by a man's ability in such a state to transcend the fear of death.

DREAM 1: I had to get somewhere by a certain time. On a diagram I saw how to get there. First I was to go along a narrow street called 65½ Street, which cut obliquely into a broad boulevard paved with many-colored, bright, glazed bricks. I was to go to a house numbered 654, a sort of roadside residence or restaurant. I was there received by a fat, semi-Oriental maid of no particular age, in a black silk dress, named Todida. She handed me a glass of orange juice. She was big and jolly, and there was a sense of rightness about her. I saw I had arrived ahead of time, 9:00 A.M. I was not due till 1:00 P.M. I asked her to have ham and eggs with me. Instead of answering, she put her face in her hands and went into a trance.

ASSOCIATIONS: The narrow roadway numbered 65½ suggests the period of training in England immediately preceeding the active period of service and the break-through of my feeling when I found I could overcome fear and enjoy my role as fighter pilot. This was the first time in my life I had the full enjoyment of my powers. In school and college I was popular but found no enjoyment in it. Sixty-five is the number of missions over Germany in which I flew successfully. One-half refers to the flight leader who "flunked out" through fear, who said he couldn't pick up the target and flew back. This was an object lesson to me. The boulevard suggests Reims Cathedral and the château where I stayed in Belgium, enjoying the favor of the general and his friends. I stayed there four months, and this may account for the number 4 following 65 on the number of the house — 654. The maid is like no one I have ever seen or imagined. Her name, Todida, suggests three other words: *Tod,* the German word for death; the English verb *to die;* and Dido, the Carthaginian princess in Virgil's *Aeneid,* who voluntarily died upon her funeral pyre when Aeneas, whom she loved, went off and left her. The glass of orange juice suggests the

hopeful feeling I had when I saw the orange groves of California
on my trip west to seek help from a psychiatrist at the advice of a
friend. I had been miserable and depressed for weeks before
making up my mind to undertake this trip.

INTERPRETATION: The narrow, oblique street represents a
breakthrough in the young man's preparation for his combat
experience, during which he learned to overcome fear. The half-
man who would "flunk out" is presumably his own self-doubt,
which was integrated or included with his experience, not merely
repressed. Sixty-five-and-a-half Street therefore stands as a symbol
for the *rite d'entrée* in its entirety — the testing period in which
the initiate, as warrior, is consciously equipped for his task and
discharges it under the pressure of command from the "fathers,"
as officers who represent absolute authority.

The successful accomplishment of the test enabled this young
man to enjoy the approval of a specific officer-father, and the broad
boulevard denotes the broadening of his own mental outlook accordingly. The many-colored, glazed bricks with which the boulevard is paved show that the experience brought him genuinely in
touch with certain new aesthetic and spiritual possibilities of development, but it was only experienced from outside, as a sightseer
might view Reims Cathedral or a fine château during a period of
euphoria.

The dream ends with his recognition that some sort of encounter with inner reality has been missing, and this is now his
present goal, to be reached before it is too late. This new need is
represented by a figure as different from the officer-father as night
from day. In his euphoric mood everything had been straight-
forward, benign, radiant, and solid. In his period of depression
everything was indecisive, malevolent, dark, and shifting. But just
as the broad boulevard makes a sensible and even noble picture
of achievement in the tradition of European culture, so the dream
apparently begins to make sense of the depression by telling him
there is something health-giving in his acceptance of it (the orange
juice). He can take hope from the prospect of discovering the paradoxical qualities of his inner feminine counterpart, an ageless
feminine principle which yet seems to offer a reconciliation of the

conflict of the opposites, Death and Life. Though she is an anima of death, she is also a bearer of new life.

The patient, then, has come to a psychiatrist to seek the inner meaning of his military initiation. Though that experience had enabled him to achieve certain commendable, manly qualities, it failed to acquaint him with the most important secret of all initiation — the experience of death and rebirth as a means of achieving inner as well as outer strength. This integration is expressed by the number four, which we know from studies in analytic psychology to represent a totality which includes or incorporates the feminine principle into the masculine principle, represented by three.

The Navaho war ceremonial, *Where the Two Came to Their Father*,[13] to which I have already alluded in connection with this dream, contains some other interesting points of comparison, two of which are especially relevant. Unlike my patient, the Twins (or Warrior Gods) are warned at the very beginning, as the first part of the *rite d'entrée*, that there is a feminine principle to be reckoned with as well as a masculine. She first appears as a woman representing Old Age. Twice the Twins disobey her warning not to walk in her path, but to walk on her right side, and they grow small and old. Presumably the lesson this teaches is that they must recognize the existence of death as a limitation to the fullness of life and that they must not thoughtlessly overreach themselves in a quest for power. Since only a full acceptance of death can lead to rebirth, they are immediately rewarded for learning their lesson by the appearance of Spider Woman, whose re-creative guidance shows her to be an anima of life, in contrast to the old woman as an anima of death. She gives them each a white feather as a talisman to lead them over the Rainbow Path to the house of the Sun, their Father, where they meet their initiation proper into manhood.[14] In this early episode, as part of a *rite d'entrée*, we have an example in miniature of the experience of death and rebirth containing the central meaning of initiation.

The outward forms of initiation in the myth are clear as day. They are aspects of the hero myth. The Twins are tested by powerful trials of strength, and as they show their fitness to pass these tests, the Sun as Father recognizes them as his sons for the first time and gives them his approval. This provides a parallel with my patient's experience, where the broad boulevard signifies approval by the father, now friendly after having ruthlessly tested him.

In the Navaho story there is reference to a room sparkling with bright colors, analogous to the multi-colored, glazed bricks of the dream, a room in which the Twins undergo their final hardening and receive weapons with which to fight the monsters. Then, according to the pollen painting recorded by Maud Oakes, the two sons become four. After this doubling they all descend through a hole in the sky and overcome the monsters[15] which appears to represent the overcoming of self-centeredness or self-indulgence (the monsters are said to be the products of masturbation). Here also, as in our patient's dream, we have the theme of fear to be overcome. Can it be that the parallel is still closer? As twins they are each one half, the two representing a whole, but they do not therefore become amalgamated into one. Instead, they become four. Do they not express then the same totality referred to in the dream, in which the number four is added to the original number, instead of one-half?

There is a significant difference at this point between the myth and the dream. Following the battle and the overcoming of the monsters, the two (now four) heroes are met and cautioned by Talking God. Here a male god represents a positive relation to the feminine principle as appropriate for the tribal life of a matrilinear culture. But our patient is the product of the patriarchal culture pattern of modern America. Indeed, he was even more paternally conditioned than most Americans, and in this resided his greatest personal problem. In his early years his mother had been for a long period absent through illness, living at her mother's house during which he was tended largely by his father. As an only son he had grown up as the apple of his father's eye, and this father now expected as many great things of him in peacetime as he had accomplished in wartime. But the psyche abhors the hubris of an exclusively masculine adaptation, and because he was in no way prepared, either by his culture, his education, or the influence of his family, to meet the feminine side of his nature, his dreams shows that he is heading straight back to the very beginning — to what the Twins in the Myth learned about walking on the right side of Old Age and thus coming into possession of an effective anima function (Spider Woman). The dream shows him at the point where his masculine, extraverted adaptation has failed him. Todida can give him something to heal his sickness (the orange juice as a life-giving product of mother nature), but she also suggests that he cannot give her anything she apparently wants (bacon and eggs would more appropriately symbolize a wholesome manly breakfast). Instead she goes into a trance. It is the function of the anima to mediate between man and the unconscious; and the trance appears to be her way of indicating that what he needs more than the temporary relief of the cheerful glass of orange juice is a willingness to follow her into those regions of the psyche which border on this unknown territory.

That he did penetrate into unknown territory of the deep unconscious was shown in a dream he had six months later, though only after overcoming great resistances.

DREAM 2: I was in a deep valley beside a swiftly flowing river. On the surface floated a white feather, secured to the bottom by a cord of some kind. I thought the river was the Rhine. Beside me was my mother, who was tired and complained of the noise of an airplane engine nearby. I went over and told the mechanic to stop it, which he did.

ASSOCIATIONS: This is a "grounding" dream. Flying has no further interest for me. I saw the Rhine from the air many times on my war missions over Germany.

INTERPRETATION: The deep valley with its river stands in contrast to the broad street of the initial dream, where everything is manmade and is associated with his new cultural interests. Here he is in nature, where the valley, symbolic of the eternal feminine, carries a river, which symbolizes a new source of creative energy. Flowing from the Alps through country cultivated since Roman times, the Rhine carries also powerful historical associations. By a kind of poetic justice, he finds peace beside that river which flows through what had been enemy country during his wartime experience.

A complete reversal of values has taken place within him since then. Then he was a sky-borne hero; now he is represented as an earthly human being. His act of having the engine turned off is an intimation that his allegiance is changing from Father Sky to Mother Earth in accordance with a voluntary intention, not (as in the initial dream) unconsciously espousing the anima of death. In the initial dream the anima is associated with the neglected feminine principle, which had landed him in a deathlike depression in spite of his outward cheerfulness. Now there is an acceptance of his psychic fatigue, represented by his real mother, who had played so minor or so negative a role in his early life. He has the engine shut off *for her,* and this heralds the beginning of a new kind of relation to women.

In relation to his mother he had been unable either to give or to receive love in any true sense of the word. (When we speak of the capacity to love, we mean, I suppose, the basic recognition which first dawns upon a child that he can receive love and also give it back to his mother.) But this man's personal problem can now be understood only against the background of nature. We can infer that the valley is an archetypal place of rebirth. Following the death of his former self, a man exclusively oriented to his father's expectation and to the larger patriarchal order of culture, he now submits to the rite of the new birth in the maternal order of nature. But why is this not purely regressive? Presumably because the maternal order, though containing the personal mother, gives birth to the river as an expression of a new masculine force, free to leave the maternal valley and pursue its course through the fields and cities of men.

There remains a strange and unexplained element in the dream, the white feather anchored to the stream bed but floating on its surface. In the myth *Where the Two Came to Their Father,* the Warrior Gods, after their encounter with the woman representing Old Age, were given each a white feather by Spider Woman as a talisman. This theme is found in many other traditions, where the questing hero receives from a special woman his protecting or guardian symbol. The patient said that he regarded this as a "grounding" dream; and we may conjecture that the feather, which may in itself symbolize his heroic, sky-borne achievement in overcoming fear, is brought down to earth, where it now stands for a different kind of achievement associated with the mother and with the restorative values of the introverted psychic life of mankind. The Warrior Gods, in contrast, go on to complete their initiation into the father's world *after* having obtained their feather. (Similarly in Case III, Dream 1, the symbol of the Queen Mother is carried by a young man as the culmination of his initiation associated with the mother, before he goes on to his initiation by the father.)

In subsequent dreams, as in the Navaho myth, there seems to be no necessity for the initiand to complete the initiation in one cycle before going on to the next, but rather of a certain oscillation or partial repetition of cycles all the way through. In the Navaho myth, when the masculine powers become too strong, the Twins find female helpers and perform duties toward the feminine, and so it is in the dream material of modern people. The chief psychological meaning of this is the distinction made in the dream between the personal mother and the feather, pointing to a distinction between the mother as a biological container of the infantile psyche and the feather as a symbol of some spiritual expectation engendered in the child at birth, the potentiality of a second birth from a primordial level of the unconscious. Perhaps the dreamer is referred back to this level again. The feather being anchored at this level may be a warning that there is some danger of fixation at this level during analysis and that he will later have to release again this symbol of his air-borne spirit.

If we ask what the mother function means in the light of these dreams, we find that in every case it is some symbolic image of woman associated with the Great Mother. But the dreams all clearly state that the personal mother and her actual effect upon the growing infant and child were crucial to the definition of a certain cultural attitude toward the feminine, and she appears in all the dreams as the personal, maternal element for which the individual in questions feels some old-new responsibility. But however carefully the personal mother problem is tended and the laws of filial piety obeyed, it is not until a suitably compensatory symbol from the archetypal psyche is discovered that the individual is free from his infantile problem.

In these five cases, as in many more, the means by which the compensatory symbol is made available to consciousness and therefore to effective integration by the ego is some form of the initiation archetype, expressed as a rite of new birth with its appropriate threshold rites of passage.

CHAPTER IV

Remaking a Man

I. *All for the Father*

WE SAW in Case V a man who had experienced initiation as the need for acceptance by suitably formal father-figures. His initial dream represented a painful emergence from boyhood into a place of ritual rebirth, an emergence which denoted his symbolic apotheosis as a hero-figure. But because he had not known his mother and had experienced no meaningful rite of separation from her world, he had first to return in fantasy to discover a mother of universal, not personal, nature. In contrast to this case, the young man described in Case III had known his mother all too well; having exhausted the experience of her personal influence, he was ready to go forward into the next stage of development by crossing a significant threshold into the father's world. This is shown in the following dreams:

Case III (continued)

DREAM 2: My mother was dying, and my father was recovering from an illness.

DREAM 3: I was climbing a mountain. Suddenly my path came to an end before a white marble house. There was no wall on the side facing me, and I could look inside as onto a stage. The walls of the house were of white marble, and the place was empty except for a marble sarcophagus at one side upon which lay a white marble figure of myself. A great doorway opened on the stage from behind in the center. As I looked, I saw a veiled priestly figure approaching, bearing a tall staff on the end of which shone a golden disc bright as the sun, flooding the whole place with light. As the disc was brought in, I saw it was divided vertically into two halves. One half represented half a man's face; the other bore the outline of an animal (a bull or ram), below which was an inscription in some ancient language (Greek or Egyptian).

ASSOCIATIONS: The dreamer stated that climbing a mountain "is like overcoming a weakness or surmounting an obstacle. It suggests to me the effort I am making in my analysis."

The white marble house and its open side suggested to him both "a mausoleum and the stage of a Greek theater," and he added: "I have learned with great interest that Greek tragedy may be understood in the light of typical complexes, and I am especially interested in the characters of Oedipus and Orestes. The sarcophagus with a marble effigy of myself made me feel terribly anxious, but this mood quickly changed to a feeling of confidence as I perceived the priestly figure entering the stage. It dispelled the mood of death suggested by the sarcophagus and I felt as if I were renewed by the rays emanating from the sun-symbol he carried on his staff."

INTERPRETATION: In Dream 2 we find a motif compensatory to the patient's conscious thoughts. It shows death or dying as being associated with the mother and renewal associated with the father: in his personal life this young man was symbolically dying as his mother's son and coming to life as his father's son. This personal equation, with its change of emphasis, fittingly introduces the archetypal theme of death and rebirth of Dream 3. That his death in this dream is associated with the mother is further borne out by his association to Oedipus and Orestes, whose tragic fate came from too great preoccupation with the mother. Oedipus married his mother, while Orestes murdered his. From this we can guess that the patient experienced emotions of love and hatred for his mother, who, in her capacity to arouse equal feelings of fascination and fear, represented the Great Goddess in her dual role as creator and destroyer.[1]

If we compare Dream 3 with Dream 1 (p. 47), we find that in each there appears a symbol carried on a staff. The carved bust of the Queen Mother in Dream 1 embodied the archetypal image of the mother in transition from a personal to an impersonal line of development, marking the shift of feeling from the mother to the father. We might therefore assume that the sun symbol of the third dream is the archetypal father image, but it is not stated in the dream and only appears in a confusingly composite form as a sun disc containing both human and animal characteristics. To get our bearings and see if our hypothesis can be verified, let us turn to Harrison's further discussion of the Kouretes.

She had already said that "the Kouretes project from their body a Greatest Kouros," and with this figure we identified the dreamer's newly found role in Dream 1. But the Greatest Kouros is subject to a higher power, the god, in this case Zeus, who came to be "all for the father." In the dream of his personal parents the patient was, so to speak, all for the father; so if the sun disc is for him a form of the father image, we must reconcile its archaic character with the mythological figure of Zeus.

In *The Origin of the Olympic Games* by F. M. Cornford, we learn that "in Crete . . . the birth of a divine child, called Zeus, was concealed from his father Kronos, who had eaten his other children. . . . The concealment was aided by a dance of young men in arms, called Kouretes."[2] Can we trace the descent of this line, which bore allegiance to the mother, to the tradition in Greece which was "all for the father"?

Cornford informs us that the Olympic Games began as a ritual foot-race of the Kouretes. "The race, we may suppose, determined who should be *the* Kouros . . . of his year. The winner received, not a prize of commercial value such as were usual in funeral games, but a symbol of his office as vegetation-*daimon* the branch of the sacred tree."[3] This was a branch of the wild olive, and the victor was crowned with its leaves. But the wild olive was a moon-tree, of which Miss Harrison has collected numerous examples on Mycenean gems, and "Minoan mythology knows of the Moon-Queen, Pasiphaë, — *She who shines for all*, mother of the holy, horned Bull-Child" — [4] to whose service the Kouretes were dedicated, as they were to the service of the Mountain Mother. "Even before it became the moon-tree, the holy olive probably belonged to Earth . . . The Kouretes 'slept on heaps of fresh green leaves' . . . in order that they might draw oracular wisdom from the Earth.

Olympia also had its Earth oracle and its cult of Demeter Chamyne, whose priestess sat enthroned in a place of honour and witnessed the Games of Zeus."[5]

Secondly, the tradition of the birth of a divine child "is firmly rooted in the monuments and cults of Olympia. The legend says 'when Zeus was born Rhea committed the safe-keeping of the child to the Idaean Daktyls or Kouretes, who came from Ida in Crete. . .' [and the holy child is] 'Zeus the Saviour' who as Pindar says honored it, with the Saviour of the City, Sosipolis . . . — The child Sosipolis . . . was represented not as an infant, but as a boy," the same figure as the "Kouros of the Cretan hymn, who comes 'for the Year,' and brings with him the blossoming of the Seasons."[6] This youth must be born anew each year.

Zeus, then, was originally a year god and as such maintains an obvious connection with the sun. Harrison indicates that he *was* the sun. Zeus and Apollo were identical in early Greek mythology; now one, now the other takes over the function of the Greatest Kouros, becoming the male god associated with the sun. In the Olympian pantheon Zeus became the Father and Apollo the Sun, but this separation of attributes was artificial and is unknown in earlier traditions. Olympian Zeus was originally the leader of the band of initiated youths and also the sun.

This argument could lead into a maze of primitive vegetation mythology, with its many false rationalizations of the type so often put forth by Frazer, but Cornford allows us to distinguish once for all between fertility rites as such and the symbolism of initiation:

> The Easter death and resurrection of the same individual is evidently at first distinct from the death of the Old Year at the hands of the New, where the two individuals are necessarily different and the death might be a real death. The death, on the other hand, which is followed by a resurrection cannot be real; it must always have been a mimetic rite.

This mimetic rite was an initiation ceremony.

> It "was in essence a ceremony of New Birth, of mock death and resurrection . . . It gives us the ritual which is needed to complete the religion of the Mother and Child and the Kouretes . . .

We conclude that, while the birth of the new Year God was celebrated in the cult of the infant Sosipolis, his Easter death and resurrection — his initiation or inauguration when he passes from childhood to youth — was marked in ritual . . . and in myth.[7]

Having accounted for the solar and anthropomorphic attributes of Zeus, we must now account for the theriomorphic component on the other side of the disc in our dream symbol. With what we already know, this is an easy step. The young Zeus was not always represented in human form, but often as an animal. "The Givers of all Increase, the Horae, bring back the God in the Spring, be he Bull or human Kouros . . . Any young full-grown creature can be the animal form of the Kouros, can be sacrificed, sanctified, divinized, and become the *Agathos Daimon,* the 'vegetation spirit,' the luck of the year."[8] That the animal in question was Zeus is confirmed by Cornford: "At Argos, Karnos the Ram was called Zeus and *Hegetor.* . . . In ancient days the leader of the annual procession might be a holy Bull or a Goat and at Athens the Kouros in Bull form and human form came in procession to the theatre."[9] Finishing this line of investigation, both Cornford and Gilbert Murray have traced the elements of Greek drama to their beginnings in early ritual, where tragedy is found to spring from the mimetic death ceremony and comedy from the rebirth ceremony of the sacrificed god.[10]

The theme of sacrifice therefore comes into our initiation series at this point. This sacrifice is an act of submission experienced as a meaningful initiatory ordeal, to be distinguished from the trial of strength appropriate to the accomplishment of heroes. The patient in question had undertaken his analysis in the spirit of heroic conquest suggestive of climbing a mountain which he associates with achieving self-mastery. His dream corrects this attitude by showing him to himself as having died, that is, having submitted to a power greater than himself — a power which then appears with its message of rebirth. In Christ's life also, as we shall presently see, we find many elements of the hero myth; but these are the humanly triumphant moments, to be distinguished from the initiatory passion leading through death to resurrection in the Father.

We are now in a position to interpret the elements of Dreams 1 and 3. In Dream 1 the dreamer ran to the head of the line of young men; this has its parallel in the ritual foot-race for a prize, the winner becoming the Greatest Kouros and receiving a prize — in the patient's case, not a wild olive branch but a carved figure of the Great Mother herself. In Dream 2 the sun symbol has in all respects the attributes of the Kouros, a sun-god, half-animal and half-human, who embodies the primitive notion of a Father. Even the confusion as to whether the animal is a bull or a ram is symbolically meaningful, suggesting their propinquity in the adjacent Spring signs, Aries and Taurus, in the symbolism of astrology. Even the antique tradition of the ritual is suggested by the inscription below the animal. This is remarkable: the patient had no conscious knowledge of the symbolic significance of the events of his dreams, yet his dreams unfold as logically as if he had produced a work of classical scholarship.

Finally, all the separate elements of the two dreams, the band of young men, the procession, the foot-race, the leader, the mother symbol, the trial of strength, the sacrifice, the image of death and entombment, and the revivifying sun disc with its correlates (new-born son, animal, and father), together with the setting of the last dream upon a stage associated with a distant but actual ritual drama of death and rebirth — all these point to the emergence, in the unconscious of a modern man, of an archetypal pattern of initiation which marks a transition from childhood to youth.

II. *Classical Antiquity and the Christian Dilemma*

So FAR we have used no anthropological evidence concerning actual initiation ceremonies such as have been reported by field workers studying the remaining tribal societies of the world in our time. Our knowledge has been taken from the history of religions which have come down to us in literary or art forms, whose massages can easily be misleading. We must examine, for instance, the possibility that these ritual forms are merely reflections of a changing social structure — in this instance, from the Creto-Mycenean period of Mediterranean culture, with its matriarchal heritage, to the golden age of Greek patriarchalism, a change which covers the period roughly from 1500 to 400 b.c. An early follower of Jung or of Freud might eagerly have seized upon this historical parallel with our dream material and used it to prove that earlier social forms survive in the individual, that ontogeny repeats phylogeny.[11] But this generalization places us in danger of losing the true psychological significance of the dream experience *for the person having it*, of reading what it means to us rather than what it meant to him.

Neumann warns against the kind of schematization in dealing with any archetype:

> The manifestations illustrating the archetype may belong to the most diverse epochs, times, and cultures; a monument of a late culture may symbolize a late phase or archetypal development. Similarly, in the analysis of a human individual, symbols and symptoms of future and later developments may appear at the very beginning, and conversely infantile and archaic elements may present themselves in stages of relatively fuller psychic development. . . . For this reason, the most that can be achieved by an exposition in the field of depth psychology is a compromise between conscious schematization and the uniqueness of the material that fills and overflows the schema. Thus it will always be possible to criticize the schema for being far from reality, and to criticize the material chosen to illustrate the schema for being accidental. . . . [But these objections will not] prevent such an exposition, inadequate as we know it to be, from helping the whole, living man toward a fruitful orientation in the living reality of the psyche.[12]

In Case V the historical parallel, the transition from the Creto-Mycenean to the Greek culture pattern, cannot be correlated with the dream material exactly because of the absence in the dream material of any conflict such as we know must have existed historically. The patient appears to have made a smooth transition from mother to father by means of an archetypal pattern of death and rebirth associated with an experience of initiation. There was no such easy transition from the matriarchal culture patterns of Crete to the patriarchal patterns of Athens. It took the Trojan War, among other things, to bring this about, to say nothing of the historical implications of Theseus' penetration into the Cretan labyrinth to overcome the Minotaur and free Ariadne. Nor did the conflict between matriarchal and patriarchal powers rest there. Patriarchal Greece was conditioned by the proximity of Eleusis and its powerful cult of the Mother and Daughter, Demeter and Kore. Even today revivals of Euripides' *Bacchae* present the indelible lesson that patriarchalism, if pushed too far, provokes the vengeance of the unconscious feminine powers. Yet the patriarchal order won out politically, and from patriarchal Rome we hear Cicero's nostalgic cry of response to the Mother and her rites of initiation:

> Much that is excellent and divine does Athens seem to me to have produced and added to our life, but nothing better than those Mysteries by which we are formed and moulded from a rude and savage state of humanity; and, indeed, in the Mysteries we perceive the real principles of life, and learn not only to live happily, but to die with a fairer hope.[13]

We are left with the very striking fact that a piece of ancient history comes to life in these two dreams and that they effectively recapitulate the inner meaning of the religious changes which transferred the balance of power from a Mother religion to a Father religion, without totally relinquishing the importance of the Mother as a prize to be won along the way of initiation, which finds its culmination in the Father rites.

I cannot but conclude that the dreams, like the sensitive scholarship I have drawn on to explain them, really mean to impart to the dreamer this message and not some other. As usual in the interpretation of dreams, we must never forget their compensatory relationship to the conscious mind. This young man was of Anglo-Saxon background and was brought up in the Protestant faith, which he had sincerely tried to apply to his life and had failed. His dreams presented him with a totally other, pre-Christian pattern of development in which could be seen the possibility of knitting together the cultural attitudes appropriate to mother and father, which he had failed to do in the Christian way. Having been deeply affected by his own mother in the early years of life, he could not suddenly swing over to the father's world without amputating all he had previously been. He had attempted this, and it had pushed him into a severe neurosis. In his analysis he was enabled to find a suitable compensation to his condition and was led by his dreams to recognize a pattern of development closely analogous to the initiation pattern of pre-Christian Greece and of the whole Mediterranean culture complex which we call classic. His dreams presented him with a pattern not exclusively matriarchal or patriarchal, nor of conflict between these principles, but a pattern in which the two are functioning in harmony, thus pointing up his need to achieve psychological unity in relation to these two principles.

This may be the inner need of all adolescents, and in a society such as we know existed in ancient times, it was given full expression in a socio-religious sense by means of the initiation rites. Since we have no adequate social medium for expressing this today, at least for young men with my patient's type of problem and orientation, he had to find the psychological equivalent somewhat belatedly in psychotherapy. Possibly what helped him most was to learn from his dreams that such a pattern of development could exist; indeed, *had* existed. This gave him the incentive to go ahead and balance his own equation between mother and father and grow up to his years.

I do not mean to imply this young man would have had no inkling of initiation if it had not been for his dreams of classical antiquity. Of course this is not so. Anyone with a feeling for history, even though scantily instructed, can sense the pattern of initiation during the adolescent period, and many of the forms it once took are still in evidence today, even though many of them appear only as fossil specimens. We are aware of the meaning of army life as a kind of trial of strength implying an initiation to the Father, reflecting that religion of soldiers from Asia which "spread like wild-fire through the length and breadth of the Roman empire in the first four centuries of our era."[14] This was the cult of Mithra, in which we find recognizable elements, among them a sun-god, a sacred animal, a sacrifice and baptism, and the ritual of death and rebirth. These rituals and others found their way into Christianity and can be studied in some of the Catholic rituals today.[15]

The fact remains that initiation as a meaningful process of

transition between Mother and Father, or between inner and outer worlds of experience, has been almost entirely lost in Christian times. Essentially patriarchal in this respect, Christian initiation begins with the theme of overcoming the Mother and/or being rescued from her clutches by the loving and approving Father, who can protect the initiate from the nightmares of childhood and bring him to a state of grace. As Neumann so aptly remarks, Father is equivalent to Heaven in the patriarchal scheme of things.[16]

Nevertheless, within this limited framework the initiation pattern may still function quite well for many people. A dream of a modern youth illustrates this and, as a corollary, shows Mother as a genuine threat to such an experience of spiritual grace.

Case VI (Male, age 24)

DREAM 1: I have crossed a stream when I am attacked by a huge eagle. I have only a small pocketknife with which to overcome the eagle, and though I fight back, I know I must fail. Then I see coming from my right a procession of men, the leader carrying a staff with a single crosspiece at the top. I feel confident that these men will somehow rescue me from the eagle, though they are coming at a slow, measured pace.

ASSOCIATIONS: The fight with the eagle seems to be associated with my fear of failure to achieve supremacy in my academic career. I am not satisfied with just getting by; I want special recognition and I seem to frustrate myself. I make stupid mistakes. I lack the full conviction that I am qualified for the career I have chosen. The pocketknife is a small, pearl-handled knife given me by my father. I like owning it, but it is too small for ordinary purposes. It only sharpens pencils, which is better done by a mechanical sharpener.

The man leading the procession impressed me by the calm dignity with which he carried the cross.

INTERPRETATION: The eagle seems to be associated with ambition, but why is this principle so aggressive or so dangerous for him? Is it unnatural for such a young man to be intensely ambitious? Actually, his vaulting ambition was motivated by an inner wish to live up to his mother's expectations that he would achieve some kind of supremacy and not simply meet the demands of a routine job. Yet he was in fact a gifted young man, who certainly gave the impression of being serious at his work and one who might go far. Perhaps, then, his qualms were unfounded. When his mother had fed his ambitions, was she not absolutely right and therefore a good mother to do so?

Looking into his relation with his father, I found the explanation of this danger from the mother. The patient had never on any level really accepted his father's view of life or that of the men who represented his father's world. They seemed to him materialistic, dull, and purely concerned with achieving practical goals. In contrast, his mother had ideals and had selflessly encouraged him to leave home at an early age to find recognition in the larger world. She had, of course, unconsciously implied that success would not be enough: he must achieve pre-eminence in whatever field he chose, and he had accordingly been pushed into the inflation of a typical *puer aeternus*. There were other dreams which showed that he had come to the end of his idealism, because it was not at bottom his; it was his mother's.

This battle with the mother represented his battle with an unreal, because unspecific, ideal, arising by compensation from his mother's own subliminal feeling of inferiority at not having achieved an impersonal goal of her own. Her husband, with his strong patriarchalism, had robbed her of any conscious incentive to make of herself much of anything beyond the role assigned to her by convention, that of wife and mother. She had never even considered the possibility that she might study something, learn a trade, or even cultivate her aesthetic and religious interests, apart from her home and her duty to him. As the deeper stratifications of this case came into view, one could see clearly into the early life history of this family in which the mother, unconscious of her own motives, had dreamed into that little boy, her son, a wish that by some special power he might fulfill the inner need to liberate her own longings, which at that time seemed forever closed to her in the sacrifice she had made to marriage.

Such psychological events conform to the strictest possible determinism. The naturally maternal woman, if she has no opportunity to develop or find recognition for her feminine capacity for spiritual understanding, is impelled to sacrifice her love blindly on the altar of the coming generation of patriarchal men in the hope that somehow, through her son, her longing for individual fulfillment will be realized. He in turn may live the first part of his life as if trying to satisfy this longing and, pushing his father's values aside, may seek unconsciously to develop those talents in himself which his mother would have wished for herself. It is also true that many men, in response to this maternal motivation, have achieved remarkable things. But the price they have paid is a loss of masculine identity, a crippling resistance to finishing their work,[17] and an inability to feel the satisfaction they and their mothers expected. A great many more men, fortunately, fail to satisfy the maternal ambition for them because the inner wish to achieve identity through the father makes itself felt strongly enough at the close of adolescence.

Such was the case in question. The analysis of this young man had made him doubt the validity for him of his mother's unconscious wish that he achieve pre-eminence in her terms, and in the dream he encounters her unconscious will-to-power as a dangerous eagle which he must overcome. But because of his lack of relation to the father, his equipment for the battle (the pocketknife) is inadequate. He cannot cope with this danger single-handed, but only with the help of the masculine group with its patriarchal leader, which comes slowly but surely to his rescue.

As in the earlier cases, the procession of men and the staff held by the leader comprise an archetypal image of group initiation. But whereas in the other dreams the symbol carried on the staff was either matriarchal or patriarchalized on an archaic cultural level, here the symbol is the cross, embodying the concept of Christian sacrifice with its love for the Holy Victim who left his mother at an early age and, after a full spiritual development, ascended at last to sit upon the right hand of the Father. The mystery of the cross as a symbol of initiation is an example of a universal theme, the initiatory ordeal.

It might be assumed that Christ's Crucifixion and his Ascension after 40 days to the Father would have disposed of all vestiges of the Mother. It is therefore surprising to learn that in the most venerable ecclesiastic ritual, in both the Roman and Greek Orthodox traditions, the events of Good Friday did not mark the beginning of this final rite, as they so frequently do in our modern Western churches. They were merely the prelude to a great ritual of initiation starting on Holy Saturday and ending in the early hours of Easter Sunday. The ritual was essentially a return to the Mother for the sake of rebirth, represented by the living water of the baptismal font; but this is not self-evident and we have to dig rather deep into Christian symbolism to find this essential meaning. Watts tells us:

> Clearly, it involves the most extraordinary complex of symbols, since the water is all in one the Womb of the Virgin, the stuff of the world, the emblem of Purity or Voidness in which the past leaves no stain, and the depths into which the neophyte descends with Christ in his death, and from which he rises with Christ in his Resurrection. All in all, Baptism represents the involution and evolution of the Spirit, the descent into and ascent from the waters being the whole "play" of God in dis-membering and re-membering himself, in dying into multiplicity and rising into Unity. . . .
> Strictly speaking, the candidates should be thrice immersed in the Font so that the water covers their heads, and at the same time the priest gives them the new Name, which is "in Christ", conjoining it with the Name of the Holy Trinity. . . . After immersion the "new Christs" are again vested in white, and given candles lit from the New Fire.[18]

Jung tells us that the Font or "baptismal bath was described as a *piscina* (fish-pond) quite early. This presupposes that the believers were fishes, as is in fact suggested by the gospels (for instance Matt. 4:19). There Christ wants to make Peter and Andrew 'fishers of men,' and the miraculous draught of fishes (Luke 5:10) is used by Christ himself as a paradigm for Peter's missionary activity."[19] We saw in Case I, Dream 3 (p. 49), how the symbolism of being caught as a fish was represented in a woman's dream by the feathers of the trout fly hooked up each nostril. Thus she experienced a sense of being "caught" by the archetypal experience of initiation.

The immediacy of water as a symbol is explained by Jung as "the living power of the psyche."[20] Von Franz points out that this "living power of the psyche," when it appears in patients during analysis, calls for a sense of containment and at the same time is a purifying experience. She observes a need to approach the unconscious creatively is often ushered in by a crying fit. This is not merely a personal expression of sadness or self-pity, but is a genuine response to an archetypal image, as in the creation myths where the initial reaction of the creator god is to cry.[21]

This was demonstrated very clearly by a woman who came to me for help because of three frightening dreams she had had over a period of several weeks. One was of an earthquake, another of a powerful wind, and the third of a threat of fire. Upon examination I found her to be in a chronic state of emotional paralysis, isolated, and fearful of undertaking any new project. Her personal relationships yielded no significant data; she was outwardly secure and should have had nothing to worry about. But she had talent as a writer which had long been neglected, either from inertia or from some indefinable lack of confidence. She was not morbidly depressed, merely suspended.

I explained that I thought the dreams showed a strong movement in the psyche to break up her stalemate and that this would of course be at first exceedingly painful. From ancient times the four elements — earth, air, fire, and water — were supposed to represent the changing structure of what we today would call the objective psyche. It is as if these elements, appearing in such a disturbed form, provided a strong activation to change her psychic condition and reestablish her creative ability and feeling. Even as we talked, I could see her anxiety emerging at the prospect of such a change, but with it came a new animation. Only three elements had appeared in her dreams. Where was the fourth element, water? At the next interview she brought some interesting drawings representing her earth, air, and fire dreams, and then, after a brief conversation, she began to cry. In her tears was the missing water, which now promised to dissolve the rigidity of her conscious thoughts.

Von Franz completes the interpretation of this type of experience in an analogy with alchemy:

> One of the beginning stages of the alchemical work is very often the *liquefactio,* the turning into liquid, in order to undo the *prima*

materia which is very often hardened or solidified in a wrong way and therefore cannot be used to make the philosopher's stone. The minerals have first to be liquefied. Naturally, the underlying chemical image is to melt and then use the metal out of the ore, but *lique-factio* has very often in the alchemical word also a connotation of being a dissolution of the personality in tears and despair . . . and that throws a light on what crying means, namely it effects an *abaisse-ment du niveau mental* through which then the creative content of the unconscious can break through. That is specially the case with people who tend to have a consolidated or rather rational conscious habitual attitude and therefore need this liquefying process in order to approach the layer where the unconscious can come up and speak to them.[22]

It is precisely such psychic liquefaction which seems to occasion the need to produce a suitable symbol of containment, wherein the subject is at once ritually purified and ritually drowned. The inevitable symbolism of a return to the Mother, while the officiating priest personifies the Father, lends to the Christian rite of baptism a sense of universality.

The theme of return to the Mother and of the need for rebirth from the Father is stamped upon the traditional representation of the Crucifixion, where the sorrowing Marys stand or kneel at the foot of the Cross. This is a memory of the pre-Christian saviors who, as sons and lovers of the Great Goddess, were yearly sacrificed and reborn among the lamentations of the throng of wailing women who roamed the hills and deserts of Mesopotamia, mourning the dead Tammuz or Osiris or Attis. These mother-son religions were in conflict with the monothestic religions from which Christianity and Mohammedanism sprang, which scorned ritual and exacted a stern devotion to an all-powerful father-god.

Around the crucified figure of Christ and the ritual of baptism experienced by his followers, there seems to have taken place a kind of metaphysical miracle through which these antagonistic traditions were joined. The regenerating power of the Mother and the spiritualizing power of the Father were for a moment balanced in an equal and opposite tension, which provided early Christians with the experience of initiatory liberation.

In the patristic tradition this miraculous conjunction of opposites is brought out clearly in the equal and opposite figures of the

Virgin and John the Baptist. In an impressive fifteenth-century icon from the School of Moscow[23] we see the figure of Christ seated between two standing figures, the Virgin on one side, John the Baptist on the other. They face Christ with open hands, suggesting their submissiveness to his superior being. Of John the Baptist, in this connection, Evdokimov tells us he is violent with the violence of Christ, the archetype of which violence is found in the figure of Elias (Elijah) of the Old Testament, who was vehement without mercy.[24] God was said to have taken Elijah to Heaven, saying, "Climb up to heaven, . . . and I will become a pilgrim on earth. For, if thou were to remain on earth, the human race, chastised so often by thee, would be reduced to nothing."[25] This aggressive emotional zeal for reform was, in the Carmelite tradition, tempered by the gentleness of the Virgin. Thus the violence of John the Baptist becomes the violence of one who is "meek and lowly in heart" (Matthew 11:29).[26]

The connection of this tradition with initiation lies in the probability that John the Baptist was the potential leader of the mystery religion of the Essenes, a monastic community living in the desert and practicing a strict asceticism. On the other hand, John is traditionally represented as a man from the desert in a "raiment of camel's hair, and a leathern girdle about his loins; and his meat was locusts and wild honey" (Matthew 3:4). This man of nature, who is also the instrument of consciousness concerning justice and the preparation for final things, is very like a primitive shaman raised to the level of a director of conscience in the old Judaic style.[27]

Evdokimov sees in this figure of John the Baptist an archetype of the masculine, as he sees in the Virgin an archetype of the feminine. In this role she is not the Mother of the Nativity; she is under the sign of the Pentecost, she who bears not the infant Jesus but the new age to come. As John presides over those who come as athletes and soldiers of Christ to receive the initiatory rite of chrism, so the Virgin withholds herself from the power of action and triumphs through the victorious purity of her being.[28] She therefore *is* the water of rebirth.

The Christ of this tradition is the universal archetype of the human being in whose mystical (we would say psychic) body is created a symbol which is both masculine and feminine for it is the place of their integration.[29] Together they provide the means of salvation in the Christian sense, forming a composite master and mistress of initiation for all who are capable of perceiving the Christian mystery as an inner process. The need for such wisdom, and the correction of the evils which its absence entails, comes to light in the dreams of patients in analysis.

Returning to Case VI — and to the theme of baptism as an initiatory symbol — the young man's dream began: "I have crossed a stream when I am attacked by a huge eagle." The end of the dream provided the image of the cross as the rescuing Christian symbol; here at the beginning we find the reference to water as a natural force at the place for a threshold crossing (i.e., *rite de passage*). We know that the patient had been exposed to the power of a negative mother which he was unable to combat. What if, instead of falling into the neurotic condition which followed, he had experienced a meaningful ritual, a baptismal purification? We have already seen the importance of the river in dreams as providing a meaningful return to the positive mother for the sake of renewal. This young man evidently needed a ritual to separate him from the negative effect of his mother's unconscious power-complex. In the absence of any meaningful rite he was vulnerable to the demonic power of the maternal archetype, exactly like an unbaptised pagan and he had not even the measure of safety provided in the rites of a peasant community.[30]

In medieval Europe, Christian baptism replaced many indigenous rites associated with purifying babies at birth, freeing them from the ritual taboos prevailing around childbirth. The newborn child was thought to be vulnerable to attack from evil spirits, especially witches (who are, as we know, negative mother figures). On the early Christian level of awareness, baptism became a rite of separation, not only from the actual mother, but also from the terrors of the pagan unconscious with its tendency to degenerate into a state of primitive participation. Even baptism was none too certain to provide a safe refuge from these dangers, since in early medieval times the cult of the Virgin had not overcome the doubtful magic of tradition surviving from the old goddesses of fertility. Christianity, with its strong patriarchal heritage and its trinitarian consciousness, strenuously opposed and finally suppressed all natural matriarchal culture patterns, and the burning of witches went on into the eighteenth century.

It is only now that the inner content of what was so thoroughly abolished in its outward form comes to light on an inner level and we may become aware of the tremendous loss we have suffered religiously from the purging of those meaningful initiatory rituals from our culture. Baptism has become a formal rite to such an extent that it has largely been pushed back to infancy and the official Catholic position is that no living psychic experience need occur.

[Baptism] confers regeneration "automatically" (*ex opere operato*) whether the candidate actually understands what is happening or not. . . . But the tragedy of merely formal Baptism is not that it is given to people without understanding . . . but [that it] remains the empty enactment of a myth to which the keys have been lost.[31]

From our studies of dream symbolism, as from our study of the early ecclesiastical traditions, we have learned to observe a certain order in the sequence of the baptismal initiation. Baptism is followed by chrism and then by communion. At one time these provided the three basic principles of an initiation of youth in the Christian sense "corresponding to the three degrees of the mystic life: purification, illumination, and union."[32]

Because Baptism and Chrism, washing and anointing, transform man into Christ, he enters into that Communion-by-sacrifice of the divine and the human which involves union with God and humanity. He is thus ready to participate in the Mass, so that after Chrism he is admitted to First Communion.[33]

In the triple rite thus outlined we encounter that universal rite of passage which accords with van Gennep's original classification basic to all threshold rites: a rite of separation, a rite of transition, and a rite of incorporation. Baynes enlarges upon this scheme as follows:

The three stages of initiation in the pagan mystery-cults were sometimes symbolized by three concentric rings. The outer ring represented the rite of purification or lustration; the middle ring, the ordeals and the sacrifice; and the inner ring, the identification with god. The same symbol could express the three stages of realization —experience, reflection, and understanding.[34]

In a subtle way this description clothes the bare skeleton of van Gennep's classification with the living flesh of initiation. The rite thus reveals, in each individual case, a psychological as well as a spiritual meaning.

This account of Christian initiation, though presented in accordance with empirical observations, may strike the churchgoing Christian or the theologian as narrowed by a dogmatic or expository approach to religion. What is lacking, from this point of view, is an apologetic or correlational approach to the subject, especially an account of the changes in Christian theology and in ritual practice through the centuries which have sought to correct the one-sidedness to which we object. (We have also not attempted to describe the valuable use which many churchmen are now making of the insights derived from depth psychology, both in counselling their parishioners and, in some cases, in providing psychotherapy.)

The whole rite, including confirmation, takes place in infancy in the Eastern church. In the West this was partially corrected by rescuing the confirmation rite from this seemingly-regressive trend and making it available to older children or adults, who had reached an age when they could be said to make a conscious choice in the direction of their salvation. In such historical sects as the Cathari (who influenced Christian ecclesiastical tradition far more than is generally known) the baptismal rite was the crowning achievement as an initiation test only for those who could forswear all sexual expression, even in their marriages. Baptism was symbolized by the Pentecostal fire. Those who were baptised were the Perfects, who made of baptism a final rite of incorporation through the symbol of bread, and whose function was to provide the Believers with the blessing of consolation. Many of the Perfects were women, and we may perceive in these rites an attempt to universalize the rite of initiation in that typically Christian spirit of the early Fathers, who believed that the doctrine should be "proclaimed upon the house tops" rather than be kept secret, as the antique mysteries had been.[35]

In modern church ritual, von Franz reminds us:

> The Protestant confirmation and the Catholic First Communion are, *mutatis mutandis,* remnants of primitive initiation rites. . . . In certain Italian villages the priest still gives the boy a hard slap on the face as a memory of the ordeals of initiation. With us Protestants, the boy often receives his first long trousers and a watch; he moves from the timeless dreaming state of childhood to time-awareness, and manhood. . . .[36]

Von Franz made these observations in a paper pointing out the dangerous increase of delinquency due to the collective appearance of the *puer aeternus* problem in our time and the failure of modern religious movements to meet it adequately. She sees an urgent need for inner psychic religious experience, begun by the Catholic mystics and the Protestants, which needs to be carried further with the help of the insights of depth psychology, especially those of Jung with his awareness of the religious need.

This development frequently leads to an exceedingly fruitful cross-fertilization of psychology and religion, the experimental nature of which transcends both the atheistic hubris of those earlier psychologists who were impelled to disregard all traditional religious systems as outworn superstition, and the unreality of those religious leaders who have been unable to accept an anthropocentric as well as a theocentric approach to problems of the spiritual life.

It is not only in a Christian context that the experience of initiation engages our interest in this new sense. Initiation in a traditional Jewish context becomes as important, at times even more important, with its living memory of the rite of circumcision as the expression of the ancient covenant of Abraham: "My convenant shall be in your flesh for an everlasting covenant" (Genesis 17:13). Unlike the Christian boy, whose baptism has usually left scarcely any memory trace except in the personal unconscious, the Jewish boy who has experienced the rite of circumcision on the eighth day after birth knows that he has been received into the religion of his fathers by the evidence of his senses. If he knows more than this, he knows that in some way he has been sexually as well as spiritually prepared for his future role as a bridegroom, with its initiatory meaning for both himself and his bride. In accordance with this ritual, Gaster tells us, "it becomes immediately clear why the Hebrew word for 'bridegroom' (viz. *hatan*) derives from a root meaning 'to circumcise.' "

Here we are not concerned with circumcision as an initiatory ordeal as it is practiced in the so-called puberty rites. The Jewish rite known as the Brit (i.e., covenant), performed skillfully by the mohel, causes no suffering to the infant and cannot be thought to represent symbolic castration, as Hobson clearly shows.[37] Even as a representation of mother-son separation, which is a basic theme in all circumcision fantasies as we meet them in analytical practice, this rite minimizes its actual meaning in favor of the symbolic meaning for the future development of the child.

Both Hobson and Seligman stress the symbolic meaning of circumcision, the latter especially in reference to the Old Testament conceptions. He points out that infant circumcision became a ritual practice only after the settlement of the Jews in Palestine. By this time the dreaded danger of the children of Israel falling under the power of the Great Goddess and her Baalim was largely in the past. "The import of the newly emerging religion of Abraham is that those powers must not, and need not, any longer be worshipped." From this time on, they practiced circumsion in a purely affirmative sense:

> [It is not] a magical means to ward off the dreaded danger . . . [but] has become the seal which they have set to the covenant. The ritual is subordinated to the Word, and the Word is the conscious realization of a meaning which had been only incipiently present in earlier forms of the ritual. Further, the forging of a link with the ancestral lineage is no longer the ultimate goal of the rite, which now finds its consummation in the link with God.[38]

Thus this form of initiation, like the Christian baptismal rite, aims at incorporation of the individual with God in essentially the same sequence of events — beginning with purification, and ending with atonement.

What is abundantly clear from these studies is the overwhelming importance in both Christianity and Judaism of the patriarchal tradition inherent in all monotheistic religions. Hobson sees the early date of infant circumcision as excluding the mother, at the outset, from the boy's spiritual life.[39] Seligman considers "that the early performance aims at consecrating the whole of the individual's life to the covenant." He also points out that "as long as the ritual does not sink to the level of sheer routine conformity, it also involves on the part of the parents the early realization that their son will be dependent upon God in a deeper sense than he depends upon them."[40]

I am inclined to agree with Seligman that the mother is not really excluded, but is even included in the true inner sense of things, since in the monotheistic religions her son's God is also her God.[41] An interesting example of this among my patients is a young Jewish woman who had been brought up as a rather half-hearted Christian until her marriage to a man whose family, though not Orthodox, had maintained a good relation to the essential traditions of Judaism. At first she felt ill at ease in this environment, but at length found her natural Jewish faith and her own religious identity in response to the circumcision rite of her first-born son.

Seligman's psychological conclusion, which does justice to the Christian baptism as well as to the circumcision rite, is apt in this connection. Because the initiation archetype can no longer be regarded merely as regional or tribal by anyone in our society, he says, the level of consciousness that was reached in the religious past calls "for reinterpretation in the light of our analytical insight; the Word of God may need to be related to a situation which we have come to recognize as an inner situation." He suggests that we must "look for the 'promised land' also in our own souls, and that we can share in God's creative power only by coming to terms with the psychic forces into which mother and father, earth and heaven have now shrunk — or grown."[42] The young woman whose experience of her son's circumcision rite I have mentioned, for example, could hardly have come to her realization without crossing a bridge provided by analytical psychology, and this was facilitated by her husband's acceptance of the psychological approach to religion for himself.

Judaism in the West, since the fourteenth century, has developed another rite which admirably complements the circumcision rite by providing in early puberty a rite of admitting the boy into the religio-social circle of his elders. This rite, the Bar Mitzvah, has stirred the admiration and frequently the envy of modern Christians because it seems to give the boy an individual part in the conscious direction of family affairs and thus seems to promote a civilizing process more effectively than the Christian confirmation, which merely initiates collectively a group of boys and girls who remain uninstructed concerning their social role and social status.

Some modern Jewish commentators, however, find the Bar Mitzvah lacking in much the same way we have criticized the Christian confirmation rite. According to Gaster:

> During the past hundred years, under the initial impetus of the Reform movement, the favorite solution has been to substitute for the individual Bar Mitzvah ceremony a collective "confirmation" of juveniles at the festival of the Feast of Weeks (Pentecost) . . . open to girls as well as boys and thus take cognizance of the fact that the social and communal status of women has indeed changed appreciably since the days when the traditional Bar Mitzvah was established.

But Gaster finds that this solution merely confuses the issue and believes that the Bar Mitzvah, even in the Orthodox tradition, fails in its ostensible promise to equip thirteen-year-olds with true socio-religious status.

> In the first place, in Western society today a boy of thirteen is not, in fact, an adult; he is still a minor. He does not marry, does not become a responsible member of a household, and cannot enter into legal obligations. Moreover, within the sphere of the Jewish community itself, he is not—as a rule—eligible for full membership in the congregation and certainly not for any active voice or executive position. . . . To be sure, the bar mitzvah boy is reckoned thenceforth as one of the ten males required to form a *minyan*, but the *minyan* itself . . . has degenerated to the level of the mere formal quorum for public devotions. Moreover, on the American scene, the boy actually is often relegated to membership in a "junior congregation" — a device which deprives him of his "civil rights." . . . What is granted *de jure* is denied *de facto*.[43]

Gaster presents some interesting suggestions as to how the Bar Mitzvah might be elaborated, in order to become a rite of "social graduation." Then "the first ceremony — the present Bar Mitzvah at thirteen — would have the force of confirmation" in the Christian sense, where confirmation is a *sacrament* pure and simple, concerned, as in baptism, with the bestowal of grace.

[This] would mark the close of initial religious education. . . . But it would not admit to adult status in the House of Israel, nor to membership in the adult congregation. The confirmand could become, however, a member of the junior congregation, which would thus acquire an organic place in Jewish life. Then, after a further period of preparation, when he is indeed legally an adult, he would be admitted to the senior congregation.[44]

In outline, this plan might be as valuable in the Christian churchgoing community as in the Judaic synagogue. Yet from a psychological viewpoint its success would depend upon the type of individual leadership which could be found to implement it. In our analytical patients we are continually reminded of the individual variations of religious response when the claims of both conscious and unconscious are brought together in a suitable dialectic. When this happens, we see some very unexpected attempts at syncretization in which both Christian and Jewish responses meet significantly to provide an initiatory threshold.

A man of thirty-seven, for instance, who felt uncommitted to his marriage and was strongly attracted by women other than his wife, had the following dream: "I am kissing a young woman standing on an open lawn. A former girl friend interrupts us and hands me a menorah, or seven-branched candlestick associated with the Jewish religion. On one of the arms I see hanging my wife's wedding and engagement rings."

His associations brought up the memory that when he was in the army, he frequently associated with Jewish men because they seemed more civilized, more sensitive, and more committed to life than the Gentile men, who seemed by comparison to be "slobs." The menorah reminded him of these Jewish men and of the mystical tradition of Judaism, about which he knew nothing but of which he had some rather numinous feeling. By way of interpretation I explained to him that I had often encountered in world mythology the number seven or nine as pertaining to initiation as an inner process. I suggested that the most important thing about his feeling, is the sense it conveys that initiation is a formal and irreversible commitment to life, providing those necessary limits to personal experiment which are the essence of true civilization.

He then immediately recognized the message of the dream — an effort to connect those rings, representing his formal commitment to marriage and to his wife, with his own inner need for an experience of commitment to himself. This connection would correct his promiscuous behavior by reminding him, in the form of an earlier anima-figure (the girl friend), that this marriage had supplanted this relationship in reality and that he should now enter into it more meaningfully. His own conscious affirmation of this came gradually, of course, as part of a process of development which brought him an acquaintance with the patriarchal principle, which was foreign to his own family pattern and its form of Christianity, in which the mother had been dominant and possessive, keeping him emotionally immature.

The case of a Jewish woman patient illustrates an opposite type of symbolization. She was impressed by the Christian doctrine of love, especially in relation to nature. The figure of St. Francis became especially congenial for her as seeming to represent this type of religious response. The importance to her of such an experience came as part of a process of freeing herself from a rigid, controlling father, who seems to have been at times paranoid in relation to the patient's mother and herself. She had to conceal from him in early years all her most important cultural interests for fear of disapproval, and this led to strong feelings of isolation from others as well as her father. St. Francis came to represent all that was freely undefended, a religion of love that dares to expose its intimate feelings even in the presence of ecclesiastical authority, and the promise that in this exposure of a naturally religious attitude one may be strong enough to triumph over all psychological injustices. This symbolizing, though it does not illustrate a pattern of initiation in any formal sense, was experienced by my patient as the kind of initiation that would be right for her, just because of its naturalness and lack of formality.

III. *The Ordeal*

INITIATORY ORDEALS associated with the rites of the Father in tribal societies are so common and their intention so perfectly evident that we can immediately recognize the likeness to our own initiatory disciplines, such as hazing, tests of endurance, and the secret brotherhoods, formed on the principle of self-sacrifice, found among our school and college communities. But we should not be misled by appearances. The modern equivalents of initiation rites are strictly secular, organized and led by boys only a little older than the neophytes. Even when the teachers are older men who may exert a formative influence of the better sort upon young boys in their athletic contests, the ideal to be attained is limited to those immediate forms of physical heroism within the reach of boys whose parents have made quite sure that their sons' lives are not going to be endangered.

How different are the tribal initiation rites, which begin with a final separation from the mother or the mother's world, in which the boy's life is considered worthless unless he can withstand the terror of believing that he may literally have to die in order to satisfy the Great God who originally gave the initiation rites to men! Eliade reports the seriousness of the boys as they learn the mythology of the rites: "The ordeal and the trial of strength are joined in one typical endurance test, the need to conquer sleep and physical fatigue" (cf. Lindberg's account of his transatlantic flight) "Not to sleep is not only to conquer physical fatigue, but is above all to show proof of will and spiritual strength; to remain awake is to be conscious, present in the world, responsible."[45] The word *spiritual* is here no figure of speech; it denotes the basic experience of the tribal initiations. As Eliade repeatedly emphasizes, the initiations are always sacral in character; they are meant to impart religious belief of the highest order. The boys are initiated, not in a spirit of play, but seriously and by the most important elders and medicine men of the tribe. The message they deliver is from the supreme or divine beings themselves. "The maternal universe was that of the profane world. The universe the novices now enter is that of the sacred world. Between the two, there is a break, a rupture of continuity."[46]

The meaning of the ordeal becomes clear in the tribal rites: it shows the initiate's ability to accept and yet to withstand death. For "passing from the profane to the sacred world in some sort implies the experience of death; he who makes the passage dies to one life in order to gain access to another . . . the life where participation in the sacred becomes possible."[47]

Analytical investigations of modern symptomatic behavior and dreams have frequently shown the essential difference in these two reactions toward initiation. I have found that I can accurately predict an unreadiness on the part of certain people to accept the responsibilities of adult life by observing that they see the initiation pattern as a purely profane experience, which can be rejected or accepted at will, rather than as an essential, spiritual experience. The only apparent exception occurs when an individual who has developed a responsible attitude is unwilling to reaccept certain secular social patterns which have been ignored in adolescence. These are elements of the trickster cycle which cannot be won over to "religious, moral and social instruction" without some outward dramatization or acting out.[48]

Actually, it is a good instinctive reaction when a young person rejects initiation if it fails to provide him with a convincing socioreligious meaning. In my freshman year at Princeton I went meekly along with my classmates to huddle upon the granite steps of one of the debating society buildings (a neo-Greek temple) while the sophomores pelted us with flour and then drenched us with water. This event, known as the Flour Picture because a photographer came at the end to take a picture of the deplorable result, was discontinued after that year simply because no one could any longer see any sense in such a juvenile proceeding. Yet originally it may have had a more valid meaning, and I have often thought since how closely, after our drenching, we must have resembled the "white clay men" of antiquity (also found among our Pueblo Indians), representing initiation as a return to the land of the dead, where the novices briefly personify the ghosts of the departed ancestors or original "titanic" men in a ritual of death preceding a rebirth into the present world of the living.[49] If the Flour Picture was ever enacted in that spirit, it may have had a meaning that was lost upon a more sophisticated generation. But I suspect it was always purely a secular rite without much archetypal content.

An initiation which involves an unexplained or unmeditated ordeal is bound to be unconvincing. An early patient of mine had such a dream, following which he quite understandably rejected any further treatment from me. In the dream he was in a dentist's chair and I was the dentist. His wide-open mouth was filled with various instruments, and I was about to perform some sort of operation not specified in the dream. Suddenly he felt that he could not bear this submission to me and, tearing the things out of his mouth, leaped from the chair and ran out of the room. Whether this failure to trust me was due to his resistance or to my lack of skill is a question I have never been able to answer satisfactorily; but as long as he saw me only in the role of dentist at this crucial period in his analysis, he could not endow me with sufficient insight into his psychological problem to go on. Yet the fact that I was a dentist in his dream pointed to a wholesome need for him to allow something important to be done for him which he could not do for himself and for which an act of submission was necessary.

This theme is expressed in the dramatic initiation rites of the Yuin tribe of Australia. The first act of submission forced upon the novices is that they must not look up but only at the ground beneath their feet.

> When they are suddenly ordered to raise their eyes, they see before them masked and disguised men, and to one side, carved on a tree, the figure of Daramulun, three feet high. Presently their guardians cover their eyes, the chief medicine man approaches dancing, seizes the head of each novice in turn, and knocks out one of his incisors with a chisel and a small hammer.

That this is not a purely surgical and therefore profane rite, nor a form of sadistic torture, is borne out in the subsequent unfolding of the meaning of the ritual:

The novices endure this ordeal with admirable indifference. They are then led to the tree bearing the image of Daramulun, and the great secret is revealed to them. Daramulun as Supreme Being "lives beyond the sky, and from there watches what men are doing. It is he who takes care of men after they die. It was he who instituted the initiation ceremony and taught it to the ancestors [in the Alcheringa Time, or Dream time, of long ago]." Hence there is a reactualization of mythical events, which enables the new initiates to assimilate the religious heritage of the tribe.[50]

What gives body and conviction to this ritual was apparently lacking in my patient's response to me. He saw me in a purely medical role, and this did not answer his need — the need of the youthful initiand to establish a transference of feeling to a suitably priestly father-figure. Where this has occurred, I have noticed a different kind of unconscious response to therapy, as shown in another case.

Case V (continued)

The young man described as Case V, having come to terms with the Mother and having reinstated his feeling for his own mother belatedly, then came to a new phase in his analysis which called for a reactivation of the Father. Since he felt that his original father and his father surrogates (his commanding officers during the war) had failed him, he now looked toward me with expectation but also with trepidation. He was afraid of finding in me another overexpectant, loving father-figure who would demand more of him than he could give. A still more alarming prospect was his fear that his love, newly awakened in his response to the Mother image, might be transferred to me in a homosexual way if he allowed himself to submit to my therapeutic influence. So he resisted taking the next step, and I did not urge him because I did not know what it should be.

The stalemate which ensued brought up once again the original passive rebellion he had exerted against his father's ambitions for him. Like the character of Biff in Arthur Miller's *Death of A Salesman*, he chose to live away from home doing odd jobs, rather than give his father the satisfaction of watching him achieve anything exceptional. He did not find satisfaction in this role himself, and it seemed to me he was retreating into a state of isolation which would ultimately push him into a serious regression. But because I was by circumstance somewhat in the role of a parental authority over him, I was quite powerless to exert any influence without losing the power to help him further.

At last there came a dream with its attendant insight which allowed him to make the necessary transference of feeling to me and, because of all he had been through in the earlier phase of his analysis, to go a long way in resolving it. Shortly afterwards he was able to get back into life and make his mature choice of work and marriage. This was the dream:

DREAM 3: Some teeth were loose in my lower jaw. When I examined them more closely, I found that all the teeth, together with the whole jaw on one side, seemed to be giving way. I panicked.

I came to you as a therapist to help me. You were dressed in a white coat like a medical doctor. When you examined me, you were firm but compassionate, and I felt I could trust myself to you.

With a syringe you injected some life-giving fluid into my umbilical scar. This made me feel revived, but it was the recovery of a spiritual, not a physical, strength.

ASSOCIATIONS: These were of no particular significance, except that the dream made a great impression upon him and relieved him for the first time of all restraint in relation to me. He felt he no longer needed to defend himself against my opinion, nor did he need to fear being misunderstood.

INTERPRETATION: The dream contains three themes closely suggestive of the primitive initiatory rite of the Father, here expressed in terms of medical treatment. The first section of the dream suggests the *ordeal;* the second, the *father-figure;* and the third, the *treatment.*

The symbolizing of the ordeal as a loss of teeth — in this case, a loss also of the jaw holding them — points to a still deeper disturbance than would have been signaled at first sight by the patient or his symptoms. We can recognize this as typical of the initiatory fear inspired in the novice during the initiation rites of tribal groups — the fear of total destruction of ego-consciousness or will power. The loss of the teeth, or the hair, or the foreskin, or whatever part of the body is sacrificed, signifies total dismemberment. "According to a myth summarized by R. H. Mathews, Duramulun told his father, or master, *Baiame*, that during initiation he killed the boys, cut them to pieces, burned them, and then restored them to life, 'new beings, but each with a tooth missing.' "[51]

The patient's acceptance of his therapist as both trustworthy and humane suggests that in his transference of feeling from mother to father, he accepts the role of the doctor as a transitional figure, a master of initiation, who is both mother and father, firm and skillful in his use of his instruments, but also compassionate. The treatment emphasizes still more clearly the ambiguous role of the doctor, who performs his operation by an act suggestive of phallic aggression yet who actually produces, as it were, the maternally nurturant effect of feeding the patient some revivifying substance, injected precisely at the place from which the embryo was fed by its mother through the umbilical cord. The homosexual fear is apparently allayed, since the erotic transference, instead of binding him, seems to be spiritually liberating.

Most important of all is the mobilization of a bisexual response as an act of integration in the formation of the new man. This is said to be acted out in certain tribal societies in which both novice and tutor (and/or master of initiation) play maternally supportive and sometimes actively homosexual roles. Layard has reported the social organization of these practices in Australia, New Guinea, and Melanesia, where the homosexual role in its religious manifestation has the function of endowing the novice "with whatever measure of 'psychic masculinity' he may have himself achieved." The rite performed by the tutor (anal penetration) is said to be performed by *"the collective spirit of the ancestors* who are the guardians of tribal morality. . . . The concept of the novice's 'femininity' and therefore potential (though psychic) pregnancy is very evident in that the whole period of initiation lasts nine months."[52] In the Hopi Snake Dance Ceremonial the antelope priests place their arms around the shoulders of the snake priests in their time of ordeal, while the latter are holding the snakes in their mouths. In Africa, as well as in Melanesia, the older initiated youths hold the exsanguinated novices, following circumcision or bloodletting, in their arms as mothers hold their children.

The most striking of all these initiatory ordeals is the rite of subincision, an operation which creates the simulacrum of a uterus or vagina in the urethral zone of the penis. The loss of blood from this region appears to represent mimetically the dis-charge of bad blood, as a woman discharges menstrual blood and thereby renews herself. To press the analogy further, we may conjecture that archaic man, in thus simulating a biological like-ness to woman, is seeking to take on her ability to experience death and rebirth literally — an experience forever closed to men, who can experience death and rebirth only as a ritual or mimetic rite.

In some tribes the novices are dressed as girls or women, or covered over by rugs, until the moment of the revelation of the Divine Being. The animal master of initiation is always aggres-sively masculine, impersonating a bear or a lion, and we might infer that the Great Father as Daramulun must also be fiercely masculine. On the contrary, Duramulun in the form of the bull-roarer is, in one of the oldest and best authenticated Australian rites, both man and woman. The central mystery of this initiation is called "Showing the Grandfather," which leaves no doubt as to its being an authentic patriarchal rite.

> [The novices] lie on the ground and rugs are put over their heads. The men approach, whirling bull-roarers. The headman tells the novices to throw off the rugs and to look at the sky and then at the men who are carrying the bull-roarers. . . . They are shown the two bull-roarers — one of which is larger, the other smaller, and which are called "man" and "woman" — and the headman tells them the myth of the origin of the initiation.[53]

Appropriate to a patriarchal rite is the recognizable assumption that man is larger than woman, suggestive of the story in Genesis where Eve is said to be made from Adam's rib. This might be a symbolic assertion that woman does not have equal status in her own right, but such an explanation seems too superficially rational.

A better psychological explanation might follow Jung's idea that man has to reckon with his own lesser feminine component, the anima, just as seriously as with his ostensible masculine identity. In the Kurnai initiation, Eliade observes, there is "no kind of operation or mutilation. Instead, the initiation is confined to religious, moral and social instruction. . . . "The peaceful nature of the ceremony in general is indeed striking."[54] One might easily multiply examples to show that the bisexual motif occurs on all levels of initiation and that what counts is a psychic, not a physical, ordeal.

What does this mean? Are the tribal fathers merely trying to endow their rites with enough matriarchal atmosphere to provide a congenial transition from the self-indulgence of childhood to the sacrifices of manhood? By this reductive reasoning, the boys would then not be so frightened that they would fail at their tests, nor would they become rebellious; mother can be given up if father is in some way as loving and as nurturant. We know from our patients in analysis how difficult it is for a person suffering from arrested development to trust the stern law of life that eventually pushes him out into the world alone. No wonder, we may think, that the fathers try to mitigate this hard lot and make of the male group itself a kind of mother substitute. Did we not find such a configuration in the rite of the Kouretes, with its protection of the holy male child, the infant Zeus, by a band of shielded nurturers devoted to the worship of a Mother Goddess?

In the light of the tribal rites, however, the transition from Mother to Father, as archetypal figures representing masculine and feminine qualities can be more effectively understood as the expression of an existential condition for which the symbol of bisexual union represents the attitude of wholeness or integration necessary to maturity. It is a desirable, permanent acquisition, not just a phase of development to be outgrown. This teleological viewpoint is supported by Eliade:

> I suggest that the religious meaning of these customs is this: the novice has a better chance of attaining a particular mode of being — for example, becoming a man or woman — if he first symbolically becomes a totality. For mythical thought a particular mode of

being is necessarily preceded by a *total* mode of being. The andro-gyne is considered superior to the two sexes just because it incar-nates totality . . . [as the] desire to recover a primordial situation.[55]

What is seen in the tribal rites is also found in individual psychology at the level of youthful initiation patterns. Over and over again, when a young man who is still too much a boy asks, "How shall I become a man?" of when a little-girlish woman asks, "How shall I become a woman?" I find in their dreams the firmly paradoxical answer: "By becoming both man and woman."

CHAPTER V

The Trial of Strength

I. *The Centering Process*

WHEN THE ARCHETYPE of initiation has been fully activated by the rite of separation, the initiate is ready to be accepted by the social group as a container for further instruction in becoming a man. (The psychology of the corresponding women's rites will be discussed later.)

In the dream of one young man (Case VI, p. 76) we saw a dream image of this type of patriarchal group, the procession of men led by a man carrying a cross. In another young man's dream (Case III, p. 67) we can see even more clearly how the anticipation of his acceptance by the Father brings forth a new effort from him to reach a temple presided over by a priestly figure representative of sacral group consciousness. In the same dream we found the patient making an effort to reach a goal described as "climbing a mountain"; in an earlier dream (p. 47) he ran a foot-race for a prize. In a third young man's dream (Case V, p. 59) there was shown a breakthrough (as *rite d'entrée*) into a broad boulevard, suggestive of acceptance in his military group.

All these examples point to the existence of an archetypal theme no less constant in initiatory patterns than the ordeal. This phase is the trial of strength.

The initiatory trial of strength is different from the trials associated with the hero myth. Psychologically the hero myth is an expression of ego identity not fully established, and the triumphant hero-figure therefore is compensated by a figure we recognize as the hero's adversary, the betrayer, or in milder form the doubting shadow or weaker younger brother. The true initiate has finished with his dreams of glory and is ready for a stronger test of manhood.* He is on the Way of Initiation, a kind of journey wholly nebulous or mystical for those who have not found it, but absolutely definite and secure for those who have. Unlike the trial of strength associated with the hero myth, the initiatory trial of strength is a continuation of the ordeal and becomes a signal that the initiate is about to transcend it. In tribal rites this is synonymous with the achievement of adaptation within the group.

This aspect of initiation has often been regarded by anthropologists as the whole of the initiation and described by them in great but misleading detail. Consider Hutton Webster's description of the Man's House, the institution which provides the setting for this initiatory experience:

> The men's house is usually the largest building in a tribal settlement . . . . it serves as council-chamber and town hall, as a guest-house for strangers and as the sleeping resort of the men. Frequently seats in the house are assigned to the elders and other leading individuals according to their dignity and importance. . . .[1]

One would gather from this type of account that the tribal rites are similar to our own public institutions for preserving masculine solidarity, legality, and the hierarchy of class consciousness. Early psychoanalysts naturally seized upon this aspect of the tribal rites to show how the Oedipus complex (as sexual jealousy toward the father) is solved by a mobilization of ambivalence toward the Father image — such as we experience in our own class system — when the tribal fathers, by a process of punishment and reward, divert the rebellious impulses of the sons into socially constructive channels.

This type of explanation, however, ignores certain basic facts. Initiation as a rite has been shown to transcend the wordly social

---

* As long as the novice unconsciously clings to the mother and to his own boyhood, he will accept the group of initiated men only if it gives him what he thinks he wants, even to becoming its leader. This inevitably leads to the hubris of the hero myth, and the trial of strength becomes an obsession, destroying the very life from which it derives spiritual regeneration. A good example of this failure with its ensuing tragedy is the figure of Captain Ahab in Herman Melville's *Moby Dick*. Not Captain Ahab, the ostensible hero, but the white whale, as an embodiment of the collective unconscious, becomes the true hero in the experience of nemesis which overwhelmed the captain.

plane of existence and to have its chief concern in relating spiritual height to psychological depth. The Australian rites of the Man's House, for example, assimilate the novice to the sky-god Daramulun by means of the symbol of a pole or tree which he is supposed to mount in order to reach the ancestors of the Alcheringa Time, whereas the Pueblo Indians descend to an underground chamber (*kiva*) in order to communicate through an opening in the ground (*sipapu*) with the spirits of the ancestors living below. An intermediate symbol is the totem pole of the Indians of the Pacific Northwest, which seems to join Earth and Heaven in an ancestral symbol of totemic nature. The function of totemism as a rite of initiation permeates all these rites in certain definite ways.

In fairness to the psychoanalysts, it is true that the roots which attach tribal man to his ancestral past may be expressed in sexual terms. The etiological myth of the Hopi Snake Dance Ceremonial is a good example: The Hopis say that long ago there was a youth who spent his time beside the Grand Canyon wondering where all the water went. He finally persuaded his father to let him embark upon the river in a hollow log. He was borne to the sea where he encountered Spider Woman. Spider Woman agreed to help the youth and she grew very small, perched upon his ear, and whispered instructions to him. She told him to go to the house of the Turquoise Woman who would have killed him had not Spider Woman told him how to behave for suddenly the Sun came down into her house, having completed his journey for the day. When the Sun saw the Hopi youth he knew he was worthy and bore a brave heart so the next day he took him on his journey through the sky. At the end of the day the youth, *Tiyo*, again went to see the Spider Woman, who told him to visit the mythic Snake People. At that moment these people were human in shape. They subjected the young man to various tests which he successfully met with the aid of Spider Woman. The Snake People then assumed serpentine form. At the instigation of Spider Woman *Tiyo* seized the fiercest of these, whereupon the reptile was immediately transformed into a beautiful girl. This was Tcuamana the Snake Maid, whom *Tiyo* then married and led back to his own country. The first offering was a brood of serpents, but later human children were born to become the ancestors of the Snake Clan. Another version states that a Corn Maiden was transformed into a snake.[2]

This myth provides the basis for a touching initiation drama for children on the day preceding the Snake Dance. Before dawn there issues from the opening in the roof of the *kiva* the calm chanting of the antelope priests, in whose hands the purificatory ritual is placed. They are chanting the story of Tiyo and Tcuamana, who are impersonated by a boy and a girl. The young novices are attended by their mothers. The boy is given a snake to hold in his hand and the girl an ear of corn as they stand on either side of an altar. The ritual suggests a form of matriarchal rite similar to some reports of the Eleusinian Mysteries in ancient Greece, where there were also a snake, a mystic ear of corn, and the significant union of a male with a female priestess in an underground chamber.

But the patriarchal aspect of the Snake Dance Ceremonial as a whole and of the snake youth myth is well marked. In true patriarchal fashion Tiyo mistrusts the Snake People, fears them, and only at Spider Woman's encouraging injunction dares to pick up one of the snakes. Spider Woman is like Athena in the Greek myth of the Odyssey, performing a function designed to protect the masculine will from being devoured by the Terrible Mother (in this case, Turquoise Woman) or destroyed by the Great Father (in this case, the Sun). The transformation of the snake into a woman in turn suggests the Garden of Eden with Adam's projected fear and his naive assumption that sex is the only avenue to relationship. Such stories reveal clearly that this serpent represents man's ancient, projected fear of being unable to join sex with feeling and thereby to humanize his instinct. He is still afraid of the incest taboo.

It is significant that the first offspring of the Snake Youth and his bride were serpents; this expresses man's uncertainty whether he can maintain his human nature in relation to his instinctual life, which forever threatens to swallow him into the belly of blind craving. But the second brood was human and became the ancestors of the Snake Clan. In memory of them the Snake priests, setting an example for their novices, return every year at the same time in late summer to the snake level of consciousness — a state of mind designed to bring about some transformation upon a deep instinctual level. This is brought out in the ceremony of the mixing basket which contains a brew made from bear's paws, puma skulls, herbs and other things. The contents of the basket are vigorously stirred and the ceremony is accompanied by singing and piercing war cries. Similarly, in the previous ceremony of the children, a bear actor thrusts a corn ear in the faces of the antelope novices and a puma actor thrusts a snake in the faces of the snake novices.[3]

The culmination of the whole ceremonial is the dance in which the snake priests, painted black, dance with rattlesnakes in their mouths. This ritual act, which is said to be an act of communion with the ancestors, is a striking parallel with the ancient mysteries of Sabazius, where "the snake also played a large part in the initiation ceremonies, under the strange title, ὁδιά χδλπου θεος (the god through the lap). Clement of Alexandria says the symbol of the Sabazius mysteries . . . 'is a snake which is dragged through the laps of the initiates.' "[4] In the Hopi ceremonial the ritual of eating the snake is stressed symbolically, while in the Sabazius ceremony the sexual symbolism is stressed, the lap representing the genital area. But the sexual nature of the snake is emphasized in the Hopi Snake myth as the theme of sexual transformation (marriage with the transformed serpent); and the Sabazius ritual, where the snake is drawn from above downward, may also denote a ritual eating of the god.

This equation of ancestor worship, sex, and food is verified in general by Eliade, who finds that a "mystical interconnection between food, blood, (i.e., kinship) and sexuality constitutes an initiatory pattern" especially associated with the sanguinary ordeals of Melanesian and Indonesian rites.[5] But here, instead of the initiatory ordeal with its painful wounds, we have a trial of strength in which the initiate, while submitting to the unknown dangers of the rite, is nevertheless a chief actor in a drama by which he wins his manhood from the regressive pull of the parental archetype.

In this type of rite, as well as in the equivalent dream of a modern individual, the retrogressive trend is represented by a suitable ritual ordeal (as ritual death) followed by the successful accomplishment of a trial of strength (as ritual rebirth). The patriarchal rite emphasizes the upward-striving impulse toward consciousness against the downward pull of the unconscious forces associated with the negative mother-image. But the positive mother-image appears to be invoked at the same time, so that the Father may not be guilty of hubris and thereby bring about a regressive return to the hero myth. In the Hopi ceremonial the Antelope priesthood appears to conduct itself in harmony with the claims of matriarchal consciousness with its agricultural orientation (ear of corn).

During the Snake Dance Ceremonial the trial of strength is foreshadowed by a ritual foot-race of young men. Fewkes' account of this race shows that it is part of the agricultural, and therefore matriarchal, rite. Before dawn the Antelope Priests assembled in their *kiva*. A maiden was brought in, given corn stalks to hold and placed on one side of a sand altar. A youth, one of the Snake novices, holding a snake in his hand, stood on the other side of the altar. She is the corn maiden Tcuamana, and he is the Snake Youth Tiyo, ancestor of the Snake Clan. They represent the mythological figures whose marriage is commemorated in the ceremony. Eight of the ceremonial songs are sung before dawn. Just at dawn naked runners started from a distant spring in the desert six miles from the village and raced up the side of the mesa in competition for a prize. When they reached the plaza each was given a corn stalk or a melon. Women rushed at them struggling to wrest these things from their arms. After a brief struggle the men relinquished their burdens and retired.[6]

This is clearly a fertility rite in which the active masculine principle transcends the passivity of the natural state. The foot-race for a prize and the climbing of the mesa at the time of the rising sun point to a typical Kouretes rite in which each man is the potential leader (Kouros) — that is, the initiate whose prowess will earn the spiritual blessing of the Sky Father and the fruitful cooperation of the Earth Mother.

The theme of a celestial ascent, which is so commonly described in association with shamantic trance states and which is enacted ritually in the ceremonial climbing of trees in Asia and America, is a still more dramatic example of the trial of strength. Eliade reports:

A tree or a sacred pole plays an important role not only in puberty initiations . . . but also in public festivals . . . or in the ceremonies and healing séances of shamans. . . . The novice during his initiation, or the shaman in the course of the séance, climbs the tree or the sacred pole, and . . . the ascent always has the same goal — meeting with the Gods or heavenly powers, in order to obtain a blessing (whether a personal consecration, a favor for the community, or the cure of a sick person). . . .[7]

In Asia the sacred pole or tree symbolizes the Cosmic Tree, the *axis mundi,* and this ascent to Heaven "represents one of the oldest religious means of . . . participating in the sacred order to transcend the human condition." Hence the candidate for initiation into a secret society "symbolically goes up to Heaven . . . to transmute his ontological status, and to make himself like the archetype of *homo religiosus,* the shaman."[8]

The importance of these rites for us resides in their psychological significance and in the fact they still appear spontaneously in the dreams or fantasies of modern people. We therefore are well advised to learn as much as we can about their origins and character. The *kiva* rite seems to come from an agricultural people who had achieved a kind of rough balance between matriarchal and patriarchal mythologies in the manner of the Bronze Age civilizations of Greece, India, Egypt, and China. In contrast to this culture and antedating it, the rite of celestial ascent is associated with the great hunting cultures of Northern Asia, Europe, and parts of Africa. The anthropologist or religious historian seeks to isolate these cultures in their purest forms and to show how they have influenced each other by diffusion. But in our psychological research in depth analysis we find a preformed syncretism in the unconscious, and this forces us to study the rites as if they had to be reconciled in personal ways which could not possibly be foreseen from the pure forms or combinations of tribal rites. This syncretism is frequently seen as a combination of shamanic magic with agricultural fertility rituals.

The archetypal pattern of the shamanic initiation combines a descent to the underworld with an ascent to Heaven, denoting not two different experiences but two-in-one, which spectacularly proves (as Eliade is so fond of observing in his historical synthesis of the initiation rites) that "he who has undergone them has transcended the secular condition of humanity."[9] The symbolism of height and depth from this initiation pattern combines with the initiation pattern previously defined as the union of opposites, of male and female. The upward dimension seems to belong to an experience associated with symbols of the spirit; the lower dimension, with symbols of sex. We have now to discover what this means empirically.

Case VII (Male, age 28)

In the paintings of a borderline schizophrenic patient I have found some excellent examples of the symbolism of height and depth combined with the symbolism of male and female. In one of these, the symbol for spirit appeared as unreal or death-dealing, whereas sex appeared as a devouring monster. These themes have their parallels in the account of tribal initiations in which the initiate is ritually dismembered at the onset of the ordeal. In my patient's drawings, the features I at first considered to be simply schizophrenic distortions or meaningless archaisms took on a new meaning as expressions of the initiatory ordeal. They seemed to show him in a place of a ritual death from which he could emerge only by a ritual of rebirth. But as is so common in such cases, where the person has been psychically injured at a very early age, the tendency to regression pushed him back again and again into the dismembered state. Pictorially expressed, he was alternately pushed down into the toothed vagina of the Terrible Mother or spirited upward on the wings of the demonic Father God. Despite considerable improvement, he remained in a psychically dissociated condition, sometimes wildly elated, sometimes abysmally depressed.

At length there came a new development in his paintings, a tendency to create a central design — round, or square, or both — between the poles of his conflict; this was combined with a radial design which seemed to reconcile the poles, not only of a vertical, but also of a horizontal dimension.[10] Another type of design, in which the vertical dimension was strongly emphasized yet conditioned by a strong central design, was impressive. Around the base of a large pole rising from the earth lay coiled a serpent. The top of the pole ended in an oval-shaped central area containing a branch with four leaf-like appendages. This area was central also to a body whose huge, male lower limbs stretched downward from the top of the pole; the oval covered what would have been the genital and lower abdominal part of the body. The upper part, which was really drawn like a separate body, lighter, and proportionally smaller than the lower part, was a sketch of a rib cage with two round, breast-like areas, suggesting a female torso. Two distorted crossed arms with ineffectual hands reached upward from the lower part of the figure, as though they did not even hope to grasp those abstract-looking breasts above. The figure had no head.

At first sight, the thick pole with its oval-shaped upper extension seemed unmistakably phallic, but the snake coiled about the base of the pole was suggestive rather of the ancestor-snake of the Hopis with its origin in the magical fraternities which create order and direction, allotment of clan moieties which determine the Social Structure of the whole tribe. The oval-shaped area with its plant symbol clearly represents the magical principle of growth, probably standing for the principle of psychic development on an archetypal shamanic level. The pole is therefore not so much a symbol of sex per se as a symbol of growth. Here it is a sacred tree as axis of the world, providing the vertical dimension of the identity as a centering and growing process (Neumann's centroversion[11]).

Another parallel may be found among the Kwakiutl, whose novices for initiation return from the forest to the ceremonial house (or *imago mundi*), where they find a copper pillar symbolizing the axis of the world. According to their myths, men can mount to Heaven or descend to Hell by climbing up or down a copper pillar. "The copper pillar is represented in the house by a cedar pole thirty or forty-five feet high, the upper half of which projects through a hole in the roof. . . . The ceremonies take place then at the centre of the visible universe; hence they have a cosmic dimension and value." The Kwakiutl initiates, like my patient, have been "broken down" mentally, terrified or

> possessed by the spirit of the Society, just as they were when they were ravished to the forest [ordeal]. This possession is equivalent to

the death of their individuality, which is dissolved in the supernatural power. . . . Identified with the spirit, the novice is "out of
his mind," and an essential part of the initiation ceremony consists
precisely in attempts on the part of the older members of the
Society to "tame" him by dances and songs. The novice is progressively cured of the excess of power acquired from the divine presence; he is directed toward a new spiritual equilibrium.[12]

The cannibal spirit from above which animates this ritual is
in contrast to that of the Hopi Snake Ceremonial, which is ani-
mated by the generic ancestor as blood-brother from below. The
snake dancers are also "out of their minds" and so need to be
carefully tended during the dance by the Antelope Priests, who
remain watchfully conscious lest they harm themselves. At the end
the dancers are given an emetic by the women and are brought
back to their normal state of ego-consciousness. The Kwakiutl also
drink salt water to cause vomiting, and "the wild paroxysm is
followed by complete prostration, and during the following nights
the initiate is silent and depressed at the dances."[13]

In like manner my patient was silent and depressed following
the wild paroxysms which had led to his "breakdown," when for
a brief period, prior to seeing me, he had had to be confined in a
mental hospital. I was thus treating him during a time of recovery,
and his paintings brought to light a review of all he had been
through. By allowing the symbols expressive of his inner experience to emerge and by giving them form in his paintings, he began
to be cured. The pole had a centering effect upon his disorganized
psychic life, restoring a sense of structure. In the same way, his
representation of the plant with its enigmatic leaves or fruit was
placed in the very center, from which it seemed to exert an order-
ing, nurturant effect.

The universal significance of this drawing is now clear. It represents the patient's ability to reorganize his psyche from below
upward, and one can predict that he is not likely to fall again into
the jaws of the world monster. The two huge legs on either side
of the central pillar refer to a strengthening of his reality function,
which had been severely crippled in his breakdown. (A frequent
theme of his earlier drawings had been animals with distorted or

injured hind legs.) The monster is now the healing ancestor-snake, whose protective coils seem to represent it as a guardian of the underworld threshold.

So far everything seems favorable, but the upper part of the drawing shows the state of human deprivation probably still existing on the personal level of his life. Those pathetic limbs reaching up toward an unfeeling, abstract kind of feminine image most probably denote the problem which remained to be solved. He had in fact suffered from considerable isolation due to emotional deprivation in early childhood, and this had not yet been adequately compensated. He had begun to compensate in a close relationship with a sympathetic older woman friend, whose interest in him he had learned to trust, but unfortunately she died before he had attained the security of a really new position. Eventually, however, he did strengthen his ego to the extent of entering into life in a new way, and he achieved success in his career. He also married and, I presume, made some adjustment on the personal-feeling level of his life. Though I did not see him again, I heard that after about fifteen years, during which time he had periods of mental disturbance complicated by alcoholism, he went into a new regressive phase, lost his capacity to work, and finally underwent a negative character change, during which he died.

His painting thus appears to have been prophetic: it indicated that he could integrate the first part of his life and develop his creative potential, but would probably not be able to go on to a higher integration of his conscious spiritual identity as a man capable of maturing in the second part of life. But this is conjecture.

All we can say for certain is that we often find the opposites, expressed as male and female and as height (spirit) and depth (sex), represented in a single design which has the potential of a mature integration of instinctual capacities. The pole of male and female as horizontal may be imagined to transect the pole of spirit and sex (see Figure 1).

Let us take each axis separately and test it by comparing the mythological images with the substance of modern dreams. As our inquiry proceeds, we may become more or less convinced of the

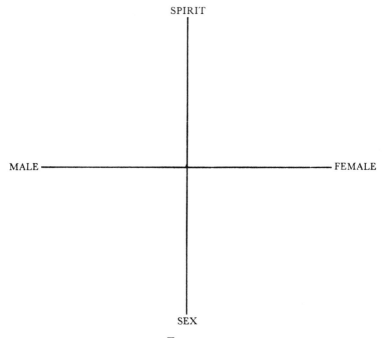

FIGURE 1

validity of this visual concept, though it will have to remain essentially unproven.

II. *The Individuating Factor*

IN THE PRIMORDIAL IMAGERY of dreams we find a peculiar identity existing between the image of the group and that of the individual; they are two in one. But in cultural forms of these images, no such identity exists. Instead of unity, there is division, separateness, and conflict between the claims of the group and the claims of the individual. There are different symbols for the group and for the individual — for the group, symbols of containment; for the individual, symbols of transcendence.[14] (I shall have more to say about these in a later chapter.)

The true interrelationship and dialectic between these two principles belong to the mature phase of life, but the young person of necessity makes some acquaintance with them in any but the most decadent tribal cultures. Our own so-called free society actually exploits these different principles of orientation by encouraging young people in the spirit of competition. At its best this is an aspect of education which may embody a true spirit of democratic social consciousness in which both group and individual claims are honored. At its worst it results in their mutual contradiction, expressed in such meaningless terms as *enlightened self-interest*. Many people of exceptional ability — to avoid wasting their powers in this seemingly futile, never-ending conflict (and because the competitive spirit so easily degenerates into a form of low cunning) — turn away from modern group life before they have adequately experienced those significant patterns which are represented in their clearest form by the tribal initiation rites.

We do, however, find many parallels with these patterns in the dreams of modern individuals who have achieved the basic conquest of their infantile tendencies and are at least firmly ego-centered in their work and their marriages. In the vertical dimension they have achieved something tangible at either a depth or a height, and they have been tested sufficiently to know that they are ready to be tested more fully, to complete the process and eventually become men on both levels.

We have previously noted that many modern people, because of arrested development, fail to achieve identity within the larger group and must wait for the moment when an individual self-affirmation can effectively compensate their lack. At such a moment the social archetype frequently appears as an image in dreams, inviting such a person to return at least in fantasy to the boyhood games he has missed, and shows symbolically how he could exercise his social adaptability *now,* in the hope of making him not just a man but a man among men. Such a dream is the following:

Case VIII (Male, age 48)

DREAM 1: If a young man of the National Guard committed an offense, he had, as punishment, to go to the stadium and win an Olympic prize. I was one of these young men. We accomplished several feats of youthful bravado which were quite nonsensical but lots of fun. In one of these we bathed in the sea at the city water-front below the quay. We found a rock which weighed 416 pounds, and each of the five hundred youths lifted it above his head in one hand, standing waist-deep in the water. I observed this from some distance and saw that the rock was the head of a statue of an ancient man which had long lain in the water.

With another young man I stood in front of a store window and looked in. Then I bent over and, with my buttocks spread apart, looked at my anus in the reflection in the window. As I did so, I made a strange expression with my mouth. The other fellow observed this, laughed, and did the same thing.

Associations: The patient thought that the events of the dream suggested a puberty rite of some kind, in which baptism, horseplay, and a test of manhood were mixed up in a confusing way. The last scene suggested to him a possible homosexual adventure, utterly foreign to his experience or taste but having the effect of loosening his inhibitions in a general sort of way.

Interpretation: These associations at once put us on familiar ground, and we can assume that this immensely exaggerated trial of strength compensated for some important loss of consciousness (the sunken head). In reality this man's education had not helped him to integrate his life with any one group, and he had not achieved a lasting vocation. Instead, he went off on idealistic and adventurous quests originally inspired by his mother. The symbol of masculine consciousness, for which his father could have been a model, had also failed him because his father's adaptation had been made on too materialistic a level for the introverted, reflective, and artistic boy. His dream therefore speaks of his having to reach down into history to recover this very real archetypal symbol of human masculine consciousness in order to compensate for his rather unreal, idealistic imaginings. Seeing himself as one of five hundred young men compensates for his extremely lonely development in adolescence.

But why is the trial of strength exacted of those committing an offense? And why is this trial represented, not as a sober initiation ritual of young men, but first as a mere act of bravado seemingly devoid of any spiritual meaning, then as another form of license with obscene gestures?

The first answer to these questions can be drawn from the personal life of this man, and again the meaning is a compensatory one. In his adolescence, a carefree, fun-loving attitude leading to uninhibited behavior was largely repressed in favor of the serious individualism of his adaptation. The dream brings in precisely those elements which most fittingly compensate his lack: identity with a group, and an ability to find in what is below a meaning totally opposite from his over-serious, spiritual attitude. Now, belatedly, his dream shows him both the importance of the crude, awkward, autoerotic masculine tendencies of extreme youth and the playful aspect of boyish friendship. But this is not the patient's personal idiosyncrasy. We find the same theme collectively expressed as the basis for an aspect of initiation which, though not incorporated in the transcendent rites and rituals with their sacral character, is nonetheless a necessary part of the whole initiation archetype.

Related to the Kouretic initiation rites, but more archaic, is the tradition of the Kabeiroi and their "profane" rites, which nevertheless contain many of the same elements as the "sacred" rites of Eleusis. We learn from Kerényi that the novice in these initiations

> had to prove that he had offended against the divine order, in order that the *Sai* [priests] might purge him of his guilt. But he *had* to be an offender, because the original initiates of Samothrace, the Kabeiroi themselves, the prototypes of all subsequent initiates, had been criminals. . . . A tradition of Thessalonica . . . tells of two Kabeiroi who killed a third and hid his head in a blood-red cloth. . . . The names of the Titans, the original criminals of Greek mythology, were listed in an invocation of the Kabeiroi.[15]

The Kabeiroi are sometimes represented as grotesque phallic dwarfs or pygmies. Their total masculinity is emphasized in the description of them as "figures who in their spectral outlines seem to us now Titanic, now dwarf like and spirit like."[16] As such they were inimical to the feminine principle represented by delicate cranes, storks, or other water birds which they killed and ate. Here they showed "the essential quality of Kabeiroi":

> They represented the antithesis to the paternal dignity of the source of life, they stand for the absurd unrestraint, and yet helplessness, of the phallic element. It is something grotesque and savage which can prove fatal; it is manifested, for example, in the wild voracity of the pygmies devouring the beautiful birds they have killed. Contrasted with such creatures, the celestial nature of the birds is all the more striking.[17]

But the birds are anima figures, heavenly nurses who seem to represent the transcendent principle which can discipline and rescue "the earthy, the wild and crude male principle, which is elevated into higher spheres by a winged femininity."[18] It was the influence of Demeter which seems to have brought this quality of the spirit to these subhuman creatures. The cult of a sacred marriage is mentioned, and we know this signifies the ritual joining of a female with a male element to create a more stable condition. But this does not make the cult a matriarchal affair. "The giant figure of the god (assimilated to the archaic Dionysos type) . . . shows that the male principle in the function of a divine father . . . was elevated to the highest conceivable rank in this secret cult founded by a goddess."[19]

In his dream this modern man had to return symbolically to the pre-Christian, even pre-Hellenic, level of "the Kabirian primeval man" to find this "spirit still in process of birth."[20] In recovering the archetypal male principle of consciousness (the head), he is enabled to recover his lost (i.e., repressed) masculine instincts. Leaning over to observe his anus and, at the same time, his mouth seen upside down suggests a ritual act of recognition that anal and oral zones of interest are interchangeable upon a primordial or infantile level of awareness and that mobilization of this narcissistic libido leads to a new awareness that what is above and what is below may become as one.[21] It then follows that mental and physical, or sacred and profane, are capable of being joined. Thus the trickster-like behavior of childhood is rescued from a destructive individualism by the rite of initiation and is redeemed by its healthy inclusion in the spirit of the group with its friendly good humor.

A variant of this pattern can be summarized as follows:

Case IX (Male, age 46)

DREAM 1: The dream has three scenes: (1) I win a wrestling match against a vigorous young man. (2) I urinate with ease. (3) I am invited by friends to join them for supper. I tell them I will join them in a few minutes. They say they hope it will not be like last time, when I came back an hour later. As I walk away, I am pleased that I have no urge for a drink before dinner.

ASSOCIATIONS: The patient's sense of ease in urinating is in contrast with the many times he has had difficulty finding a urinal.

INTERPRETATION: The three scenes represent, respectively, a trial of strength, an autoerotic element, and incorporation with the male group.

The wrestling match in this context points to a successful over-coming of Kabeiroic violence in an acceptable sporting act. It is compensatory to this patient's characteristic reserve and inactivity, exemplified by his sedentary, intellectual occupation as a professor and writer. Urination, in dreams, is a frequent sign for a wish to liberate all those aggressive masculine feelings (desire for power, for sexual domination, etc.) which would not be acceptable on a gentlemanly social level unless properly channeled (finding a urinal). In this case, such a need had been frustrated in the past but now is fulfilled, as shown in the final scene, where his friends ask him to join them at supper. His ambivalence toward taking this final step is due to his arrested development at the point where autoerotic feelings conflict with the experience of group initiation. That he does not need a drink points to his readiness to give up this autoeroticism (oral dependency), and his healthy response to his friends' humorous reference to his former delay has a liberating effect by pointing out a fault (lateness) which he can presumably correct consciously. Thus the dream carries the prob-lem expressed in the previous case further and shows a man who is ready to give up boyhood, or adolescent, patterns of ego-centered feeling in favor of achieving a new sense of identity as part of the contemporary social group to which he naturally belongs.

These dreams frequently suggest the activities of secret societies in tribal cultures, emphasizing a difference from the so-called puberty rites. In the secret societies the role of Celestial Beings is less important than the role of the ancestors who originally formed the society. The image of the community replaces the God, as when Themis replaced Moira during the emergence of Greek culture. We may conjecture that this type of ancestrally oriented community probably became the prototype for the emergence of the city state with its hierarchy of nobles. Kingship then became an attempt to actualize the original Supreme Being as a reconciling principle between the sense of individuality and the organized social group.[22]

Meanwhile, we must not forget that Frobenius and the historico-cultural school of anthropology claim to have found evidence that the men's secret societies were originally a creation within the matriarchal cycle. The men are supposed to have segregated themselves and gained power over the women by terrorizing them. Male death and rebirth ceremonials would thus be a reflection of the men's desire to imitate the women and to attain the sense of immortality which a woman may feel through the exercise of her maternal function.[23]

Eliade makes it possible for us to see these facts in a wider perspective by showing that the rites of puberty and the rites of the secret societies are basically the same but that, in spite of much borrowing, there is a real difference between the rites and functions of the men's and women's groups:

If men in their secret rites have made use of symbols and behaviors proper to the condition of woman (e.g. the symbolism of initiatory birth), women too . . . have borrowed masculine symbols and rituals [(e.g. hunting magic, secret lore concerning the Supreme Beings, shamanism and techniques of ascent to Heaven, relations with the dead)]. . . . [This] tension between two kinds of sacrality implies both the antagonism between two magics — feminine and masculine — and their reciprocal attraction. . . . [The female societies] organize themselves in closed associations in order to celebrate the mysteries of conception, of birth, of fecundity, and, in general, of universal fertility. . . . The antagonism and attraction between two types of sacrality [show] above all a strong and essentially religious desire to transcend an apparently irreducible existential situation and attain a total mode of being.[24]

In modern women's dreams the theme of belonging to a group is much less marked than in the case of men, but it is no less important in its bearing upon the woman's individual life pattern. The idea of identifying with a women's group does not seem to appeal to most women except as a transitory phase. They may belong to women's clubs or other organizations, but these do not enjoy the solidarity of the men's equivalent groups. What a woman seems most frequently to need is a sense of her own individuality *as woman* in such a way as to feel developmentally contained in the mother-daughter archetype with its cyclical rhythm of union and separation, so beautifully exemplified in the myth of Demeter and Kore.

Case X (Female, age 40)

A woman who had suffered deeply in early years from a sense of alienation from her mother and who in later years experienced a conflict between her duties as wife and mother and her duty to her own introverted nature came to some interesting conclusions some years after her analysis which throw considerable light upon women's initiation experience. I will let her account speak for itself before commenting upon it:

> I used to have a recurring image of a large rock in the center of a stream, the water flowing smoothly around it. I seemed to be the immobile boulder, not being carried along by the stream but only gradually being worn away. The stream always flowed from left to right. I was simply "stuck." In an early dream my analyst was reading back to me a summary of my case to date. "The mother is at the bottom of it all, but that isn't the whole story." In another dream I was saying to someone, "My parents wrapped me in cotton batting when I was little, then when I grew up they unwrapped me and expected me to stand on my two feet." An image came to me early in my analysis of a rosebud with a wedding ring around it. The bud could not possibly open because it was restricted by the ring, although at the time the ring was simply resting against the closed

petals. I especially remember the wonderful idea which soon became a custom during the time of my analysis of taking off a whole day for myself usually during my menstrual period. This was first suggested to me by reading in Harding's *Women's Mysteries* about the menstrual hut in primitive societies where women live in seclusion alone or with a few other women during their menstrual period. I especially was interested in reading that, when going into the menstrual hut for the first time, all their old clothes are taken from them and they are dressed anew as a symbol of giving up their former life and entering a new one. I had numerous dreams of this type representing my need to acquire a new sense of myself as a woman. But the basic value of this initiation fantasy lay in feeling I had permission for the first time to have an introverted time alone and it did me worlds of good. In fact, the whole analytical process was like a sojourn in a place for deep introversion. Even now a recent fantasy of a castle represented a time of removal from the demands of outer life in order to re-enter it later on a higher plane, so to speak. I had another type of dream later in which it seemed I was trying to find my larger "function" or "vocation." This did not have anything to do with entering the man's world to work at something which would have to be organized. This sort of thing I had done and had no wish to repeat. My new need was represented in a dream where "I was returning to the interior of China to a position of great responsibility having to do with women," and this I felt as a call to initiation in which the need for introversion (interior of China) is combined with the idea of being a responsible woman in my own right as different from my mother's idea of the kind of woman I should be. I feel sure the "position of great responsibility" was simply my own responsibility to myself as an individual. I do not think it implied my doing anything for people or with people, except incidentally or naturally; and the "woman" part was just finding my own way as a woman. I still look back on that as the biggest dream I think I ever had. . . . But none of this could have taken place without the analyst in the role I must have assigned him as "medicine man" or some such figure. Certainly this transference was the biggest part of my analysis, as initiation. At first I had negative father-feelings to get rid of. Then it was a gradual transition from a hard, defensive shell protecting the organism within, through the stage of being completely unprotected and vulnerable — willingly so — then finally the growth of an inner strength like a bony structure to give form but not hardness to the new soft creature. still vulnerable but not easily crushed. The "medicine man" has to be the protection during the vital period of metamorphosis, he is the initiand's *only* protection. I am sorry I am so utterly incapable of putting this into words.

In this account we see how very sensitively yet definitely the woman's initiation succeeds in establishing her identity as a woman without any need to borrow images of masculine authority to support her in creating this identity. What she needs perhaps more emphatically than does a man is the feeling of being contained in a meaningful relationship to a person who can carry the sense of its being a transcendent, not just an ordinary, experience of relationship. Therefore she made the transference of a medicine man upon her analyst for this phase of her experiences.

The first dreams of this woman show the uninitiated state of her emotional life, which had been carried over into her marriage so that the rosebud of her girlhood feeling could not unfold. This indicates the quality of the young girl's initiation as an unfolding or sense of awakening, in contrast to the boy's corresponding trial of strength. While women also undergo ordeals and trials of strength in tribal societies and women's mysteries, the specifically feminine experience seems to arrive at some form of inner containment which gives rise to a new confidence in being herself renewed in the world (the new clothes).

In the light of this type of experience, it is shortsighted to assume that women's initiations are merely institutions for instructing them about sex, childbearing, gardening, or the lubricious rites for insuring fecundity. Still less are they rituals for competing with men or for seeking to possess them illegitimately. They contain their own special meaning for women who are engaged in the adventure of self-discovery, as necessary as the heroic exploits of the men, which, apart from exceptional "heroines," get all the world's acclaim.

It is therefore highly gratifying for the psychologist to have the observations of a really skilled religious historian, such as Eliade, by which to check his own observations. What appears to be an insoluble problem on the plane of sociology becomes religiously and psychologically understandable. Thanks to this type of research, one can call a halt to the eternal, boring debate among the anthropological schools and show how *transcendence*, or *depth*, or *process*, or any of the other psychological power words of our time may express different yet ever the same realities, according to whether we apply them on the extraverted social level or on the individual plane of introverted awareness. This is so because they have a psycho-religious common denominator.

The attraction/repulsion between the male and female secret societies has its psychological counterpart in the inherent bisexuality in men and in women, which is to be understood as a difference not of sex but of gender, or symbolic sex.[25] As Eliade so rightly observed, this difference of gender is sacral in character, and therefore it transcends either pole. Men have a feminine response in their psychological constitution (*anima*), just as women have a masculine one (*animus*). Thus Spirit and Sex are common to both men and women though operating on different planes of experience; and if men and women often disagree in their minds, their hearts recognize an affinity. What is above speaks to what is below, and male and female find the same initiatory answer to their different questions.

Case XI (Male, age 36)

This oscillation between masculine and feminine symbols is seen in the material of our patients. A man of thirty-six brought me the following dream: "I am in a room with my grandfather, who is dead. I enjoyably eat a hard-boiled egg, suggestive of Easter."

His associations led to the following interpretation: He is now assuming greater authority at his job, but is doubtful of success, yet sure he will assert himself to the utmost. He is divorced and is trying to decide whether to marry again. He is afraid he may fall victim to a woman who wants to marry him, rather than make his own free choice. He is in a position to make such a decision, but still is hesitant. The dream tells us that he is in the power of the initiation archetype, where the death of his grandfather is compensated by the symbol of rebirth (the Easter egg). It also tells us that, the authority figure of the family being dead, he can rely upon his own authority — indeed, that he *must* do so from now on. Eating the Easter egg, a symbol of wholeness in the feminine sense, shows his ability to ensure his own pleasure and the future of his chosen wife; he knows that he can do what he wants in this respect and need not allow his mother or his first wife (who was a mother-figure) to tell him what he should do or how he should feel in his relation to women. The inner meaning of the dream shows his readiness to acknowledge his own masculine feeling in a spirit of understanding wherein both masculine and feminine principles are related. Finally it shows that, being unafraid of death, he can enjoy the fruits of rebirth.

Case XII (Female, age 48)

Sometimes the theme of a man's initiation is found spontaneously in a woman's dreams. One forty-eight-year-old woman, whose husband had died after a long illness, was left in charge of two late adolescent children, a son and a daughter. Being an essentially feminine woman, she understood more or less consciously what to do in preparing her daughter to find her way through the labyrinth of love into marriage, but in relation to her son she was at a loss. Her dream came at the beginning of an analysis which she had undertaken to help her find a new direction for her own life and to help her understand the new role she had to play.

DREAM 1: My son has some kind of little wheel-tool knife-sharpener which a friend has given him and which initiates him into some club or competition. The prize to be won is another of this same kind of wheel-tool knife-sharpener, which seems to me unnecessary and ridiculous. I tell him so, but he is enthusiastic about going.

INTERPRETATION: The son was in late adolescence, on the threshold of having to choose a career. The wheel-tool knife-sharpener suggests two of the most important inventions of early man, the wheel and the knife. Here, as in the dreams of the previous two men, the helpful friend as alter ego and the initiatory group provide both the original motivation and a trial of strength which utilizes a specific masculine faculty, his inventive or creative mind. That the woman who has the dream sees this as unnecessary and ridiculous is expressive of the fact that the woman, purely as mother, cannot see the reason for the masculine initiation, which touches upon things outside her immediate experience of the feminine world with its emphasis on relatedness. For this reason the masculine *Logos*, as a discriminatory function, tends to be antithetical to the feminine *Eros*, as the function of relatedness. Yet her dream insists upon the fact that in spite of her disapproval he will retain his enthusiasm for this activity. Subsequently this youth became a successful doctor and a responsible married man, thus satisfying in his chosen vocation and his married relationship the basic conditions for a man to find satisfaction for the first part of his life.

The patient's interest in this son led to another dream which represented the beginning of her own initiation into the independent masculine world — an attitude requisite for her if she were to live as a single woman in a new way appropriate to the second part of her life. For her the wheel-tool knife-sharpener came to represent her own need to learn how to develop her animus function in a more effective way.

The cleavage between the psychological problems affecting people in the first half of life and those in the second half of life has been so strongly emphasized in much of the literature of Analytical Psychology that one might expect initiation to mean different things at the early and later stages of life. It is therefore interesting to see that the basic pattern of the archetype functions uniformly throughout the whole of life. A mature woman may have to learn from an adolescent boy the essential piece of wisdom concerning the archetype she needs, just as in the Kabeiroic symbolism we found that the crude masculine principle (as phallic dwarf) had to submit to initiation by tutelary maternal spirits in the form of storks or cranes.

What becomes increasingly clear is the essential bipolarity of the initiation archetype with its emphasis on the group experience as one pole and on the individual experience as the other. It is this polarity which in the Jungian sense first expresses the true challenge of individuation. Granted that individuation cannot be realized consciously till the second half of life, we nevertheless find in studying the initiation archetype that in young people the basic polarity of the individual and the group is already being 'activated. In one case it may be the individual component that meets the initiating challenge; in another it is the group. The archetypal image is common to both, but the pattern of behavior changes with age and experience. When the conflict between the claims of the individual and those of the group finally breaks through into consciousness at the upper level of youth, we may find individuation at the moment of its inception. The dream of a young man who had reached the threshold of the second half of life and was about to feel the full force of its individuating challenge may illustrate this point.

Case XIII (Male, age 34)

DREAM 1: I am in the village where I lived as a boy. I had been going down a long street from west toward east, downhill, when suddenly I turn right and start south (*see Figure 2*). Then I am going down a short street at its point of bifurcation with the longer street. This means going down a rather steep, short hill to the level part of the village. There is a moment of doubt. Should I go a third way indicated by an invisible line making a 45° angle with the two streets (*see Figure 2*)? This line in southwest direc-

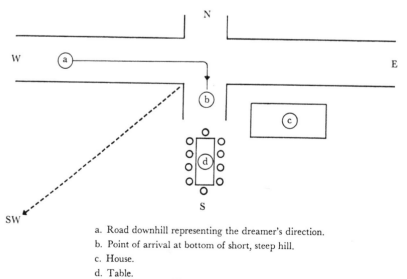

a. Road downhill representing the dreamer's direction.
b. Point of arrival at bottom of short, steep hill.
c. House.
d. Table.

FIGURE 2

tion extends off into space, which seems dark and mysterious. Then I see myself as lonely and weak. How can anyone like me or respect me? I have accomplished so little in life! Then as I am about to descend the hill, I suddenly feel I have a terrible ordeal to undergo — an ordeal impossible to describe. It is like being in a madhouse where everything is diabolically mechanized; the machines are grinding and whining all about me. But I sit calmly enduring it.

Then imperceptibly I slip down to the lower level at the foot of the short hill. It is near the house of some very humble people whom I used to know as a child; their home life was cozy, warm, and human. In the street a long table is set, and I take my place at the right hand of the host at one end. My wife and many other people are there. Before me, instead of a plate, there is a round object like a clock made of gold. On the face of this clock, where the number VIII should be, there is a medallion with a beaded border. In the center is the figure of a winged horse with a man or god on its back — a very beautiful thing to see. It has some direct connection with, or some inner meaning of, the situation I am in with the other people at the table.

ASSOCIATIONS: The associations to this dream were not significant, but the patient's life situation at the time of the dream is important to bear in mind. He had only recently begun to make good at his chosen work as an architect, and he still had some doubts as to whether he would continue to be successful. His associates and superiors regarded him as having a very promising career ahead of him. His doubts were chiefly subjective: he had made a late start and was an introverted, thinking type with a rather weak support from his other functions.

He had recently married, and two weeks before the dream his wife had borne him a son. This had been a happy occasion, and he now felt every incentive to make a solid place for himself and his family in the community. He was, however, plagued by a fear of falling back into his previous neurotic pattern, which could be described as the self-protective device of the introverted man, which is so successfully erected that he suffers from self-isolation behind it. The supposed freedom to think his own thoughts without interruption, which such a man has insured for himself, finally leaves him with a feeling of dry hopelessness, so well described by T. S. Eliot in "Gerontion" as "thoughts of a dry brain in a dry season." In fact, the subject of this dream bore a psychological likeness to the combined characters of two of Eliot's protagonists: Prufrock, with his outworn infantilism and mistrust of feeling, and Gerontion, who has exhausted his spiritual life in an attempt to reduce everything to a rational, intellectual common denominator.

An early period of analysis had largely rescued the patient from the neurotic aspect of his problem, but he had still to come into possession of his full capacity for extraverted adaptation in life. Though he had taken some big steps in that direction, he had not yet taken the final plunge (an example of how boyhood in our society frequently ends only at thirty-five). This plunge would necessarily entail a commitment to life in which there could be no further retreat into the sterile situation of one whose thoughts, like those of an Eliot protagonist, "flow into an imaginative 'inquisition' of his own situation."[26] One would think that such a man would be more than happy to relinquish his morbid thoughts, but it is not so easy. At the juncture between the first and second halves of life, not only the introvert but all men experience a sense of failure and a sense of panic that they may be unequal to the task of becoming truly mature.

From a subjective point of view, the man of our time looks out upon a world which really is quite terrible in its ruthless mechanization and depersonalization. To this patient, who had been brought up in the country among pleasant surroundings and who thought of himself as a nonconformist as far as worldly city values were concerned, the world seemed especially terrible. He tended to forget that he would have been a misfit in his community if he had stayed there. By going to live in a city, he had actually found a great deal more real freedom — or, at any rate, more time for himself — than he would ever have found in the country, no matter how idyllic. But still he cherished, like so many men of his type, the illusion that there is a haven of security in some part of the world where the noisy machines and the hurrying crowds can be forgotten in the eternal present of a pastoral countryside. He made the mistake of so many other Englishmen and Americans who, because they were reared in prosperous country families, are convinced that they belong basically to an agricultural civilization,[27] forgetting those great factories of the Midlands or of New England and the Midwest which stamp their culture as an industrial civilization.

INTERPRETATION: With this background, let us look again at the dream. The patient is back in the community into which he was born, which presumably activated the original archetype of the group. As in reality, so in the dream he is somewhat aloof — on the hill above the town, though part-way down. He is also at a crossroad, which metaphorically expresses the urgency of a decision to come down, either the long way (slowly) or the short way (quickly). There is a hypothetical third way, as yet only an imaginary line, bisecting the angle of the two main roads and leading in a southwesterly direction to a place full of darkness and mystery. This hypothetical way may represent the way of escape through an imaginative flight into future possibilities as yet unconscious, the sort of flight which characterized so much of this man's previous neurotic escapism. He is now called upon to accept an ordeal before he can come down to the level of the natural community of men.

This ordeal of being in a mechanized madhouse is suggestive of his having to accept the world of over-rational collectivity without letting it demoralize him. The fact that this is expressed as a psychotic threat shows that he perceives the actual madness of the purely collective mass man, and this awareness is his safeguard. Such a scene is a representation of the truth, so often expressed by thoughtful psychiatrists and analysts today, that there is a sickness of society as well as a sickness of the individual and that they are interdependent, so that it becomes a necessity for the individual to understand and protect himself from the sickness of the society. The need is expressed in this dream as an initiatory ordeal, rather than as a purely local reaction to environmental conditions. I suspect that the need has always existed for the man who is ready to become an individual.

Having experienced the ordeal, the dreamer imperceptibly

slips down the short hill to the main level of the town. This slipping down to a lower level is a frequent theme in the initiation dream and shows the salutary effect of an irrational happening in contrast to an over-rational effort to achieve release. It speaks of a letting-go by which a more essential level of experience may be reached, and this is especially meaningful and necessary for the intellectual type of individual.

This patient had been brought up by parents who kept somewhat snobbishly aloof from simpler people. His change in the dream brings him to those people's friendly home with its genial memories; and the dream relates him to that family pattern, not as from above, but on its basic human level at the table. In other words, he is immediately rewarded for his willingness to sacrifice the superiority of his intellect by a new promise of healthy contact with his fellow men, as a communal group experience in which he and his wife participate (that is, he in his own new identity as a family man). The host is unspecified, but we may assume he is some form of the master of initiation appropriate for this type of transition.

But even with this communal experience, the idea of the dream has not unfolded to the utmost. The dreamer is presented with a final image which is totally unexpected and, in the dream, unexplained. A golden clock suggests an intrinsic value (gold) united with a mechanical representation or sign of that collective need for conformity which causes us to be conscious of our orientation to time, place, and person — in short, our ego-consciousness.

Here, then, we have a mechanical symbol of the rational aspect of the extraverted collective, which is as positive as the mechanistic madhouse was negative. Having given up his false isolation with its attitude of superiority, he now symbolically throws in his lot with the collective man on a natural communal level and sees, as if for the first time, the value of the collective culture in which he lives. After all, it *does* make sense as a system of outer orientation in relation to the things which can be achieved on the plane of everyday life.

But what about the medallion of gold with its winged horse and his god-like rider? Clearly this does not fit in with the clock representing his extraverted orientation. It is not a sign, such as the clock, but a symbol which conveys an imaginative message out of time, placed at the numeral VIII. Number eight is a double four, and we know its impressive history as a symbol of psychic (as opposed to physical) orientation.[28] Presumably such an important symbolic number, though not actually separate from the numeral of this clock, emphasizes a direction away from mundane reality towards psychic reality expressive of an inner symbolic content. We may also conjecture that the mysterious line to the Southwest may also express this content. The winged horse has a particular meaning as a symbol for the instinct which, though normally earthbound and in need of considerable control, here acquires the wings which mark it as having a capacity for liberated movement. The god-man is of course the superior man as hero image in relation to the vertical dimension. But the big surprise in this dream is to find that the winged horse is not a Pegasus embodying a sublimated image of triumph. The symbol does not here mean any heroic flight or any escape from reality. As the patient understood it in the dream it meant "the sharing of a common life with others and the sense of communion with my other fellow men at this table." So we are left with a paradox, as is so often the way with dreams, and it may take months or years to figure out the full meaning which they present and, at the same time, gently withhold.

In this case the conversion of a vertical experience (the winged horse) into a horizontal experience (the communal table) does not, however, seem too difficult to grasp. Having lived too fully in the world of his intellect and imagination, this man now comes down to share the communal life of his fellow men; and so the symbol which once meant individualism, aloofness, and escapism is here found at his place in a new collective group experience. The symbol finds its true function by forming part, not a whole, of life's design for him.

Every educated young person comes out of childhood with the impossible expectation of achieving some kind of godlikeness. I have already called attention to the immense social danger of this illusion unless it is corrected. What we can excuse in a boy and even admire, because of the enthusiasm with which he may enliven his elders with his divine discontent becomes both a private and a public danger in a grown man. It is fortunate if this tendency is punished by nothing worse than a neurosis, especially if the sufferer of the neurosis has the patience to find a cure for it in his dreams.

The patient in question understood, though dimly at the time of his dream, that in some way he had to lose his life in order to find it. But the dream symbol also told him that nothing of true value is ever lost, though it may find itself in strange company from time to time. He knew that his winged horse must be kept to the business of life in this world and that if he was ever to fly again, it would not be through any denial of his basic social contract.

Four years later it was reported to me that another type of symbolism had appeared in this man's dreams, suggesting that he was ready to embark upon a different — and, for the first time, truly an individual — journey of initiation. The invisible line at the bifurcation of the two streets in the dream, with its dark and

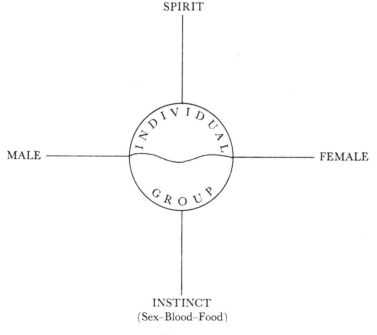

FIGURE 3

mysterious extension toward the southwest, began to come clearer to him. Its affinity with the golden winged horse at Number VIII of the clock which was suggested by the fact that it forms with each of the streets an eighth of a circle, began to open up a new vista towards the spiritual life, appropriately connected with the real banquet of life in this world. This is the essence of individuation in a psychological sense.

It is for this reason that we analysts discourage young people from taking the way of individuation until they have completed their adaptation to the communal archetype and have found their place in the real society of their peers. Only then does the symbol of godlikeness take on the features of a truly inward experience. To set the stage for this process in reality and to present the guiding line of its direction to consciousness is the aim of initiation at the onset of the second half of life. To denote this in a general visual image (*see Figure 3*), we may take our former diagram of the vertical and horizontal dimensions and add to them the potential dimension of mature development, a center in which are combined the inextricable components of the individual and the group meeting in such a way as to suggest a dynamic interchange.

CHAPTER VI

The Rite of Vision

I. *The Journey of Initiation*

THE CENTRAL SYMBOLS of the phases of initiation which we have examined so far are associated progressively with the Mother, the Father, and the Group. Each of these symbols has seemed to provide a rite of passage and a safe haven for further development. The change through which the novice passes appears to be, not so much a reshaping through instruction, as a process of transformation. In this, initiation differs from education in its formal sense.

Education does, of course, lead us through the outward forms of behavior appropriate to each of the central personifications with which we identify in youth: actual mothers, fathers, and teachers. But, as the case material has shown with increasing clarity, allegiance to any one person or group carries with it a strong element of doubt. Thus we have had to postulate the existence of another factor — individuality — which stands outside any parental or group authority and, through some mysterious kind of imagery, transcends it. Without this factor, history would be one long, unbroken chronicle of conformity; in fact it records many rebellious acts by those heroes who have periodically changed the culture patterns of the world.

We have also seen that the transition from family to social group is managed very indicisively in our society. In the interest of family piety we insist upon preserving the tie between the young and their families indefinitely. If we achieved thereby a condition of true *pietas* in the old Roman sense, with every adult shouldering a clear responsibility, there would be no complaint. But we all too often preserve the family tie by encouraging young adults to laziness and dependency, with the mature, responsible members carrying an ever larger burden of immature people, the deadwood of the family tree. It is also apparent that an individual does not break his infantile family ties merely by leaving home; some form of the initiation archetype must be activated appropriately. In response to these dangers it becomes of the utmost importance to gain further knowledge of individuation — how it may appear, and how it may be cultivated.

In dreams or myths, individuation most frequently presents itself as the lively, urgent wish to undertake a journey of initiation alone or, at most, accompanied by a friend. It is apparently the absolutely unpredictable goal of such a journey that provides its charm. In the Navaho myth *Where the Two Came to their Father,* the twin heroes at the onset of the journey of initiation say, "We will know where we are when we get there." Loneliness, depression, and fear of failure are all present, but all are triumphantly overcome by the twins' curiosity and enthusiasm for embarking upon a journey which offers so great a stimulus for the discovery of individual resourcefulness. That the youthful journey in reality has this inner meaning is borne out in many accounts of actual journeys of the type once known in Germany as the students' *Wanderjahre* and in England as the "Grand Tour" of privileged young men; these find more elaborate literary treatment in the many examples of the picaresque novel and even in travel books. As W. H. Auden remarks in his preface to *Italian Journey* by Goethe:

> One reason we enjoy reading travel books is that a journey is one of the archetypal symbols. It is impossible to take a train or an aeroplane without having a fantasy of oneself as a Quest Hero setting off in search of a princess or the Waters of Life. And then some journeys — Goethe's was one — really are quests.[1]

But we should not delude ourselves into thinking that because we understand the obvious archetypal journey as a Hero Quest, we therefore understand its meaning as an initiation. This distinction is complicated by the fact that the unconscious does not itself distinguish between the gross phase and the subtle phase of initiation. It is questionable to regard the archetypal journey purely as a hero's journey, a pattern of conquest over the regressive forces which would hold a young man back from achieving a sense of his identity.[2] On the other hand, we can see it as a journey of individuation undertaken at the zenith of life in order to allow a mature person to come into possession of that psychic wholeness by which the claims of the ego are subordinated to the claims of the Self. The latter journey leads to maturity as self-integration, whereas the former leads to the ego's conquest of worldly prestige. This symbolism in terms of myth is universal; but, for an actual individual's experience, universality is not enough. The experience of the symbolism must also be specific in defining the position of his personal development.

In accordance with the archetype of initiation, the individual undertakes his inner quest without any heroic show of strength and achieves it, not as a triumph, but as a submission to powers higher than himself. He accomplishes nothing by guile, which would be merely another form of heroic trial of strength. He is essentially a suppliant, not a man of power. He can count only upon his own intrinsic human worth and is of necessity his own teacher. He may be allowed to see the object of the heroic quest but not to possess it, or he may possess it briefly before losing it again, or he may derive spiritual insight from it as a talisman which comes and goes.* The boon is not to be shared with the group. Like the guardian spirit of the North American Indians, it is to be cherished, tended, and kept absolutely secret from all men.

Case XIV (Male, age 25)

The main feature of those who undertake the initiation journey is that they have exhausted the absolutism of their group identity — temporarily, if they are young; more or less permanently,

---

* That the initiation in this sense is itself the meaning of the quest, not possession of the quest object, is seen dramatically in two types of story, one of which represents the failure of initiation and the other its success. Two examples of stories representing the failure of initiation are the final part of the Gilgamesh epic and the initial story of the quest of Gawain or Parsifal for the Holy Grail. Successful initiation is represented in the story of Tobias from the apocryphal book of *Tobit* and in the initiation journey of that lowly but admirable fellow, the Snake Youth, Tiyo, of the Pueblo Indians (leaving out those elements which relate this story to the hero myth). A journey of initiation combining failure and ultimate success is Virgil's story of Cumae in the *Aeneid*, which we shall have occasion to study in some detail later in this chapter.

if they are older. A young patient who was being told from all sides that he must adapt to the social mores of his family and their friends and that in this would lie his salvation, had the following dream:

DREAM 1: I am in a huge football stadium. It is completely empty. I turn down one of the ramps to leave, breathing a sigh of relief.

ASSOCIATIONS: The stadium was the scene of many exciting football matches I watched as an undergraduate. I was carried away by enthusiasm when our team won, cast into gloom if we were defeated. Nothing more glorious ever seemed to happen to me than to participate in a triumphant "snake dance" when our team won. I was completely one with the crowd. Now all this seems like a kind of mass madness, and leaving the stadium, alone, seems the sane and sensible thing to do.

INTERPRETATION: This man, though still young, was in the process of outgrowing adolescence, and the group identity associated with the university years is now empty for him, especially the part associated with the image of a conquering hero as its central symbol (the team). I had the impression he was unable to transfer his allegiance from the college group to his social group for the simple reason that he felt the social group supported by his family was itself unconsciously patterned on the hero myth in its competitive struggle for supremacy. If so this would account for his complaint that he felt at times quite disoriented or demoralized as a result of trying to conform. Was he about to become a social renegade, or was there a place for him to contribute out of his own ability, not just from the abilities of his class? To these conscious doubts and fears, the dream in its compensatory manner answers unequivocally: he must for the time being turn his back on the collective symbol of the group and go his own way, and then he will feel right with himself.

Analysis of his dreams first brought to view the unconscious elements of his life in relation to his parents and the social group to which they belonged. The dreams showed these elements of his personal life history alternating with archetypal patterns. At a later stage these elements and patterns were mixed together and organized in such a way as to show very clearly the characteristics of a myth of the Hero Quest. Then, surprisingly, instead of pursuing this quest through an ordeal leading to a triumph or an apotheosis, the dreams suddenly veered away from the classical hero myth, and a dream of initiation took its place.

DREAM 2: I was about to leave my childhood home when I saw upon a hillside nearby a lot of people in strange costume, like South European peasants, emerging from the ground. I did not distinguish any faces or other individual qualities, nor could I tell which were men and which were women. Some of them seemed as yet imperfectly formed or stunted in their growth. Yet they pushed their way up out of the ground vigorously.

The scene changed and I was traveling alone through strange, beautiful country. Sometimes I was walking through woods, sometimes along the edge of a lake, and my way led towards high mountains which I had to cross. I noticed that the country, though cool and autumnal, was also in places warm and spring-like. Spring flowers were growing side by side with the fungi one associates with autumn or early winter.

The scene changed again and I was well along on my journey over the mountains. In fact I had passed the summit and was descending on the other side by a winding path with many upward and downward bends. At one point an ugly old woman placed a huge stone in my path, but I managed to push around it and continued on my way down to what promised to be a warm and sunny country similar to the Alpine slopes of northern Italy or southern France.

The scene changed again and I was at sea level, walking along a sandy beach with my father. We were enjoying the calm sunny weather and there was good feeling between us. Then suddenly I slid down a sand dune into a kind of valley away from the sea but with an inlet or bay forming a narrow calm body of blue water. The scene I beheld on the other side of this bay from where I was standing was extraordinary. There were four green hills symmetrically arranged around a central, higher, cone-shaped mountain. As I looked at this mountain, two large birds, one black and one white, flew from the crest of this mountain, and I realized that it must be a volcano. The flight of the birds created an atmosphere of danger from the volcano, and I felt alarmed at realizing I was entirely alone in this beautiful but sinister landscape.

The scene changed and I found myself in a square house consisting of one room and no windows. I must have entered by a door but I remember none. The place was dark, and though still alarmed at my predicament, I had some sense of security in this place.

The scene changed again. The danger had passed and I found myself in a narrow passage between two rather steep slopes. There were spring flowers, especially lilies, and the place was green. Coming down the hillside, I saw on my left a brown beast walking very slowly until it stood before me, beside a rough wooden gateway. The beast then appeared to be a young bull bison with beautiful kind eyes, and I felt I could see in them the power to change the beast into human form. I remained for a long time looking into the beast's eyes and enjoying the beauty of the place, which had the same atmosphere as the earlier part of the dream — the autumn and spring combined.

ASSOCIATIONS: Leaving home suggests the effort I have been making in analysis to solve the problems of early childhood that have inhibited me from finding myself and my own way of life. The people pushing their way out of the earth suggest the emergence of some form of life much deeper than anything I had previously experienced; they seem to be independent of my personal problems. The lake reminds me of Lake Geneva, through which the Rhone River visibly flows on its way to the mountain pass by way of which it ultimately reaches southern France and the Mediterranean Sea. I visited this place on a summer trip when I was seventeen. I think of it as having been a haven for many famous people who had to flee from political or religious tyranny in the eighteenth century, people such as Voltaire, and as having been associated with such founders of Romanticism as Rousseau and Byron.

The old woman barring my way on the mountain road reminds me of a woman who made a strong impression on me recently because of her almost mediumistic power of seeming to know what I was thinking. I benefited from some of the things she told me but was mistrustful of others. She was not in reality ugly, and she showed nothing but kindness toward me. The good feeling between my father and me as we walked along the beach together suggests the actual situation at present, in which I have regained much of the good feeling I had for him as a boy. In recent years I have been in conflict with him and with the principles of life he has embodied. The changes of scene, the final ones especially, where I saw the four hills and the volcano, the little house and the strange bison, seem like visions rather than dreams — as if I might have seen them as waking fantasies. They were very real and I could see the colors clearly. They carried no personal or historical associations, and the dream landscape seemed aboriginal and timeless. Upon awakening I immediately thought of the beast in *Beauty and the Beast* and of *The Frog Prince* in connection with the animal of my dream.

INTERPRETATION: The associations confirm that this young man had learned to accept the fact of his arrested development and that, far from being a true social deviant, he was unconsciously still somewhat bound to early family patterns. This had caused him to live provisionally, unable to commit himself wholeheartedly to any one vocation or social group. But in this dream we see his inward readiness to leave home and family in a significant act of separation.

He states that the people pushing their way out of the earth represent an activity independent of his personal problems. Thus he himself defines the new activity as coming from the collective unconscious. The people remind him of South European peasants, from which we can infer that the psychic layer of the unconscious which is emerging at this point relates to an historically ancient pre-cultural level. Peasants of this sort are living in a culture of their own which maintains many pre-Christian, perhaps even pre-classical, patterns of behavior to this day.[3] In America too we can find these deeper levels of culture clearly represented in the myths and ceremonial chantways of our Indians, a living expression of Bronze Age mythology such as existed four thousand years ago in the Mediterranean world. There is a demonstrable connection between them.

By diffusion these fragments of myth probably found their way through Asia across the Bering Sea and down into the southwestern part of the North American continent, where they retell the old story — how mankind was created in a deep underground place of darkness and only emerged upon the unformed face of the earth after traversing four worlds. The Pueblo and Navaho Indians have a myth of emergence which recalls the earliest Greek myths of creation before there was any Father-God. The myth of emergence implies creation out of Mother Earth, reflecting a primordial condition of mankind before cutlure became conscious of itself.

Following this historical direction backward in time, we find that our symbolism of emergence may lead us to a still deeper stratification of early culture in the old Stone Age. Archaeologists have taught us that megalithic architecture evolved from a much earlier period in which the architectural prototype was the cave, serving Paleolithic man as a burial place, a temple (especially for animal worship), and the place where significant initiations of the shamanic type were originally performed. These caves appear to have had a peculiar significance for the earliest hunting tribes, and much of the art found there was apparently meant to promote hunting magic. But there is another theme of this art which seems to make the animal itself a symbol of fertility, designed to further reproduction not only of animals but perhaps also of human beings.

In stone bas-reliefs and figurines we find, during at least one part of the Paleolithic period, an abundance of feminine figurines with breasts, buttocks, pelvic breadth, and sexual triangle grossly enlarged. The true significance of these figurines has not been fully determined, especially since they show a remarkable variety of forms. But at a much later stage the unmistakable reality of a Mother cult appears — the tree-and-pillar cult of the Aegean civilization. Gertrude Levy tells us that the pillar is presumably used instead of a figure of the Mother Goddess herself, flanked on either side by "worshipping demons or emblematic beasts."

Such a conception may underlie the creation of stone architecture (which we now know to date, in Anatolia, for example, from Neolithic times), as successive to the excavation of rock sepulchres with roofs vaulted in memory of the cave. Such stone-cut chambers might themselves be regarded as holy — the cavern-form of the Mother Goddess. These, in Minoan analogies, might then become shrines of a pillar, a concentration of chthonic energy like the stalagmite whose contemporary sanctity is attested in offerings found in actual caves.[4]

These architectural chambers served a triple function which seems to carry on the original Paleolithic function of the cave: they were tombs, temples, and healing shrines. The last is suggested by the discovery of cubicles in Maltese temples, "like the Temple of Asclepius at Epidaurus, where incubation was practiced in later days."[5] We can infer that these temples, as tombs where the dead were buried (and occasionally contacted ritually as spirits of the dead), were the same temples that provided the ritual of rebirth as a healing rite. Hence they must have been places of initiation also, since initiation at this stage of human awareness appears to acknowledge the simultaneous experience of death and rebirth as, in essence, being at one and the same time concerned with finding new life in this world and new life in the next. The old Paleolithic assumption that nothing ever really dies but only transmutes its ontological status, still seems to hold firm in this period, during which the cult of the Mother Goddess stood for an original source of chthonic energy to be transformed by the initiate into the particular requirements of his human need.

The dream we are considering introduces the dreamer to this symbolism as the emergence of new life from an ancient source, and in this connection we can already catch a powerful allusion to the whole message to be conveyed: that death and rebirth are experienced most meaningfully in one and the same moment, during a season not known to exist in our mundane calendar but one that is nonetheless symbolically real, a season in which autumn and spring are going on simultaneously as death and rebirth struggle for supremacy. But in the mood of the dream there is no struggle between these forces, such as would be found in conscious waking life. There is a kind of balance achieved within the archetype of death and rebirth which unemphatically promises that in the end initiatory death, as a way of nature, will give way to initiatory rebirth, just as spring follows autumn and winter.

This symbolism is combined in the dream with the theme of an initiatory journey. The place through which the dreamer walks is strange and beautiful country, "sometimes . . . through woods, sometimes along the edge of a lake," and here the mythological mood of death and rebirth is first experienced. But his association to the lake evokes a personal memory, his real journey to the Lake of Geneva when he was seventeen. When questioned, he recalled that he had been supervised on the trip by two older cousins, but had been allowed to take some excursions on his own, one of which was a trip by boat around the Lake of Geneva. His account of this period was not remarkable; it was the usual picture of a youth in his period of naive idealism and hypersensitivity to social injustice. While this pointed to his own backwardness due to having grown up in an overprotected environment, it also pointed to an affirmative countermovement forwards. This comes out in his positive response to such men as Voltaire, Rousseau, and Byron, who dared to express their disapproval of the bigotry of their times and, especially in the case of Rousseau, to liberate a feeling for nature from its bondage to social conventions. His interest in this region as a place of exile also points to a peculiar tendency or need of the late adolescent to experience a time of withdrawal during which he can seek the new identity he will need in order to reach maturity.

Erik Erikson refers to this as a period of rapid change in the loyalties and rebellions of youth, in response to which "societies, knowing that young people can change rapidly even in their most intense devotions, are apt to give them a *moratorium,* a span of time after they have ceased being children, but before their deeds and works count toward a future identity."[6] Because modern education has become in many ways so active and so competitive, it frequently frustrates rather than furthers this natural moratorium, which is a desirable period of introversion in the psychological sense. The young may then experience strongly in fantasy the historical immediacy of those great figures who have been forced at significant times into periods of inactivity, during which they have had to turn inward and experience their loneliness and the anxiety of separation unaided. The adolescent can partially identify with such historical figures as the patient mentions and can imagine that he too, someday, will come gloriously out of this period of inactivity and present his own unique contribution to the problems of his time. Erikson recognizes this as a legitimate phase of development in youth.

> Youth stands between the past and the future, both in individual life and in society; it also stands between alternate ways of life. . . . Ideologies serve to channel youth's forceful earnestness and sincere asceticism, as well as its search for excitement and its eager indignation, toward that social frontier where the struggle between conservatism and radicalism is most alive. In that frontier, fanatic ideologists do their busy work and psychopathic leaders their dirty work; but there, also, true leaders create significant solidarities.[7]

But the identity crisis of late adolescence may have a larger meaning for cultural life as a whole, as Erikson has so interestingly demonstrated in his studies of the development of George Bernard Shaw and Martin Luther during their twenties and well into their thirties. It seems to be axiomatic that the identity crisis of a young great man will not be solved until he has made his first major contribution and that as soon as this becomes visible, he will settle into middle age. The historian Arnold Toynbee has pointed out the regularity with which the famous men of history have demonstrated the "movement of Withdrawal-and-Return." At significant periods they were forced, either by political and social accidents or by their own natures, to withdraw into inactivity, during which they underwent a process of creative introversion. From this they returned to periods of renewed and heightened productive activity.[8]

Although this analysand was not a young great man, he had encountered a similar identity crisis, a challenge to individuate, and his dream at this point takes him back to a time he had experienced that challenge in fantasy. But the lake of his dream is only the beginning of his journey, as if to remind him that the comfortable, romantic moratorium of youth is to be superseded by a much more crucial test of his identity without known historical figures or landmarks to guide him. No river flows out of this lake through a natural mountain pass. Presumably he has to climb over the mountain to reach his destination.

The journey continues by a road over the mountains, which becomes on descending, a winding way down. As he descends, the dreamer's progress is impeded by an old woman who has placed a large stone in his path. He gets around this obstacle and continues on his way, which eventually leads down to sea level, where he meets his father. They walk along the beach together on a calm, sunlit day in a spirit of friendly reconciliation. A familial problem has been solved. But there are no familial associations to the old woman placing a stone in his way. She is not a mother-figure in any personal sense; she is merely an old woman, quite unlike any real woman he had known, except for the association with the mediumistic powers of a certain woman acquaintance.

The old woman in the dream embodies the archetypal content inherent in the Oedipus complex.* The dreamer appears to escape from a negative mother-figure and to come into a positive relationship with the father, a reversal of the story of Oedipus, who first overcame his father, then married his mother. A similar reversal of the Oedipus story may be found in such figures as Orestes, who slew his mother to avenge his father's death by her hand, or Hamlet, who had to overcome his ambivalent feelings for his mother in order to avenge his father's death at the hand of his stepfather. But in this dream there is no question of jealousy or vengeance. All we have from the dreamer's associations is the picture of an

---

* Freud's conception of the Oedipus complex is justly famed because it opened the movement of depth psychology, from the very beginning, toward a deeper historical substratum of psychic activity than could have been supplied by the associations of purely environmental family influences. It was a misfortune both for Freud and for the future of psychoanalysis that he did not follow the historical direction beyond the tacit assumption, all the way from *Totem and Taboo* to *Moses and Monotheism,* that it is the Father who is at the bottom of all cultural change. Freud's followers had no choice but to accept this view or to deviate, as Jung and later many others, notably Erich Fromm, did because they knew too much about the origins of culture. Since those deviations we have learned a great deal more about cultural origins, especially from the remarkable discoveries by archaeologists and anthropologists during the past three decades, and we are now much better equipped than they were to interpret this aspect of mythology.

Oedipus complex in childhood, which is normal for boys brought up in a family which respects the patriarchal authority of the father in matters of principle or discipline but accepts the mother as nourisher and container for the years of childhood; the companionship and joy which may accompany this relationship with the mother are hard to relinquish in adolescence.

The dream, then, on this level, presents a resolution of the original Oedipal pattern. Here the mother has become strangely impersonal and negative, while the relationship to the father becomes personal and human, reviving the pre-Oedipal feelings of harmonious relationship, in strong contrast to the later ambivalence. This had all taken place in response to the patient's positive father-transference to me as his therapist. Both he and I recognized the applicability of the dream symbolism, but it did not add anything new to his insight or to my knowledge of his psychological need. We had discussed all this before in connection with previous dreams.

If taken symbolically, however, the old woman in the present dream continues the original theme of the birth of humans from the earth. *Old* then means old in a mythological sense, and the old woman with her stone is a Tellus Mater, or Earth Mother, whose intention to impede the young man on his journey evokes an archaic pattern which can be traced back to the Old Stone Age. One of its later versions is found in the Greek story of Deucalion and Pyrrha, who had survived the Flood.

> [When they] prayed to the gods for companions, they were told . . . to throw stones behind their backs, and these stones became men and women. Why stones? The version known to Ovid gives the answer. It says that the instruction was given in oracular form, for what they were in fact commanded to throw behind them was "the bones of their mother." Pyrrha was shocked, but Deucalion saw what was meant, and explained to her that their mother was the earth, and the bones in her body were the stones. To recreate the race of men, recourse must once again be had to her from whom they had their first beginning.[9]

In the Old Stone Age culture of Australia, the ritual approach to this Earth Mother is based on the mythology of the labyrinth as a "winding path of conditional entry" to a place of death (cave as tomb) where the novice is tested by a powerful female personage. This is an initiation test combined with an ordeal. The Melanesian natives of the Malekula Islands enact an impressive ritual "upon which the history of the community and also that of the individual is founded":

> *The Journey of the Dead,* as mimed in the ritual dances of Vao, bears the closest relation to the literary legends of our own civilisation, suggesting some common foundation in a universal ritual descended from the Stone Age of Europe and Asia. In Vao the newly-dead man is believed to arrive before the entrance to a cave on the seashore, where he encounters the dreaded Guardian Ghost. . . . At his approach she obliterates half the design, which the dead man must complete or be devoured. "The Path" has of course been trodden in ceremonial dances during all his adult life, and knowledge of the whole pattern proves him to be an initiate of Maki.[10]

This aspect of the myth and its accompanying rite is described by Layard as low Maki, the first phase of initiation,[11] and since this is presented as a rite for the newly dead man, there is no question of a rebirth to follow in this life. Indeed, there is no question of rebirth at all because the living, in a sense, never really die. As William Perry reports:

> The peoples of the archaic civilization tend to claim descent from a race ancestress, one of the forms of the Great Mother . . . found in the land of the dead. . . . Interment is the means of returning the dead to the place of origin, the underworld. . . . A tribe in upper Burma . . . who inter their dead, claim that their ancestors came out of the underworld by means of a cave. . . . They believe that the deceased go into the large hill whence man first emerged. . . . Certain tribes believe that their ancestors came out of stones. . . . They inter their dead and place a stone on the grave.[12]

These archaic men thought of themselves as true earth men in accordance with their belief in the origin of children. Eliade tell us:

> Before the physiological causes of conception were known, men thought that maternity resulted from the direct insertion of the

child into a woman's womb. We are in no way concerned here with the question of whether what entered the woman's womb was thought to be already a foetus — which up till then had lived its life in caves, crevices, wells, trees, and such — or whether they thought it merely a seed, or even the "soul of an ancestor," or what they thought it was. What we are concerned with is the idea that children were not conceived by their father. . . . Man has no part in creation. The father was father to his children only in the legal sense, not the biological. Men were related to each other through their mothers only, and that relationship was precarious enough. But they were related to their natural surroundings far more closely than any modern, profane mind can conceive. The human father merely *legitimizes* such children by a ritual which has all the marks of adoption. They belong, first of all, to the "place". . . . The mother has only received them; she has "welcomed" them, and at the most, perfected their human form. . . . We might say in a sense that *man was not yet born* . . . that at this stage his life was in a pre-natal phase. . . . He had, we might say, a "phylogenetic" experience of being, which he only partly understood; he felt himself to have emerged from two or three "wombs" at the same time. . . . [All this appears to have been the mythological pattern of the Neolithic people, antedating any religious evaluation of the earth such as] can only have occurred later on — in the pastoral cycle and, above all, in the agricultural cycle, to talk in terms of ethnology. Up till then, what one would call the "divinities of the earth" were really "divinities of the place" — in the sense of the cosmic surroundings. . . .[13]

Hence the myth of emergence at a later date served to commemorate man's emergence from the unconscious state of at-oneness with nature.

With this amplificatory background we can see how initiation at this level is not clearly marked by thresholds and how death and life are also in a state of at-oneness. At such a deep level of psychic awareness, "what we call life and death are merely two different moments in the career of the Earth Mother as a whole: Life is merely being detached from the earth's womb; death is a returning 'home.' "[14] Presumably, therefore, it was this Earth Mother with all that she implies that the patient met and rejected in his dream. Like the Malekulan initiate for the rank of low Maki, he has traversed "The Path" with its meandering passage over a mountain threshold and has encountered the woman with her stone of life and death.

We must now take into consideration the analysand's association to the old woman: she reminded him of a real woman who, in a friendly spirit, had used her intuition in guessing certain things about him that she could not have known factually. This quality makes of the old woman not merely an Earth Mother but a kind of spiritual guide or mentor whose wisdom he alternately admires and mistrusts. We find a mythological and ritual pattern for this stage also. In the Malekulan initiation of the "dead man," those who are to qualify for the higher Maki rank do not regard the cave of the ancestors as a final habitation. "Beyond it the dead man finds himself on a lonely shore, where he kindles a beacon to summon a ferryman (or woman) known as 'The Guide.' "[15]

We know this spirit guide in many literary traditions and can trace the feminine aspect to the first detachment of the feminine soul-image from its fixed habitation in the stones of the Earth Mother to its final resting place as the message-bearing function in the masculine psyche, as an archetypal image. This function presages the appearance of "a male deity who is the object of no cult, but only of aspiration." For the Malekulans "he 'represents their conscious striving,' and is explicitly connected with the idea of height attained in Maki, and therefore with the temple-tower and its mythological counterpart, the fiery mountain of Ambrin which for devotees of the higher culture, lies beyond the Cave."[16]

We know the female spirit guide as the Grail Messenger of later traditions in Western Europe, but her tradition extends back to Sumerian times. In the Gilgamesh epic she is Sabîtu, whose first name, according to Knight, "has been translated 'ale wife,' and who has in her gift some kind of strong drink. Her Greek equivalent was originally thought to be Calypso, but lately she has been regarded as nearer to Circe, who also dispensed a strong drink, which effected magical transformations."[17] Knight suggests that Sabîtu's second name can be equated with "the name of the 'Jewish Sibyl,' and a form of the word 'sibyl' itself."[18] Sabîtu, Calypso, Circe, and finally Virgil's Cumaean Sibyl follow in direct historical sequence as a long line of sibyls who belong to what may be called a stone daemonology . . . born in a cave, in which were statues of the nymphs; they belong to a very old layer of belief, and like sibyls . . . are only in part divine, for they are liable to death. The Idaean sibyl prophesied standing on stone. With her in her cave was a stone Hermes . . . Among other things he is a grave stone; obviously a monolith "spirit house," half remembered in the "herms" of classical times . . . It is not surprising that in classical myth he guided ghosts to Hades, or evoked them from there.

Apart from the traditions of classical antiquity Knight mentions:

> a descendant of the female petromorphic spirit . . . called "Cailleach," which means "old woman," by the Celts. . . . Like the madly prophetic sibyls, there is a Cailleach with a "roaring mouth" . . . and she appears before a hero as a repulsive hag and suddenly transforms herself into a beautiful girl. Sibyls too had an ambiguous longevity in myth.[19]

Returning to the Cumaean Sibyl, Knight reminds us that she once had "the apotropaic name of Taraxandra, 'she who alarms men.' "[20]

The function of the sibyline archetype, then, is apparently to indicate the point at which a message coming from the unconscious disturbs that form of consciousness in men that is unaware of itself, unaware especially of its truly masculine nature. Thus her strange prophecy points to the discovery of a new form of consciousness to be first found in the region of the unconscious itself.[21] This sequence of events, described as an initiatory descent, is beautifully told in Virgil's *Aeneid,* where the goal — the same as that reached by the patient in his dream — is a new encounter with the personal father.

> Near Cumae was the supposed access to the world of the dead, controlled by a priestess of Apollo and Diana, the sibyl, who guarded a temple of Apollo and a cave. Aeneas went to the temple; and stayed "reading" the picture of the Cretan labyrinth on the gates. Then the sibyl appeared, and told him not to waste time, but to offer sacrifices. He obeys; she prophesies his future to him; and he asks to be shown how to visit his father Anchises in the world of the dead . . . he must find and pick a "golden bough" as a passport,

etc. . . . He obeys and . . . is guided through the cave by the sibyl. . . . He sees evil spirits on the way and hears about the punishment suffered by the wicked in the depths of Tartarus. . . . Eventually he finds Anchises in Elysium, open country. . . . Anchises shows him a vision of Roman history and explains the moral government of the universe. . . . After the great experience, there is a change in Aeneas; he is firmer, with a stronger faith.[22]

Aeneas' journey and his descent to the underworld, then, mark the transition between two cultural modes of being; and Anchises, his father, is the image of an old authority which has been (or is about to be) superseded by a new one more appropriate to the rites of a patriarchal order. Through Aeneas, Rome is to be founded out of the destruction of Troy which symbolizes a matriarchal community which was to be succeeded by a new form of patriarchy in the historical destiny of the Hellenic world.

This transition, of course, was not made only at the comparatively late date which we associate with the rise of the Roman Empire. Patrilinear forms of culture alternated with matrilinear even in Malekula. This suggests that men in the Old Stone Age had begun to evolve an alternative religious symbol to that of the Earth Mother — the father as a solar deity. In Malekula there was a male deity of no special cult who was associated with the whole solar system, as opposed to the earth principle. "Taghar, the people say, is the direct light of the sun and stars, and lives in the moon, though he is not himself the moon."[23] Levy notes also that "there is a strong solar element in the Sumerian myth. As in Egyptian mortuary belief, where there is even more emphasis on this element, the dead seem to follow the path of the sun." All solar heroes travel westward, the road of the setting sun. "Like Shamash, the Sumerian sun-god, Hercules, or Heracles, has crossed the waters of death before . . . and it was Heracles who travelled over the ocean in the 'cup' of the sun, which corresponds to the boat of the sun in Egyptian myth." The land of the sun god becomes, in the Greek tradition, the abode of those who are reconciled to death. The old ancestral cave of the Earth Mother is replaced by the bright sunlight of Elysium.[24]

Although the slender dream fragment we are discussing leaves out much of the symbolism found in even the most condensed

form of the ancient initiation pattern, the basic landmarks are all
present: the crossing of a mountain threshold, the meander suggestive of the labyrinthine approach to a sibylline representative
of an Earth Mother with her stone, the rejection of the old woman
and her stone as an obstacle, and a further descent to a seashore
where the dreamer meets his father in an open place under a
beneficent sun. The harmonious relation he now feels with his
father is suggestive of the sun-hero at the moment of his apotheosis.
In retrospect we may conjecture that the young man has rehearsed
in his dream the pattern of development by which a boy overcomes his fears of childhood dependency and tests the durability
of his ego to meet the initial requirement of manhood, where the
father and the group are paramount.

The material of this dream takes us deeper, however, than
would a simple recitation of the hero myth. Initiation is sometimes
successfully accomplished by descent to the underworld, as in the
story of Aeneas and its modern parallel in the analysand's dream-
descent to find his father. But more often the great initiation
stories begin only after the Hero Quest has initially ended in failure. This was the fate of Gilgamesh, of Gawain, and of Odysseus
in many of his exploits. The theme of failure of initiation seems
to imply some tendency for the initiate to forget to honor (or even
to notice) significant vestiges of the old feminine religion of the
earth. Gilgamesh failed to notice the seven loaves of bread baked
by the wife of Utnapishtim, a demigoddess, on each of the days of
his initiation sleep; and failing thereby to appreciate the true nature of his initiation, he lost the plant of immortality. Gawain,
after healing the fisher-king's wound by asking a significant question concerning the first objects he saw carried in the Grail procession, falls asleep, and the secret of the Grail is lost. The Grail —
like cauldrons, stones, and other magical, food-producing objects
— is a symbol for the ancient wisdom of the Earth Mother and her
sibylline connection with the unknown powers. Where these are
unknown to the initiate-as-questor he is tempted to revert to the
security of the hero myth and its consoling religion of the Father.
Consequently the true initiate cannot remain a father's son only,
any more than he remained a mother's son in the beginning.

And so our modern Quest Hero, in the next episode of his dream, leaves his father and pursues his journey alone into still stranger archetypal country at a deeper level than before. This episode does not belong to a culture pattern but is a visionary primordial experience. The dreamer has taken a step backwards in historical time beyond the configurations of the hero myth, but he has taken a step forward in defining his individual relationship to the archetype of death and rebirth and to the principle of transformation. Sliding into a valley presents him with a threshold experienced in the same irrational manner as in the dream of Case XIII, Dream 1 (p. 125). This is typical of an individual initiation. No comfortable flight of stairs leads him down (that is, there are no consciously devised rules of procedure). The initiand has to "slide" into it.[25]

This unconscious symbolism is matched on a conscious level by the feeling so often expressed by analysands that they have "let themselves go" and do not know what is happening to them. Very often this involves acute anxiety, but they may regain confidence when they understand that this is the only way to experience anything new. Most reassuring of all to the analysand is the observation frequently made by his friends and relations that he is changing for the better — that he is freer and perhaps more truly himself when not so well defended by his social personality. Yet in spite of these reassuring signs, the strangeness of such a close contact with the unconscious and an apprehension of peril are strongly felt throughout the period of change, and it takes many months to return to the full stability of conscious identity. The reasons for this we must now explore in a comparative study of shamanic initiations, the most individual type of initiation to be found in tribal societies.

The central rite of shamanic initiation is preceded by some form of overpowering shock to conscious identity. In ancient Crete this was the "Rite of the Thunders."

> Long before Zeus was Zeus, thunder and lighting were . . . divine potencies, their vehicle was a thunder-stone. . . . After describing the din made by the . . . maddening hum of the *bombykes,* the clash of the bronze cymbals and the twang of strings, Aeschylus goes on, "And bull-voices roar thereto from somewhere out of the unseen, fearful semblances, and from a drum an image as it were of thunder underground is borne on the air heavy with dread."[26]

This passage expresses the essential identity between the thunder rite and the dream image of the volcano. That it is a volcano rather than thunder in the dream is not an inconsistency, since both are cataclysmic natural events which may be equally experienced as supernatural. Moreover, "an image as it were of thunder underground" is simply an allusion to an earthquake, which belongs to the same order of terrestrial disturbance as volcanic activity. The volcano is also a traditional symbol for the Earth Mother's manifestation as goddess of fire.

Campbell tells of an Ainu goddess of fire whose name, "Fuji," appears in the name of the sacred volcano Fujiyama. In Hawaii the goddess Pele is the goddess of the dangerous yet beloved volcano Kilauea, where the old chieftains dwell forever, playing their royal games in the flames."[27]

The thunder rite, however, implies the existence of a strong masculine force which is released in the manifestation of a thunderstorm or volcanic activity (cf. the Greek gods Zeus and Vulcan). The Malekulan material, which so often has seemed to clarify our conflicting symbolizations, again reminds us that masculine and feminine are artificial distinctions when applied to basic archetypal images.

> The initiate, as "dead man," is ferried safely to the island volcano, "Source of Fire," in whose flame some say that even Le-hev-hev may stand upright. Upon its summit, in certain accounts, the dead dance as skeletons all night long. At every dawn their heads fall off, and the bones rest on the ground till sunset. The corresponding mortuary rites resemble the occasional Palaeolithic practice of decapitating the corpse, which is buried at sundown, so that its owner may join the dance immediately after the required conditions have been fulfilled.[28]

Le-hev-hev, though frequently identified with the Terrible Mother, as the Female Devouring Ghost, cannot "be completely disassociated from Taghar," the male deity, whom we have found to be associated with the mythology of the sun-father. The two birds in the dream, one white and one black, suggest a movement, probably of the shamanic type, for spiritually transcending either the Terrible Great Mother or the Great Father.

The dream experience met with in the valley points to a rite of vision, and the threatened eruption seems to prepare the way for a series of events illustrative of the archetype of initiation. The patient felt, in discussing this dream, that he had in a sense been deserted by those previously helpful powers of protection provided by his father and the social class to which he had belonged — powers which the young man had now, regretfully, to leave in order to find his own way alone. His taking refuge in the little hut seems at first like an attempt to regain an illusory sense of security in this wild place. But in the images of the dream world we are always dealing with important symbols even when they appear in an abridged or distorted form; from this viewpoint his refuge in the hut probably has a ritual meaning which completes the thunder rite. The sequence of events suggests that because he found the hut, he was spared from the danger of the volcano, and because he experienced the seclusion of the hut, he then met a transforming animal.

We know that the thunder rite in tribal communities culminates in a rebirth ceremony. The initiates are segregated in the house while the thunder spirit is abroad. Later they leave the house and are taught to become thunder spirits themselves (i.e., to twirl the bull-roarer). Among certain tribes the house itself is built in the form of a dragon, and the youths are led in through the mouth as though they were being devoured. According to whether the threatening monster is female or male, the entrance to the hut is dragon-shaped (vagina dentata) or shaped like a bird's beak (the threatening father). When the youths emerge, they have new names and are treated as little children (i.e., reborn).

In contrast to these collective huts, the one in the dream — and the dreamer's experience there — is solitary. Eliade describes this type of individual initiation as found chiefly among the aboriginal societies of North America and Australia.

> Between the ages of ten and sixteen years, the boys isolate themselves in the mountains or the forest. Here there is more than separation from the mother, which is characteristic of all puberty rituals; there is a break with the community of the living. . . . The novice's introduction to religious life is the result of a personal experience — the dreams and visions provoked by a course of ascetic

practices in solitude. The novice fasts, especially for the first four days . . . purifies himself by repeated purges, imposes dietary prohibitions on himself, and submits himself to numerous ascetic exercises. . . . It is after these prolonged efforts that he receives the revelation of his spirit. Usually the spirit makes its appearance in animal form, which confirms the cosmic structure of the novice's religious experience. More rarely, the spirit is anthropomorphic (when it proves to be the soul of an ancestor). The novice learns a song by virtue of which he remains connected with his spirit throughout his life. Girls retire into solitude on the occasion of their first menstruation; but for them it is not absolutely necessary to obtain a tutelary spirit. . . . The novice's solitude in the wilderness is equivalent to a *personal* discovery of the sacredness of the cosmos and of animal life. All nature is revealed as a hierophany.[29]

One of these groups has been reported in detail by Jaime de Angulo, who was able to converse with them in their own language. They are the Achumavi Indians of Northern California.

Of tribal initiation rites there is no evidence (except a rite at the time of a girl's first menstruation) . . . but when the time of puberty approaches the Achumavi youth is instructed by the elders in the following words:
"You will soon become a man. Where is your *tinihowi?* You are no longer a child. Soon you will possess a woman. Soon you will go hunting with the men, you will take part in games of chance. But if you have no *tinihowi* you will be good for nothing, you will only be an ordinary Indian, nobody. If you have a *tinihowi* who gives you luck you will find game if you are a hunter. If he is good for hunting he will lead you to your game. . . . Go look for your *tinihowi*. Go into the mountain. In the evening when the sun is setting and the mountains are all red, begin to climb, climb quickly, running, without stopping. Try to reach the summit before the sun disappears. Near the summit you will find a lake [These lakes are always ancient volcanic craters, not very wide but extremely deep. . . .] It is a terrible place, a place of fear. Many *tinihowis* live in this lake. They do not like you to make a noise. Do not say anything, do not shout or sing. Do not roll stones. . . . Dive into the lake head first. Do not be afraid. You are going to die. But if you are destined to see a *tinihowi* he will pull you out. Many things are there which look at you without your knowing it.

Perhaps you will be pleasing to them. Perhaps it is a stone, or a lynx, or a bird, or a fly. And it will say, "This boy pleases me. I will make a brother of him. I will pull him out." Then the *tinihowi* will pull you out of the water, put you on the bank and bring life back into you. It will awaken you and say, "Wake up — I will protect you." And then you will return. But you mustn't speak of this to anyone, not to your father or to me or anyone. Tell no one what your *tinihowi* is. It is yours, for no one else. Go to see it from time to time. It will teach you its song. Call it, sing its song. Soon it will come out of the woods. It will hear. It will say, "There is my brother calling me." That is the way it will get to know you little by little. It will become your friend. . . . Never lead it to the house. Go to see it outside. . . . Be quite clean when you go to see it. Take a hot bath and when you have sweated much go dive in the river. Also fast before going to see it and eat no meat. Above all, do not touch a woman when you go to see it. It would quickly smell that. But perhaps you will have no luck. Perhaps no *tinihowi* will want you for its brother. Not everyone has luck, not everyone has a *tinihowi*. In that case you will be an ordinary Indian, a common man, nobody."[30]

The image perceived by the Achumavi as *tinihowi* is remarkably like the early Paleolithic drawings of animals on the caves recently discovered in Spain, France, and Africa. It is perhaps from these endopsychic perceptions and their concretization in pictorial or sculptural form that arose the whole panoply of primitive culture — the song, the dance, the hunt, and lastly the arts of the group: agriculture, medicine, magic, and the bands of Kouretes.

Characteristic of the American Plains Tribes are the sweathouses, small huts with single doors and no windows, situated at varying distances from camp. To these huts not only medicine men but other initiates go alone at certain times.

Thus among the Algonkins in North America, a Fox man in telling a missionary of his experiences in the sweat lodge said: "Often one will cut oneself . . . through the skin. This is done to open up many passages that the *manitou* (the Algonkin equivalent of *mana*) may get through. The *manitou* comes out of its place of abode in the stone. It becomes raised by the heat of the fire and proceeds out of the stone when the water is sprinkled on it. It comes out in the steam, and in the steam it enters the body wherever it can find entrance. It moves up and down and all over inside the body, driving out everything that inflicts pain. Before the *manitou* returns to the stone, it imparts some of its nature to the body. That is why one feels so well after having been in the sweat lodge."[31]

In this account we have in a very condensed form the rites of purification by fire and water, combined in a rebirth ceremony of an individual kind, by means of which the initiate not only sees the primordial spirit but is able to procure it, manipulate it, and store it in himself. This is essentially different from these sacrifices and sacraments which "tend to go over to the public, ceremonial, recurrent contacts effected collectively."[32] We have here an individual, private, isolated effort to contact it.

The little hut in the dream thus serves the function of providing a transitional stage of containment between the purificatory thunder rite and the transforming rite of the encounter with the animal. The youthful initiate, following his first lonely pilgrimage, finally thus accomplishes the rite of vision.[33]

What is to be transformed by the animal in this dream? The answer first appears in the patient's associations. *The Frog Prince* is a fairy tale in which a maiden promises to marry a frog if he will retrieve her ball, which has rolled into the pond. The frog does so and, against her will, holds her to her promise. In revulsion against making the slimy creature her husband, she hurls it against the wall, whereupon it turns into a prince whom she is well pleased to marry. The erotic theme introduced in this story is similar to the Hopi myth of the Snake Youth, in which sexual fear is overcome by an ambivalent act in which attraction and resistance are combined.

A more significant example of the myth of the transforming animal is found in the fairy story *Beauty and the Beast*. In her gradual perception of Beast's hidden human qualities, Beauty's erotic feeling is freed from an incestuous bond with her father and becomes transformed into the mature capacity to love humanly without thought of herself. It is therefore probable that Beast's transformation into the prince, which occurs when the maiden accepts her animal lover, indicates the passage from a virginal state to the awakening of her sexual instinct. But the sexual explanation of such stories is a little too narrow, since, as we saw in the case of the Snake Myth, the power of transformation inherent in the animal symbol contains always the larger sense of self-discovery and the coming into consciousness of a capacity for relatedness over and above the purely sexual urge.

The heroic power of sexual assualt is, however, a powerful image in the masculine approach to Eros. A masculine myth equivalent to the feminine myth of *Beauty and the Beast* is the story of *The Loathly Bride*, found among the Arthurian legends. In this story a knight is forced against his will to marry a bestial hag. Overcoming his aversion in an act of knightly gallantry, he embraces her, whereupon she changes into a beautiful woman, a princess whom he is happy to have as his wife. In an early episode of the Snake Myth, the Snake Youth is received by Turquoise Woman, the Sun's wife, who allows him to sleep with her. At night she is beautiful and desirable, but when he awakens in the morning, he finds her a hideous old witch. Here sexuality is represented as an incest-wish alternating with an incest taboo which turns beauty to ugliness, just as a boy experiences the ambivalence of his feeling for his mother. But if it happens the other way round, as in the Snake Youth's courageous handling of the snake at Spider Woman's advice, the incest taboo is forcibly overcome by an assertion of ego strength which transforms sex into Eros. Then the power of transformation residing in the animal symbol may be evoked in such a way as to free him for his first truly human response to love. This is initiation through sex.

Such was the type of experience made available to the patient in question. His dream and the insight derived from it actually represented a turning point in his development, a true rite of passage. The passivity of his unconscious bond to his mother and to his childhood world (which also included the protective, loving aspects of his father's early treatment of him) and the protective walls of his social identity created for him by the cultural traditions in which he had grown up were shattered in his response to this experience.

It is significant that his associations are concerned with stories which might be more appropriate for an initiation of the feminine psyche. But at the level of the initiation archetype, masculine and feminine are interchangeable; and it is just as appropriate for his feminine nature (as anima) to respond to the transforming power of the animal in a kind of erotic awakening as it is appropriate for the maiden in the fairy tale to experience a call to action of her masculine nature (*animus*), such as we saw in the story of *The Frog Prince*.

In a peculiar blending of masculine and feminine attitudes the erotic nature is changed. This young man's sexual response changed first. The symbolic animal seems to have imparted a certain wisdom which allowed him to experience sex not as a conquest so much as with a feeling of submission. Sex under the aegis of the hero myth is, for young men especially, experienced as a triumphant act. Under the aegis of initiation it becomes rather an act of communion and liberation. But the effect of this transforming experience did not end here. It carried him into a new and very active period of his life in which he began to realize his capacity for receiving and giving love, and discovered that this capacity is a far more valuable acquisition than the illusory charms of the loved one, since it is part of a civilizing process in general.

True, he met this civilizing process on a level associated in the dream with a bull bison, a wild animal of tremendous importance to the great hunting cultures of Paleolithic prehistory; and the dream landscape itself suggests a primitive sense of nature alive with magic power. But these facts do not confront us with an insoluble paradox, for the transformation is imagined to take place from animal to man, not the other way round. As a result of his dream experience he is to become less animal, as his animal, whose eyes have a human look, promises to become ultimately human. The meeting takes place at a significant threshold where we find traces of human culture — a wooden gate and the probable cultivation of special plants, such as the lilies he observes in this valley-like place.

Here we have again the universal symbolism of rebirth, first encountered at the beginning of the dream, suggesting simultaneously the Annunciation or Easter symbolism, in which the lily stands for the original birth or for the reborn state of Christ, and (more deeply buried in history) the Minoan One Goddess, who "stands above the spring meadows, or descends from the air into the midst of her ecstatic votaries, or, seated beneath her tree, receives offerings of lilies and poppy-heads, the first-fruits of her own bounty."[34] In the course of this dream the old Earth Mother with her rigid cult of the dead has imperceptibly changed from stone into the vegetable cycle, whose meaning is verified by the dreamer as the process of change we call death and rebirth.

II. *The Cup of Dionysos*

THE DREAM-LIKE AWAKENING to a natural experience of rebirth represented in the preceding case becomes in the dreams of older people, especially women, a more elaborate form of initiation evoking a type of symbolism which in our Western tradition had its origin in Greco-Roman antiquity. Fairy tales of the type of *Beauty and the Beast* still enjoy wide popularity because they smuggle into modern civilization at least part of that message from the natural unconscious, a message which in its entirety has never ceased to shock devout Christians and which they have habitually suppressed as far as possible. In pre-Christian times this was part of a widespread mystery religion associated with the god Dionysos. What shocked the Christians was the orgiastic character of its popular celebrations; yet this also fascinated them unconsciously, and it reappeared in such manifestations as the witch cult of central Europe with its many scandalous practices, but chiefly with many tall tales, copiously illustrated by artists of the Renaissance, of a witches' sabbath in which the central male figure was the devil, worshipped as a goat.

But the late medieval assumption that this form of rite was purely drunken and lascivious was erroneous; the error sprang from a guilty conscience caused by the strenuous repression of certain natural and joyful impulses. Beast in the fairy story awakens Beauty to a reconciliation of goodness with erotic love; the Dionysian religion went much further. The central rite took its initiates into the innermost sanctuary where the union of the god with his feminine counterpart, Ariadne, represented an experience totally beyond the principles of good or evil. The initiate temporarily lost his reason, but he found the spirit of god in nature to make him whole. What appears to be orgiastic in this ritual is actually a symbol of man's willingness to allow the spirit of nature to speak to him in a language totally different from reasonable logic. Hence the cup of Dionysos, which he extends to all his followers, is not the giver of drunkenness, if rightly tasted, but the container of a priceless secret knowledge better conveyed in ritual gestures than in words.

This point of view is not self-evident, of course, and it is no wonder that such wisdom expresses itself, not in psychological theories, but in the colorful visual imagery of the unconscious. Some of this material has been illustrated in paintings originally produced by patients of Jung and his followers, such as Adler, Harding, and Wickes;[35] but they are not exceptional. Whenever a certain threshold between the conscious and the unconscious is reached, there is a tendency for people to produce fantasy material which engages their interest in returning to the pre-human, animal level of being. This at first may cause apprehension or panic because of the strange forces lying below the threshold, forces whose impact might dissociate an unstable ego. For this reason, analysts carefully watch the dreams and the products of active imagination to see whether the unconscious is likely to be overwhelming.

If the unconscious presents itself in a discrete and comprehensible procession of visionary events, and if each of these events awakens in the patient an emotional capacity to understand and partially assimilate it before going on to the next, we have in therapy a modern equivalent of the ancient initiate's experience of the mysteries. But this can take place fully and be brought to completion only if the therapist can empathize with his patient's experience and mediate it for him in the attitude of one who knows it also from his own experience. He must be able to carry the transference of the priestly function, which the patient will inevitably place upon him, for at least a part of this process; and he must be able to help his patient resolve the transference in such a way as to free him for the new life which is opened up to him as a result of his experience of initiation.

The relevance of the Dionysian archetype in the modern unconscious is illustrated by a series of paintings by a patient which Jung reproduced in *The Archetypes and the Collective Unconscious: A Study in the Process of Individuation.* Jung tells us the patient was an American woman with a Scandinavian cultural background, which presumably means that she was psychologically as far from the cultural archetypes of the Greco-Roman world as it is possible for a Western person to be. Yet it was perhaps for this reason — to melt the phlegmatic conscious control of that recently Christianized Icelandic culture-complex — that she needed to drink (like Keats) "a beaker full of the warm South." Her initial response to the unconscious was felt to exist through her personal relationship with Jung as her doctor; but he appeared in her fantasy not as a doctor but as a sorcerer with a magic wand, suggesting Hermes, or Mercurius, as the spiritually phallic leader of souls.

In the first picture the patient shows herself caught or stuck among the boulders on a rocky shore from which she needs to be liberated. In the next picture, Jung tells us, "one of the round forms has been blasted out of its place by a golden flash of lightning. . . . The personal relationship to me seems to have ceased; the picture shows an impersonal natural process. . . . Lightning signifies a sudden, unexpected, and overpowering change of psychic condition." This apparently means that though the sexual symbolism remains implicit in the figure of the lightning flash that has blasted her out of some form of unconsciousness, the liberation comes from above, and the experience is spiritually liberating rather than sexually fecundating. She is thus inducted into the process of individuation by an initiatory experience. This is borne out in the next two paintings, which show a serpent behaving like a phallus, penetrating the round earth that was blasted loose and is now floating in the air. The serpent penetrates from above with a pair of wings near the head, showing it to be the instrument of a spiritual, rather than a sexual, awakening.[36]

Case XV (Female, age 45)

A similar symbolism somewhat more humanly descriptive of this cosmic assault was related as an active fantasy by a patient of mine.

FANTASY 1: The scene is in some remote mountain area. There are bulky mountain peaks and deep ravines. The atmosphere is dark and stormy, and a fierce wind is blowing. A great giant of a man is making his way across the moors and peaks in a wind so fierce that the vegetation is nearly torn up by the roots. Underneath him he propels the recumbent body of a naked full-bodied woman who has long dark hair. There is a sense that the two are moving along together but propelled by the strength and power of the man. Now, as he reaches the brink of a dark ravine, all nature trembles, the wind heightens, the sky is rent with bolts of thunder and lightning. As he enters into its depths with the woman, the earth quakes and opens up. Rain pours down from the heavens into the earth.

INTERPRETATION: In this fantasy the sexual symbolism is clearly apparent and was explained by the patient herself as a picture of the erotic storm in her own nature when she is out of touch with the humanizing presence of real men. Yet this cosmic storm and violent union of man and woman, which ends in fertilizing rain from the heavens into the earth, signifies much more than sex. It expresses a need for the awakening of her earth-bound nature in some obscure but absolutely compelling way. In contrast to the mere threat of the volcanic eruption in the previous patient's dream, she is in the presence of a true *mysterium tremendum*.

In the origin of the god Dionysos we find a similar symbolism. At Thebes the legend of his birth described him as the son of Semele, the goddess of the Moon, as Keraunia ("Earth the thunder-smitten"). Euripides in *Hippolytus* describes Semele as "the Bride of the bladed thunder," who died as a result of her simultaneous impregnation and delivery in producing Dionysos. In the *Bacchae* Dionysos identifies himself as the one "whom the brand of heaven's hot splendour lit to life, when she who bore me, Cadmus' daughter Semele, died here." Such a birth is clearly not natural but spiritual, a new-birth appropriate to the rebirth of the initiate in a rite of passage. This initial birth is clearly the result of an impregnation from a sky-spirit, "a sort of Ouranos later effaced by the splendour of the Hellenic Zeus." The thunder-stricken place where Semele died became a sacred monument and was associated with a belief in the efficacy of a thunder rite as an initiatory event of great importance. But in the Greek legend the Mother symbolized as a fallen aerolite, a thunder-stone, " 'had power to purify from madness.' She had power to loose as well as to bind. In this she was like her son Dionysos. . . . Orestes was purified . . . from his madness, mother-sent, by a sacred stone. Pythagoras when he was in Crete met one of the Idaean Dactyls, worshippers of the Mother, and was by him purified with a thunderbolt."[37]

In another form of this legend we hear the famous account of Dionysos' birth from the thigh of his father, Zeus:

> When from out the fire immortal
> To himself his God did take him,
> To his own flesh, and bespake him:
> "Enter now life's second portal,
> Motherless mystery; lo I break
> Mine own body for thy sake,
> Thou of the Two-fold Door, and seal thee
> Mine. . . ."[38]

Clearly this too refers to a second birth, or new-birth, and fits into the initiation rites as a final passage from Mother to Father, an archetypal event reflecting the puberty rites of primitive antiquity.

The god in this legend is called the Dithyramb, which means literally Zeus-leap-song. The word "leap" is interchangeable with "beget," so we have here a fertility rite represented as a dance of initiation in which Dionysos is the central figure either as a bull or as human Kouros, i.e., initiated youth. From this rite arose another tradition which linked the Dithyramb with the goat; and from this, Aristotle has told us, arose tragedy, the Goat-Song.

In both of the cases described in this chapter, the same kind of power is expressed in fantasy as we have seen in the legend of Semele — the violent yet healing effect of a thunder-rite. The second patient was especially ready to understand this event as a sign of renewed ego-strength after a particularly disturbing onslaught from the powers of the collective unconscious, which she had experienced sometime earlier. She would have been particularly impressed with the truth of the statement that such a visitation of nature "had power to purify from madness" and the "power to loose as well as to bind."

The symbolism of these fantasies and their corresponding rituals emphasize a powerful experience of death which contains within its imagery the equally powerful promise of rebirth. But the symbols of rebirth do not unfold until we reach that aspect of the material which emerges from the darkness of the mystery into the light of nature, by which the mystery can be understood. This is not the full consciousness of daylight, but the half-light of an awakening to consciousness from the deep unconscious, the light of dawn or a meaningful twilight. Paracelsus, that great psychological doctor of the Renaissance, called this consciousness the light of nature, *lumen naturae*, an alchemical expression which conveys the sense of coexistence of spirit and sex, male and female, in an individual type of experience.

The peculiar radiance of the *lumen naturae* as a form of psychic consciousness is admirably represented in another painting by Jung's patient. Jung himself refrains from commenting upon this picture, which was one of the series which only came to him after the patient's death. Whatever may be said of it is therefore speculative, but it seems to me to represent most beautifully the experience of the final stages of the Dionysian initiation, of which the initial picture of the lightning flash was the first. A central sun-symbol is surrounded on all four sides by a beautifully designed series of eight vines with their clusters of grapes. The background is divided into eight radial segments colored delicately in the graduated shades of the spectrum, blue merging into green, yellow, orange, red, and violet around the circle. The background of the picture is all black.[39]

Expressed in terms of the mysteries of Dionysos, one may say that the black background represents the darkness of the mystery proper, the midnight consciousness during which an inner sun brings to light a symbolic consciousness, Dionysos, in his sunlike aspect as the Dithyramb, reborn son of Zeus, the thunderer. The grapevines stand for the growth, from the thunder-smitten place where Semele died, of that fruit which of all others, when made into wine, is the giver of inspiration; that fruit, in turn, represents the initiatory secret contained in the cup of Dionysos, telling of the existence of spirit in nature. This picture is, I would say, the essential symbol of this experience; but since it does not specify its meaning for the analysand, we naturally wish to know what this might mean in the living texture of a woman's life.

The answer, or a part of the answer, to this question is suggested in the dream of my patient which immediately followed the fantasy of the storm in the mountains, the giant man and his woman, and their erotic immolation by the powers of nature let loose in a modern representation of the thunder-rite.

DREAM 1: It is early morning. The atmosphere is tranquil. I awaken in a household which is built around a square courtyard which has an open gate. In the center of this courtyard is a well where all people come to fetch water. I seem to be a member of the household, and my role is that of a woman who knows her place in the rhythm of life. My senses are keenly aware of this new-born day. The sun filters through a patch of blue sky; a bee is buzzing already in the morning sun. People begin to stir as the rhythm of everyday life get under way. In the moment of awakening and reflection, there is a feeling of attunement in me to the dark life mysteries and to everyday living, which seem to interweave one with the other. I prepare to arise and live this day.

ASSOCIATIONS: Nothing specific or personal.

INTERPRETATION: In this communication there is no suggestion of Dionysian frenzy or violence; in fact, the mood is not Dionysian but classically Apollonian, with its calm, ordered, rational conception of life. It is a rebirth after the ritual of dismemberment representing symbolic death. But the rebirth is not wholly spiritual. It comes into being gradually in the half-light of dawn against the background of dead night. As daylight emerges, it is not very bright and therefore produces, not a euphoric state of bliss, but a sober acceptance of the human being and her appropriate place in relation to the community as a whole. Hence the cup of Dionysos has given not just animal awareness, dissolution of consciousness, and the ecstasy of sexual assault. It has also given the ability to live in nature with spirit and finally the wisdom to understand life as a communion with others in the light of an inward consciousness symbolized by the sun.

It is easy enough for us to follow the transition from Dionysian chaos to the Apollonian spirit of order. The triumph of Apollo is just what our education has led us to believe should always take place. But it is borne in upon the psychologist, as analyst, again and again that this view is insufficient for modern men, since it may cause us to miss the deeper import of the Dionysian initiation. This patient's fantasy of finding her role in the ordered community and her new determination to live more fully in the present remained with her for a time, but later fantasies forced her back into the chthonic world of the Earth Mother, where the dark powers lie concealed. In a still later fantasy she thought a serpent came from below and entered her body, permeating in its course all parts of her in a way that made her feel again the fertilizing powers of the earth. At another time she experienced a sequence of fantasies leading to a ritual union of male and female elements, first as animals, then as man and woman, taking place in a sacred precinct. Out of this union, in a series of meaningful images, there came not a new-born animal or human being but a sheaf of wheat. All these fantasies recall the theme of the sacred marriage and carry it to a more essential level, where *coniunctio,* or joining together of opposites, expressed as male and female in an inner sense, produces a new thing.

This was also Dionysos, who was not merely the vine but the god of all growing things and at Eleusis, as wheat, was frequently called Iacchus. The products of nature as plants are symbols of metamorphosis. "Apollo is the principle of simplicity, unity and purity, Dionysos of manifold change and metamorphosis."[40] In the popular festivals reaching back to the festivals of Osiris in Egypt there was a vulgar, orgiastic element to the Dionysian religion, but even this acted on the minds of the celebrants to increase fertility and therefore the productivity of crops, animals, and women. The sacred marriage basket was a winnowing fan, or *liknon,* filled with fruits and phallic-shaped objects, which also symbolized the initiatory new-birth. Later this symbol was raised so far above the vulgarity of the collective rituals of the solstice and of spring as to lose all connection with the spirit of god in nature. It became purely spiritual — that is, ascetic — and divorced from the Dionysian religion, which maintained its connection with animal man to the end.

This alienation, which began to be experienced historically in the late Hellenic world with the rise of Orphism and neo-Platonism, became a fixed article of faith if not of practice in the early Christian period. Eventually, in the Renaissance in Europe and again in the period of Puritan Christianity, it brought about that condition of asceticism whose excess led to a compensatory need to re-experience the old Dionysian initiation. In our own time it has taken the form of the Freudian revolution of sexual morality with its rediscovery of the Pleasure Principle.

Case XVI (Female, age 20)

Sometimes modern dreams with their sly, humorous childlikeness, yet with a streak of divine wisdom, expose the true state of affairs to be corrected. In a dream a modern young Englishwoman was sitting in the congregation of a fine Christian church at night. To her amazement the roof of the church came off, and its walls were gradually destroyed by strong grapevines which were visibly growing in from outside. Quite unperturbed by this event, the clergyman announced, "And now we will have the pagan part of the ceremony," which in the dream seemed quite natural. Here, as in the Dionysian rite of initiation, was the act of bringing joy to the devout — the essential element lacking in this woman's conception of church religion.

Of Dionysos, Euripides wrote in the *Bacchae* that his was not just an earthly joy, but a joy combined of spirit and nature:

> By his own joy I vow,
> By the grape upon the bough.
> No grudge hath He of the great,
> No scorn of the mean estate,
> But to all that liveth, his Wine he giveth,
> Griefless, immaculate.
> Only on them that spurn
> Joy may his anger burn.[41]

In all the modern products of the unconscious which exhibit this symoblism, we see the same tendency to join emotion with ordered thought into one significant and transcendent experience, illuminated by that eternal democracy of joy in which the Dithyramb of Dionysos and the Paean of Apollo are brought together.

The Dionysian religion is not, of course, only an initiation ceremony for women, preparing them for sex and marriage and motherhood, though these elements are predominant in the symbols of Dionysian creativity. It is no less important for men to participate in the rite of the new-birth and to submit to the power of the sacred marriage. A woman needs the mediation of the god in her initiation rite of self-discovery; but a man no less needs the mediation of the goddesses, as anima-figures, to free him from his own kind of materiality. For him, even more than for a woman, it is sometimes necessary to find the archetypal means of bringing sex and soul, or spirit and nature, together in one experience. We see this especially in modern men who have inherited the Judaic or the Puritan tradition and have become too rigidly patriarchal and monotheistic. They may also have the habit of *thinking* about life instead of *feeling* its vital impulse as it might have been felt in the rites of Dionysos and the Eleusinian Mysteries.

Case XVII (Male, age 36)

A patient of mine who had achieved his appropriate natural autonomy as a man among men, along with a successful career, had yet a great deal of hesitation, doubt, and discouragement in his relations with women. A first marriage had ended in divorce. He was in love with a second woman but feared to enter into the deeper commitment of marriage, yet sensed that his life was unsatisfactory because of this lack. By way of association to a dream he remarked that he had been surprised to find in himself a longing for children of his own. The dream was as follows:

DREAM 1. I am reading an article in a scientific journal. Although it is obviously based on technical research, the article is written in an easier, semipopular style. Its purpose is to describe a new, more accurate method of measuring time. Through a series of diagrams and accompanying explanations, it points out that the older methods were based upon mathematical calculations from astronomy. It then indicates that the new method is much more precise: in the course of one year the error is less than 1/1,000 to

1/10,000 of a second. This new technique consists of attaching an electrode from a large electronic machine to a single grain of wheat. Each spring, at exactly the same moment every year, the germination process begins with a slight sound, which is magnified electronically. It is this moment which establishes the beginning of that particular year.

As I read the article, I speculate on the many reasons that this method should not work. It seems to me that climate, soil, different strains of wheat, and even individual differences in grains from the same strain would result in considerable variations as to the time when germination begins. I then refer back to the article and find that it discusses all of these objections, concluding that even though one might anticipate such sources of error, the actual research has established definitely the accuracy of the new method.

ASSOCIATIONS: Given in the description.

INTERPRETATION: The effect of the dream was to convince this modern rationalist, with his Protestant background, that a new and different orientation to life would be necessary in order for him to fill his life with meaningful emotional content. Because the dream expressed itself in the scientific language he was accustomed to use, he could not avoid accepting its persuasive argument. Because he had to accept this as *his* dream, not science fiction, he also had to accept what he described as "the validity of subjective time, as contrasted to objective time, and by implication, the validity of the emotional or intuitive as contrasted to the purely intellectual, scientific, or rationalistic approach to 'reality.'" In this roundabout yet authentic manner, a modern man re-experienced the initiation at Eleusis with its wonderful product, the Child (αζερὸς Κοῦρος) "the sacred ear of grain."[42]

Elsewhere I have presented material showing how the dreams of certain modern people reveal, instead of a Dionysian symbolism, images reminiscent of the Orphic pattern of initiation, with its asceticism combined with a love of nature.[43] In that connection I spoke of Orpheus as the figure who remembers Dionysos but who anticipates Christ. Thus Orphism represents the last great mystery religion of the Greek period whose main predecessors we now can recall — the cult of the Earth Mother with her

Journey of the Dead, the cult of the vegetation goddess and the Mountain Mother of Crete with her bands of Kouretes, and finally the cult of Dionysos. In a strange way Orphism seems to represent a culmination of these traditions and at the same time to make a break with them.

The legendary figure of Orpheus has recently been identified by scholars with the traditional figure of the shaman. According to Eliade, the tradition of shamanism in Greece was brought "from the North, from the land of the Hyperboreans, from Apollo's country of origin." Two such shamanic figures, Abaris and Aristeas, exhibit characteristic features of shamanism, such as the "magic flight," the ability to appear at the same time in place far apart, and features of the shamanic trance, in the ecstasy of which Aristeas "journeyed to great distances and brought back 'much mantic lore and knowledge of the future. . . .' " Also, Epimenides of Crete is said to have learned the technique of ecstasy, from which he learned "his magical cures, his divinatory and prophetic powers."[44]

> As to Orpheus, his myth displays several elements that can be compared to the shamanic ideology and techniques. The most significant is, of course, his descent to Hades to bring back the soul of his wife, Eurydice. At least one version of the myth has no mention of the final failure. . . . But Orpheus also displays other characteristics of a "Great Shaman": his healing art, his love for music and animals, his "charms," his power of divination. Even his character of "culture hero" is not in contradiction to the best shamanic tradition — Was not the "first shaman" the messenger sent by God to defend humanity against diseases and to civilize it? A final detail of the Orpheus myth is clearly shamanic. Cut off by the bacchantes and thrown into the Hebrus, Orpheus' head floated to Lesbos, singing. It later served as an oracle, like the head of Mimir. Now, the skulls of Yakagir shamans also play a role in divination.[45]

In spite of the myth, Eliade finds in Orphism "nothing that suggests shamanism, except perhaps . . . in the funerary geography of the Orphico-Pythagorean plates, the substitute for a soul-guiding of the shamanic type." Yet he also tells us that "an ascent to heaven by ceremonially climbing a ladder probably formed part of the

Orphic initiation." The mystical ladder also plays a part in the Mithraic mysteries and in the monotheistic religions; for example, Jacob's dream of a ladder whose top reaches heaven and Mohammed's vision of a ladder "rising from the temple in Jerusalem. . .". The mystical ladder is [also] abundantly documented in Christian tradition.[46] (It may also be asked whether the winged boy, Phanes, liberated from the Orphic world egg may not suggest the magic flight.)

Most important in the shamanic pattern is what Eliade calls the "primary phenomenon" because we see no reason whatever for regarding it as the result of a particular historical moment, that is, as produced by a certain form of civilization." While Orphism maintained its connection with the symbolism of the Dionysian mystery religion, it acquired from the figure of Orpheus an immediate spiritualizing influence which partially ruptured continuity with the old religions stemming from the original Earth Mother. The change introduced the idea of an autonomous form of consciousness which knows no allegiance to earth but only to the supreme wisdom of a single "celestial Supreme Being." It comes from above and by a process of evolution in the way that the great earth religions were built up, as the temples and tombs (e.g., the pyramid and the ziggurat) which were built to simulate mountains which aspired from earth toward heaven. For all we know, the shamanic experience with its descent to the underworld, its belief "in concrete communications between heaven and earth," and its peculiar ability both to remember and to prophesy concerning spiritual matters, belongs to this ideology and is just as archaic as the religión of the Earth Mother with her cult of the dead.[47]

For a few centuries these two traditions seem to have fused into a specially liberating, yet also traditional Orphic initiation rite such as we may see pictorially represented in the beautiful series of frescoes from the Villa de Misteri uncovered at Pompeii. And it is the memory of this type of balance, so rarely achieved or so rarely maintained, to which a certain type of over-civilized modern individual returns in fantasy for refreshment and release.

CHAPTER VII

Thresholds of Initiation

THE SYMBOLIC MOVEMENT of the dream images which announce alternating themes of death and rebirth appropriate for each rite of passage may now be reviewed in the light of our original postulate (p. 37). In Chapters III–VI the archetype of initiation was demonstrated from mythological and psychological material with no attempt consciously to separate its structure from its function. This was done intentionally so as to convey to the reader the universal, living quality of the archetype as it is filtered through the experience of individual, living people. For theoretical purposes, however, we need also to separate the various elements of the archetype just enough to demonstrate its true form and its internal dynamics more clearly.

The diagram in Figure 4, though it does not pretend to do justice to the rich experience of human history it represents, may permit us to mark schematically the probable range of initiatory thresholds. In the column are represented six central archetypal figures into which or from which significant symbolic rites of passage are made. The curved arrows a, b, c, and d (on the left, reading up) represent the rites of passage associated with the mythological progression of hero-figures from the trickster-figure at the lowest level to the classical hero-figure in the middle levels and to the redeemed hero at the highest level, becoming at each threshold more fully an initiate than a hero-figure. Arrows a', b', c', and d' on the right reading down) represent the rites of passage signifying a meaningful descent or return to the previous forms of archetypal conditioning. These are not regressive trends but genuine initiatory experiences.

Roughly, the mythology associated with the ascending rites

form the prototype for initiations of the youthful sort, so-called
puberty rites. The descending forms are associated with the mythological patterns found in esoteric initiations, such as in magical
fraternities and in the mystery religions.

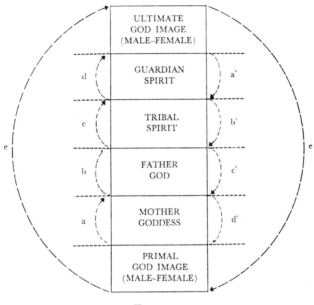

ULTIMATE
GOD IMAGE
(MALE–FEMALE)

GUARDIAN
SPIRIT

TRIBAL
SPIRIT

FATHER
GOD

MOTHER
GODDESS

PRIMAL
GOD IMAGE
(MALE–FEMALE)

FIGURE 4

The God image as defined by Jung is: "A term derived from
the Church Fathers, according to whom the *imago Dei* is im-
printed on the human soul. When such an image is spontaneously
produced in dreams, fantasies, visions etc., it is, from a psychological point of view, a symbol of the Self (q.v.) of psychic wholeness."[1] The distinction between a Primal God-image and an Ultimate God-image is my own conception based upon dream or fantasy
material in my possession and of which a good example will be
reproduced in the fantasy material of Case XVIII, (p. 203) as well
as by the religious iconography referred to in this chapter. No
tribal rites of passage are associated with either of these God-images
yet the individual experience of the shaman or yogin or prophet
— and, as we have seen, of average individuals at special times —
is expressed by a myth of transcendence, such as the magic flight,

which involves crossing an invisible initiatory threshold that separates ordinary consciousness from consciousness of the supernatural. Thus the shamanic type of initiation provides the mythology of a circular experience, descent to the Primal God Image (e') followed by ascent to the Ultimate God Image (e). In this form of mythology the intermediate thresholds of initiation are of little importance, yet the idea of stages, grades, or degrees of initiatory experience is also found in this form of the archetype.

The structure of the archetype of initiation, then, combines a series of levels, stages, grades, or degrees. As I have previously shown in *The Wisdom of the Serpent*, this structure is found in mystical traditions of initiation as having seven stages, represented graphically by the ladder with seven rungs (found in Egyptian or Mesopotamian tombs) and by the seven steps of the alchemical process, leading up to the water bath in which the King and Queen, as human representatives of the Ultimate God Image, are partially immersed, or joined in the creative union of masculine and feminine archetypal principles (*coniunctio*).

Literature pertaining to the subject of reincarnation abounds in imagery derived from this archetype, persuading us to believe that the soul in its migrations learns the capacity to transcend its previous incarnations and perhaps, through death and rebirth, to reach some ultimate or penultimate goal of spiritual perfection. This was most perfectly expressed by Carl Gustav Carus as "the old Indian teaching of the perpetual training of the soul through endless forms of existence."[2]

Romain Rolland uses the image of a staircase: "I have just recovered the key of the lost staircase. . . . The staircase in the wall, spiral like the coils of a serpent, winds from the subterranean depths of the Ego to the high terraces crowned by the stars." The archetypal nature of such utterances is expressed in reiterated statements that there is something eternal which is yet familiar. Rolland concludes: "But nothing that I saw there was unknown country. I had seen it all before and I knew it well."[3]

Even scientists have recognized the basic rational validity of such images of thought. The Darwinian champion Thomas Huxley wrote: "Like the doctrine of evolution itself, that of transmigration has its roots in the world of reality, and it may claim such support as the great argument from analogy is capable of supplying."[4]

Stories concerning initiation proper usually describe the stages of initiation as moving from a lower to a higher sphere of enlightenment, on the assumption that the novice must learn to overcome, by transcending, his animal nature. This type of story is found in *The Golden Ass* by Apuleius and in such modern reflections of this as the libretto of Mozart's opera *The Magic Flute,* with its initiatory goal in the archetypal image of the Father God and the Tribal Spirit. This Tribal Spirit is expressed as a form of group solidarity, the principle of masculine friendship whose model (for Mozart) was found in Freemasonry.

In contrast to this stepladder or evolutionary view of initiation, our material has shown a distinctly cyclic character in which a return to old patterns is of no less significance than a sense of progression to new ones. Each threshold provides a new goal to be reached, involving a rounded sense of totality thus arriving at a new center by means of the ritual sequence of separation, transition, and incorporation. Furthermore, rites of separation leading to incorporation are reciprocal in any given myth cycle. Mother and Father rites are reciprocal, and totemic rites are reciprocal with the rites of vision leading to the myth of the Guardian Spirit.

The prototype of individual initiation, as outlined in Chapter VI, is represented most fully by the shamanic type of initiation with its sense of liberated movement; but this frequently includes (or is included in) some image of containment, which must come from mythic patterns of the *temenos* associated with rites of the Group. In our material, the theme of the Sacred Marriage points back to the Return to the Mother, while the experience of the Thunder Rite points back to the Father Rites. The symbol of peaceful Apollonian incorporation with the community was found to be continuous with the Dionysian frenzy of liberation. At one end of this cycle we have a myth suggestive of rupture with the community of the living; at the other we have a myth of reunion with it. The opposite poles of containment and liberation are bound in one inevitable spirit of complementarity.

Joseph Campbell wisely suggests that we should apply this Jungian concept of complementarity to the study of the mythological hero cycles. Jung frequently evokes a term used by Heraclitus — *enantiodromia,* "running the other way" — to describe a tendency for any myth or "any psychological or historical and cosmogonic overbalancing" to go over into its opposite. Campbell clarifies this term in relation to the epics of Homer:

> On one hand, [we have] the *Iliad,* with its world of *arete* and manly work and, on the other, the *Odyssey,* the long return, completely uncontrolled. [Having completed his 'manly work' in the *Iliad,* he (Odysseus) finds himself compelled in the *Odyssey* to come back to] "that other mind" which is woman: the mind that in the earlier Aegean day of those lovely beings of Crete had made its sensitive statement, but in the sheerly masculine Heroic Age had been submerged like an Atlantis.[5]

The punishment for this kind of forgetting is the same for all excessively patriarchal men who are still partially identified with the youthful hero cycles. When, by the law of *enantiodromia,* the tide starts running the other way, the feminine principle is re-encountered as a doubtful, or fear-inspiring, or even sinister figure. In time the journey of initiation replaces the hero myth; and these figu..es which appeared so unfavorably in the form of Circe or Calypso, begin to turn positive in the figure of Nausicaä. Odysseus is then ready, as a result of his initiatory experience, to re-encounter Penelope as the mature man he needed to become.

On a purely mythological level of understanding, as Campbell shows, Odysseus is a solar hero and Penelope is a moon-goddess. Their union "would bring together in one order of act and realization the principles of eternity and time, sun and moon, male and female, Hermes and Aphrodite (Hermaphroditus), and the two serpents of the caduceus."[6] It is interesting to see how Odysseus on his journey wavers from being a trickster, the wily one, to the hero and finally is forced somewhat unwillingly into the role of the initiated man. In his last exploit, throwing the suitors out of his house, he still enjoyed to the full his murderously heroic powers. At the moment he was about to spring forward "like an eagle in free air [after the enemies], then did Athene cry to Odysseus, 'Back with you, heaven-nourished son of Laertes, Odysseus of the many wiles. . . . Move not farsighted Zeus to wrath.' So

Athene said, she the daughter of aegis-bearing Zeus. Odysseus obeyed, inwardly glad. . . ." Here Athene acts in the role of a superior anima-figure, and at last the hero submits to a master (in this case, mistress) of initiation, instead of having to go on proving his strength forever.[7]

At this same juncture, a transformation of the hero myth by initiation may first lead to the feeling of a failure of initiation, which has been widely commented upon in connection with Gawain's, or Parsifal's, quest for the Holy Grail. The same theme concludes the Gilgamesh epic, where it is clear that Gilgamesh fails to achieve his initiation because he was too identified with the hero role and could not yet acquire the insight which his initiation sleep should have given him. He was still too egoistic, expecting to acquire literal physical immortality, instead of accomplishing the healing rite of vision.

In the cases of both Gawain and Gilgamesh, the healing image was some form of the Mother as symbol of rebirth and renewal, promising something much more sustaining than the magical quest object. For Gilgamesh this was the seven loaves of bread baked on each day of his initiation sleep; for Gawain it was the Grail with its magical food-producing property. Thus both of these great stories point to the final stage of initiation, which van Gennep has told us is ritually represented by a rite of incorporation. Here occurs an inner reacceptance of the Great Mother — a realization that what was first shall become last in the eternal cycle of death and renewal, if only we do not fall asleep at the crucial point (i.e., regress to a preconscious state).

This important theme of the failure of initiation emphasizes the cyclic nature of initiation. The Quest Hero fails, like Gawain, because one can sustain the consciousness necessary for initiation only for a short time. But the fact of having known, or of temporarily possessing, the object of the quest, as Gilgamesh possessed briefly the branch of the immortal plant, has in itself a partial initiatory effect. One knows from such stories as that of the Quest of the Holy Grail that the Quest Hero will never forget his experience of being partially initiated and will therefore inevitably prepare himself to complete the quest at some future time. (Hermann

Hesse's compact novel *Journey to the East* is a beautiful modern version of this theme.)

There is, however, a great psychological wisdom to be acquired from a feeling of the failure of initiation. If the initiate had no further doubt about his status as an initiated man, he would either become an unbearable prig or else subtly return to the role of hero. The feeling that he has partially failed insures his humility and his human group identity, so that in his later life individuation will be real for both worlds, inner and outer, and will not deteriorate into empty individualism or eccentricity.

Stories of ancient Hindu, Buddhist, and later Zen Buddhist initiations convey the impression that initiations are to be regarded as cyclical. After each experience of enlightment, a return to the base line of human experience is indicated until all tricksterism, all heroism, has been refined away and only the true adept remains. In Richard Wilhelm's commentary on the *I Ching,* the ancient Chinese *Book of Changes,* we read that Hexagram 40, which represents Deliverance (suggestive of the thunder rite), is "a time of deliverance from burdensome pressure" and therefore "has a liberating and stimulating effect on life. One thing is important however: in such times we must not overdo our triumph. The point is not to push on farther than is necessary. Returning to the regular order of life as soon as deliverance is achieved brings good fortune."[8]

In the Tibetan *Book of the Dead* the last initiation is imagined to take place immediately after death. The initiate's task then is to throw off the regressive pull back to life and free himself from all earthly involvement. But even this can only be achieved by those who have lived through many lives and presumably have given all they were required to give to outer reality. This formulation applies to any true experience of initiation in life understood subjectively: by its very nature, the next initiatory threshold may not be crossed before the adept has absorbed (i.e., incorporated) all he possibly can from the previous cycle.

In a Christian tradition reflected in a Gnostic story reported to me personally by Prof. Jung there is a dialogue between John the Baptist and Christ in which John warns Jesus not to give away the secret of the mystery to the people. He argues that they will not understand it and will cheapen or falsify it for their own ends. Jesus replies there is no use having the knowledge of the mystery if one cannot give it forth to others and live it openly. This difference of viewpoint has never been and probably will never be resolved, but in its application to the initiation of youth the words of Jesus certainly outweigh the words of John. The secret knowledge of initiation may cause older, more experienced people to withdraw once more into the desert and be able to live on locusts and wild honey in the expectation of learning about final things. For the young, however, the importance of the rite of baptism lies in learning to *live* for the spirit, not to die for it. Thus even the historical Jesus may represent too transitory a figure, still too much the hero-figure who has to die to prove his point. For people in full maturity the Christ-figure becomes a transfigured image of the Self.

From the material of our study it does not appear that the modern problem of finding a new religious orientation finds its most reliable answers in either the ancient East or the modern Christian West, but in an indeterminate place where, during the seven pre-Christian centuries, the traditions of the East met the small tribal cultures of the West. Into the formation of this nucleus there seems to have come from Siberia or Africa, or both, the ancient tradition of shamanism, with its belief in transcendence; this was joined with the more recent tradition of an agriculturally oriented priesthood with its emphasis on rootedness.

Whatever the origins of this tradition may have been (and we can expect much more information about them from the combined work of archaeologists, anthropologists, and religious historians), the living tradition comes to us from no fixed religious dogma. It is spontaneously carried in the stream of those "unsuccessful" but deep initiation patterns which reappear briefly from time to time before disappearing again from view. But the stream continues to flow underground, and we find its contents in the dream images of the modern unconscious as fresh and vital as ever, just as they formerly appeared in the secret traditions of the alchemists, the kabbalists, the Gnostics, the Orphics, and the Pythagoreans, back to the religion of Dionysos-Apollo with its mysterious power of reconciling the religion of transcendence with the religion of containment — in the "light of nature."

Returning to Figure 4 with these considerations in mind, it becomes quite clear that both patterns are present: initiation as a series of levels or stages, and initiation as a cyclic experience. We might describe it paradoxically as a series of developmental cycles. What is equally striking is that the stepladder theory is not characteristic of only one type of initiation (e.g., the puberty rites), nor is the cyclic theory characteristic only of shamanism. Both patterns appear to coexist and even to be inextricably bound together. As was implied in Romain Rolland's statement that his "staircase in the wall [is] spiral like the coils of a serpent," the stages of development which we call initiation are progressive degrees of achievement and, at the same time, cyclic patterns of return in which the same experiences are repeated endlessly. Both patterns are equally valid for the understanding of this archetype.

This understanding of the nature of the archetype is essential as the starting point for any further study of its phenomenology and of its application to the relevant problems of life. Having established the basic image of the archetype, we may turn next (in Chapter VIII) to examine the series of initiatory stages which must be traversed in the effective development of ego-consciousness. This development corresponds to the youthful phase of life, in which initiatory thresholds are mainly to be correlated with socio-biological development. Then (in Chapter IX) we may more fully discuss the individual form of initiation, which replaces the degrees of ego-development by a single cyclic, spiritual experience. In this type of initiation the quest for power or love tends to be replaced by the quest for meaning, and we shall try to discover what this threshold of initiation may teach us about the psychology of individuation.

CHAPTER VIII

Initiation and the Psychology of Ego-Development in Adolescence

I. *Initiation and the Theories of Ego Formation*

THE ELEMENTS OF INITIATION in general show a coherent design in which psychosocial and psychosexual impulses are brought together in the formation of something which is not just an ego-structure but an ego which has the capacity for individual response and the power of individual choice. But this is precisely what the adolescent cannot achieve except at those nodal points of growth where insight and the power to act in accordance with it become temporarily accessible to consciousness. Far more often the adolescent ego is pressed upon, molded, or even dissolved by the family or social group surrounding him.

In attempting to free himself from the early family influence, he becomes the victim of what Erik Erikson calls *identity diffusion.* This usually becomes manifest when the young individual finds himself exposed to a combination of experiences which demand his simultaneous "commitment to *physical intimacy* (not by any means always overtly sexual), to decisive *occupational choice,* to energetic *competition,* and to *psychosocial self-definition.*"[1]

This may be a "time of breakdown," which entails a regression to infantile patterns; or it may lead the adolescent, in his "longing for intimacy," to seek a master or mistress of initiation. This search frequently fails or only partially succeeds because the object chosen for this intimacy is not up to the job or because the adolescent expects the impossible. Erikson expresses this failure as follows:

> Young persons often indicate in rather pathetic ways a feeling that only a merging with a "leader" can save them — an adult who is

able and willing to offer himself as a safe object for experimental surrender and as a guide in the relearning of the very first steps toward an intimate mutuality, and a legitimate repudiation. To such a person the late adolescent wants to be an apprentice or a disciple, a follower, sex mate or patient. Where this fails, as it often must from its very intensity and absoluteness, the young individual recoils to a position of strenuous introspection and self-testing which . . . can lead him into a paralyzing borderline state . . . a painfully heightened sense of isolation . . . a basic mistrust, which leaves it to the world, to society, and indeed to psychiatry to prove that the patient does exist in a psychosocial sense, i.e., can count on an invitation to become himself.[2]

From our case material relating to initiation, we can see how easy it would be for a young person in the crisis of adolescence to choose a "negative identity" and to return to the form of identity diffusion which we have described as the trickster-figure with its intricate play of dissocial attitudes, at times appealing, at times malevolent and self-destructive. We have also seen how this regression may, if properly guided, become an experience of initiatory return to the Mother, as archetype, for the sake of rebirth. It is interesting that the values we have found to emerge from such a regression, experienced archetypally, are essentially verified genetically by Erikson from the clinical point of view. He finds that the original relation of an infant to its mother creates a psychosocial crisis between "basic trust" and "basic mistrust" as the growing child experiences a sense not only of unity but also of separateness or division.[3] If I read Erikson's chart correctly, a regression to this stage would lead the adolescent back to reaffirm whatever basic trust he had originally acquired from his actual mother. If he had acquired a greater degree of mistrust, he would perhaps learn belatedly to acquire basic trust in a psychotherapeutic relationship of some kind.

It is significant that Erikson also stresses the bipolarity, or reciprocal relationship, which should mark the normal infant's transition from the mother-world to the object-world, i.e., from a state of oral dependency to a state of relative autonomy in the second year of life. He lists the psychomodality of the first stage of life as the combined impulses "to get, to give in return."[4] We can verify this modality, as well as the psychosocial crisis of trust vs. mistrust, by the observation that the cases I have cited, in their return to the Mother, all exhibit the need to discover or rediscover not just the mother's love for them but also their own *capacity to return love to her* as the basis for an adult behavior pattern in relationship.

We can also fully corroborate Erikson's observation that the identity crisis of adolescence is normally followed by a new (or renewed) capacity for achieving "intimacy" as against "isolation." At the same time he inadvertently corroborates our thesis that the changes brought about in such an initiatory experience have a basic spiritual character, and he sees that for the most effective "mothering" some form of religious faith must transcend the personal life of any individual mother.

> It seems worth while to speculate on the fact that religion through the centuries has served to restore a sense of trust at regular intervals in the form of faith [which entails] the demonstration of one's smallness and dependence. . . ; the admission of inner division and the consequent appeal for inner unification by divine guidance. . . . Whosoever says he has religion must derive a faith from it which is transmitted to infants in the form of basic trust; whosoever claims that he does not need religion must derive such basic faith from elsewhere.[5]

In terms of the initiation archetype, this "religion" or this "elsewhere" is probably found in the experience of a universal conjunction of opposites, a union with and a separation from the Mother, which comprise the first stage of initiation. No wonder it is so frequently represented in the ritual forms of art and architecture as a labyrinth which annuls the divisive nature of the rational, patriarchal mind. It seems to say that one must lose onself to find oneself at a significant threshold where the original experience of birth is transmuted into a psychic experience of rebirth. This need not be regarded as a religion, but it is in fact the basic experience from which one important type of religious ritual is formed — rites of purification, lustration, and baptism. Erikson's view of religion is therefore limited to this first rite of passage and ignores the higher religions of the Father or the Holy Spirit.

Erikson's analysis of the subsequent stages of development leading up to the identity crisis of late adolescence shows parallels, first to the hero myth and then to the later developmental stages arrived at by means of the initiatory "ordeal" or "trial of strength" associated with certain father-figures, masters of initiation, and the corporate life of the group. In a religious sense, the kind of confidence achieved as a psychic experience of rebirth provides the foundation for rites of confirmation. This stage would provide the basis for a religion of the Father as well as a religion of the Mother.

When the crisis of adolescence reaches its peak of intensity, Erikson envisages the stages of "sexual identity vs. bisexual diffusion," "leadership polarization vs. authority diffusion," and "ideological polarization vs. diffusion of ideals" as comprising the full range of inner and outer conflicts to be experienced and, if possible, resolved. Our study of initiation confirms that sexual differentiation is a central problem which presents the initiate with an apparently insoluble conflict or play of opposites which it is the task of initiation to resolve. This includes the psychic experience of sex which underlies all religious conceptions of divine union in which male and female are significantly unified or significantly separated. Behind the rather cumbersome headings "leadership polarization" and "ideological polarization" can we not sense the working of an individuating factor through which individual and group experiences are meaningfully separated or reconciled? Erikson even recognizes the historical importance of

> *initiations* and *confirmations:* they strive, within an atmosphere of mythical timelessness, to combine some form of sacrifice or submission with an energetic guidance toward sanctioned and circumscribed ways of action — a combination which assures the development in the novice of an optimum of compliance with a maximum sense of fellowship and free choice.[6]

Although this is expressed largely in terms of group initiation, with no mention of the purely individual, shamanic type of initiation, Erikson nonetheless appreciates the importance of an individual form of development which, even in adolescents, may transcend the claims of a purely egocentric, socially minded adaptation. In fact, he comes very close to conceptualizing Jung's Self and its role in the process of individuation:

It is this identity of something in the individual's core with an essential aspect of a group's inner coherence which is under consideration here: for the young individual must learn to be most himself where he means most to others — those others, to be sure, who have come to mean most to him. The term identity expresses such a mutual relation in that it connotes both a persistent sameness within oneself (selfsameness) and a persistent sharing of some kind of essential character with others.[7]

Erikson's observations are especially valuable because they are derived from his work with children and adolescents representing the entire social spectrum of American life. Being himself foreign-born and -educated, he is in a position to distinguish purely local differences from the larger picture of Western culture and its effect upon the young. My own cases, in contrast, are extremely limited, since they all come from a class of older people with sufficient socio-economic security and educational status to afford the time and expense of, and the desire for, a quite complete individual analysis. It is therefore especially gratifying that the stages of initiation outlined in this work correspond so closely with Erikson's clinical stages of identity development. The similarity seems to confirm the validity of the Jungian form of depth analysis, besides showing how well the Jungian approach complements the Freudian approach to problems of early ego-development.

But though Erikson is concerned, like Jung, with the end products of archetypal conditioning, he nevertheless remains firmly within the Freudian tradition, which denies any such conditioning except as it comes from the culture pattern, i.e., from outside the individual psyche. The contrasting Jungian position has been expressed by Michael Fordham.

Accepting the archetypal structure of the unconscious a priori, Fordham explains that this leads us to look for "a predisposition . . . in the child to develop archaic ideas, feelings and fantasies without their being implanted in him." He emphasizes Jung's view that such fantasies cannot be reduced to simple biological conditioning. The archetype itself is bipolar; it has an instinctual root and a spiritual root. In this sense Freud's concept of "infantile sexuality" is archetypal because it grows from this double root; Fordham quotes Jung's observation that "while perceiving in infantile sexuality the beginnings of a future sexual life, I also discern there the seeds of a higher spiritual function."[8] The polymorphous nature of infantile sexuality, with its transition from an oral to an anal and then to a phallic phase, is one of the most important forms of archetypal activity in the service of establishing identity. Having a spiritual as well as an instinctual root, this activity is creative and experimental and is not merely narcissistic self-gratification. It does not only try to get; it also wants to give, as Erikson so rightly observes.

Fordham sees the infant's first experience as the separation from the mother at birth, which has a disruptive or dissociating effect upon the developing embryo. Recent biological evidence for this event is put forth by the biologist Adolf Portmann, who regards the human infant as remaining an embryo during the first year of life. After birth this embryonic infant must re-establish its identity with the mother in her nurturant role. Its relation psychically to the mother's breast, together with the awakening of an oral and kinesthetic response, re-establishes the original totality of mother and child, which becomes the infant's first experience of unity (Erikson's "unipolarity").[9]

This unity is presumably to be derived from the Jungian Self as an archetypal image which Erich Neumann identifies as the *uroborus* and which in my diagram I have identified as the Primal God Image. Fordham sees it as a condition to be "deintegrated" in the process of ego-development. Just as Erikson regards the original condition of unipolarity as changing into a condition of bipolarity when the infant recognizes its separateness from the mother, so Fordham sees the original self-image becoming fragmented into various ego-images. The final mature ego-image developed in full maturity, then seeks to be reintegrated with the Self in the process of individuation.

Approaching this problem of ego-development in adolescence, Edward F. Edinger, following Neumann, provides an alternative conception of the dynamics by which ego separates from Self. The advantage of his theory is that it gives an explanation for the inevitable conflict which occurs between ego- and Self-images during the period of the adolescent crisis. In this theory the Self is a primal absolute from which the ego separates and to which it later

returns to establish an increasingly conscious relation. The formation of this "ego-Self axis" provides the identity necessary for the
ego to relate meaningfully to the Self-image (atonement) and to
maintain a polite distance from it (avoidance of ego-inflation or
megalomania).[10]

Just as Erikson defines identity as a unique self-determining
core of being in relation to the social group, so Edinger seems to
envisage this identity as the crucial experience of discovering an
individuating factor such as we have found in the process of initiation. Fordham's theory has the advantage of providing an explanation for the early stages leading up to the initiatory experience
in which we may perceive an image of the semi-divine quality of
childhood, not yet dissociated entirely from the original Self, as
the *puer aeternus* or *puella aeterna*. His "deintegration" of the
Self produces a series of ego-images which, after traversing several
successive stages of tricksterism, finally give birth to the hero myth
and the images associated with it.

In spite of their differences, the images of ego-formation described by Neumann and Fordham seem to represent the first
configurations of the hero cycle. The hero-figures are images of
ego-ideals fostered by watchful guardians. These hero-makers (as
I call them) are personifications of the original Self image maintaining a partial control in limiting the hubris of ego-inflation.
Thus, in contrast to the trickster myth, which emanates from a
center within the archetypal mother-child world, the hero myth is
centered within the archetypal father-child world.

The behavior patterns of these two cycles come much later,
during late childhood or adolescence, but the art products of young
children already prefigure them.[11] What is most striking in childhood is the imaginary interplay of the two cycles and the alterna-
tion or oscillation between them, which finally combines trickster
and hero cycles in a kind of evolutionary or devolutionary rhythm.
In other words, we do not find normal children developing in a
measured, progressive forward direction; they show equally a
chaotic, retrogressive need to recapitulate old patterns. Presumably they would progress and regress equally and interminably if
the influence of some strong educational agency from without or
some strong motivation of the archetype of initiation from within

did not instigate a new cycle. We cannot, I think, derive one of these cycles from the other at our present stage of knowledge, but must consider that they are coexistent and dynamically interrelated.

Premonitions of initiation, like the images of trickster and hero, may occur very early in life, long before the behavior patterns appropriate to them can be developed. But as long as they function unconsciously, the ego is essentially identical with the image, and no development of ego can take place beyond the psychobiological stage of development. Moreover, this relatively autonomous activity tends to sweep the developing ego into its orbit, carrying it back to those dim beginnings of life where instinct and spirit are wrapped in a single blanket.* This original state of at-one-ness is bound to be essentially totalitarian and hermaphroditic, and fosters the original god-likeness of the trickster image. Thus the whole cycle returns to repeat itself, as it seems, forever in a kind of myth.[12]

Neumann and Edinger have each enunciated a principle denoting the ability of the maturing psyche in late adolescence to put a stop to this eternal return of the basic trickster and hero cycles. Neumann speaks of the "personal evocation of the archetype," and Edinger postulates the formation of an "ego-Self axis." The individuating factor ceases to remain an image and becomes

---

* Hence the interest of certain Jungians in the view of Melanie Klein that archetypal symbol and physical organ (i.e., breast, penis) are identical in the child's consciousness. No doubt this is true, but such a way of expressing what a child (or a regressed adult) really may be experiencing in depth is curiously awkward and conveys the impression of a pathology at work rather than of a developing ego-consciousness. In a recent paper, "Individuation in Childhood," Fordham exposes the fallacy of this attitude toward childhood and redefines individuation as a primal condition. Fordham, as a child analyst, is able to verify from his experience that the ways in which troubled children, in therapy, solve their problems and move into the next developmental stage are not uniform nor biologically predetermined. Instead, these solutions to apparently insoluble problems convey the impression of something new and freshly spontaneous and are individual for the child at his level of growth. However, this use of the term *individuation* creates needless conflict with the classical use of the term; and while agreeing with Fordham in spirit, I prefer to use the term *individuating factor,* as I have throughout this work. The full distinction I wish to convey between the individuating factor and individuation will be taken up in the final chapter.

an active pattern of behavior at the threshold between adolescence and maturity. In a different way, each of these concepts denotes the ability of the youthful ego, at some significant point in its self-development, to refuse to continue to identify with the images of the trickster or of the hero and to separate itself temporarily from the effects of all archetypal Self images. Edinger's concept especially seems to imply that the ego at this point is able to put a significant distance between itself and all other images without annihilating its connection with them. In fact, it implies that the ability to place the right distance between ego- and Self-images is the basic condition necessary for the appearance of individuation in later life. And all this, appearing at the point of an adolescent identity crisis, marks the first effective appearance of the archetype of initiation.

II. *Psychotherapy in Adolescence*

THE PSYCHOTHERAPEUTIC significance of initiation in the adolescent period is substantially the same as in later years; and a problem is treated in much the same way, whether it is encountered at its inception or reappears later in dream material. There is, however, one distinct difference between the approach taken with older people still suffering from arrested development and the approach taken with adolescents. In the latter case, the analyst is inevitably cast in the role of a parent or educator, and some acting-out of this role is necessary to elicit the young patient's confidence.

One cannot, as with older people, rely upon the adolescent's ability to see a problem as a sickness to be cured and, at the same time, as an opportunity to learn scientifically to acquire an objective knowledge concerning this sickness. Initially one cannot talk to a young person at all about transference and resistance, nor count on his acquiring the insights to be derived from such an interaction. And when he does acquire significant insights, he may keep them to himself for a very long time — in fact, one may never know what finally brought about one's therapeutic success. Unlike the older patient, the adolescent patient presents his problem mainly in the form of patterns of behavior, seldom in the form of inner images.

There are also many external obstacles to carrying out a full analysis of these cases. Because young people are not in a position to pay for therapy, they may exploit the situation to remain unconscious and irresponsible. Their need to adjust to their contemporary teen-age culture forces them into all sorts of evasions and imitations, and they feel a very understandable need to break off therapy as soon as they, or their parents, feel they are again adapting "normally" to educational expectations for their age group. Hence educational and religious influences are supremely important in treating the disturbances of youth and, hopefully, of their families concerning them.

In spite of these difficulties, the role of psychotherapy in adolescent disorders seems to be making a progressive stride which is extremely heartening. In my limited experience, this stems from the fact that many adolescents applying for psychological treatment are prepared to feel at home with — and therefore are partially transferred to — a psychotherapist of their parents' choosing. Most of the patients of this group whom I see are the children of people who have had analysis themselves, or friends of such people. A whole new generation has grown up trusting the depth psychologist as it formerly trusted the family physician or the clergyman. Furthermore, this modern type of young person has already absorbed, consciously or unconsciously, a good deal of psychological knowledge from parents or educators and is eager to learn more. He senses that he may cross the appropriate initiatory threshold for his age with the help of this psychological educator-therapist better than with anyone else, for the patient knows that his exposure of his inner thoughts and feelings will be safely tended and protected in this process.

He may also, as frequently happens, need to understand from an impersonal source what this thing called psychoanalysis, or analytical psychology, or individual psychology, may have meant to his parents and what a totally different thing it is bound to mean to him. This may facilitate the process of parent-child separation more effectively than any other method available today. One must, however, remember that the method is nothing if it is not applied by a therapist who can approach his patient fresh, individually, and as free as possible from educational prejudices of his own. And he must have the capacity to make his young patient feel cherished long enough and in such a way that he later can accept that very personal and painful type of criticism that will plunge him into his initiatory ordeal in a wholesomely unprovisional manner.

The young do not want to be spared this ordeal, and at this point, where the shell of their pretenses begins to crack, the therapist can see a new configuration of the inner image as clearly as he can in his older patients. Thereafter therapy of this type promotes the possibility of insuring not just ego-strength but also some awareness of Self-strength — in short, *stature*. What I feel most strongly in talking to a young person is my wish to convince him of his latent capacity for achieving stature *as a person* and, as a means to this end, to help him look forward to becoming a man capable of revealing his inherent shape. Although there cannot be any rules for this type of therapy, any more than for other types in which the individuating factor is evoked, it may help the therapist to bear in mind the succession of probable initiatory thresholds to be traversed, as outlined in Chapter VII. Then he may find himself cast in the role of the Mother, the Father, the Tribal Master of Initiation, or the Guardian Spirit; and he may be guided while his patient makes his initial therapeutic surrender, opening himself for the first time to the healing power of unconscious forces.

Then, at the first sign of true resistance or opposition to this cradling, the therapist must be the one who in some way actively pushes his patient out of this state over the next threshold, even when it may be a wrench to his own feelings to let go of a transference (or counter-transference) which has called forth his fullest capacity for parental love or educational concern.

An instructive and beautifully written account of such a therapeutic encounter is found in May Sarton's novel *Mrs. Stevens Hears the Mermaids Singing*. It is all the more convincing because the therapist is a woman in no sense concerned with professional therapy, and the patient is a boy not formally in treatment. Yet what happens between them evokes the pattern of initiation in a remarkably convincing way, as a model for this type of psychotherapy.

It should be borne in mind that what these characters — Mrs.

Stevens, a poet, and her protegé, Mar — call "poetry" might be expressed in psychological terms as a creative openness toward the unconscious, with the intent to acquire self-knowledge. Thus Mrs. Stevens says, "Poetry has a way of teaching one what one needs to know . . . if one is honest."[13]

Mrs. Stevens is well aware of the risk involved in encouraging anyone, especially a young person, to "listen to the mermaids singing," as she calls this kind of introspection, since instead of finding a source of healing magic, he may be tempted to drown in his own narcissism. Mar's problem presents itself, in fact, as such a danger: the autoerotic component of an initially creative homosexual tendency.

Hence, after encouraging the boy enough in his talent, she wisely but firmly, even passionately, steers him away from "poetry" toward the living of life for its own sake. She insists that if he, as a man, is ever to become a true poet, it must be the expression of his fullest capacity for being and becoming himself. In the course of their association it becomes clear that, just as Mrs. Stevens is something of an anima-figure for the boy, he in turn is something of an animus-figure for her. It is her eventual realization that he is, in this sense, her "muse" that enables her to call forth the man and father in him as the wished-for liberation of her own creative talent, to become more mature than it had been and better prepared for the inevitable misunderstandings and criticisms which an important writer must expect. In other words, she looks forward to a new coming-of-age for her work as a writer, as much as for the boy to be launched into his life as a man.

Throughout this novel the theme of bisexuality recurs, as if to remind us that the sensitive thresholds of initiation always involve a meeting of opposites which force people to face both sides of their natures. The novel also reminds us that the first true, though tentative, resolution of this opposition occurs at the peak of the adolescent crisis.

At this point a therapist may for the first time really doubt his work because the young patient suddenly seems removed from all that the therapeutic relationship has meant to the therapist. In the novel Mrs. Stevens realizes that Mar cannot become a good poet if he does not "live out his life to the full as a man."

She was afraid because of all she had told him, asked of him, believed could be possible for him, as if he were herself. Here she ground her teeth to keep from swearing aloud, so fierce was her sense of failure in regard to him. He must have a whole life, grow up, marry. So she knew in the very center of her being. How to set him free? How persuade?

"I'm an old woman, Mar. You must grant me that."

"Do I have to?" He came back toward her, smiling. "You talk about it a lot, but you don't seem exactly old. Or young either. Just yourself," he said, considering her with evident pleasure.[14]

So, in the end, she convinces him not with arguments or interpretations or counsel but by her own individuation, which appears to the boy, as yet too young to have any experience of this himself, perfectly natural. Upon a new basis of mutual understanding he then shows her that he is ready to take the step from the Mother to the Father, and to the world — not to find another therapist as father, but rather to discover the father in himself. Mrs. Stevens registers this in her own reaction to his standing over her like "a father-figure."

Finally she leaves him with the sense that such a threshold crossing is not final, and merely means "peace, order, poetry, to be won over and over again, and never for good, out of the raw, chaotic material. . . .

" 'All I meant to say, Mar, is that every end is a beginning.' "[15]

Without belaboring this analogy between the novel and psychotherapy, it is apparent that Miss Sarton shows cleverly the precise extent to which Mrs. Stevens acts out the role of parent-educator without implying for an instant that she could have a permanent intimate relationship with her youthful protégé. She has her life, the boy his; and although they have a friendship of real depth, there is no indication that, even if she were a much younger woman, it would be therapeutically right for her to encourage him to love her as a woman and to enter into a love affair, which she could so easily justify on the grounds that this would be the best way to rescue him from his homosexual tendencies and make a man of him.

This method of physical involvement has been tried, not only in life situations, where at least it is well-meant and occasionally successful, but also in some professional psychiatric relationships with older but still undeveloped patients, where it can only confuse and ultimately ruin the patients' chances to learn how to take the initiative for their actions and to separate these from their inner understanding of the male-female balance in their own nature, viewed archetypally.

There is also, as I have indicated earlier, a qualitative difference in the erotic response of girls and boys. But the sex of patients or of the therapist is not so important as the therapist's ability to respond to the individual needs of each person to be treated. We generally find a uniform need for both boys and girls to be allowed, even forced, to find the essential answer to the problem themselves, and not to have it handed to them ready-made.

When these dangers are avoided, as they were in Mrs. Stevens' treatment of Mar, the young person is capable of an experience of analysis in depth, shorter but no less authentic than a more mature person's analysis. But, as Mrs. Stevens indicates to Mar, its end is his beginning.

CHAPTER IX

Initiation in the Process of Individuation

IN PEOPLE of real maturity, dreams reflect a personal mythology appropriate for individuation. But the cases we have studied so far had not reached this level of maturity; they had not fully accepted individuation as a way of life, though some of them were making a significant approach to it. Many of these cases also illustrate Jung's observation that in young people psychic energy is directed instinctively toward the living of life for its own sake, in order that they may become rooted in reality, learning their capacities and limits as they proceed. In my experience this usually continues well into middle-age.

Jung maintained categorically that no one should, or even could, undertake the way of individuation before the second half of life. A psychological study of the typical course of an analysis, however, frequently throws doubt upon this assertion.[1] Anyone may need at any age to become disentangled from the claims of outer reality and to withdraw once again into himself for individual reorientation. As we have seen, young people caught in the identity crisis of late adolescence may experience a foretaste of individuation, just as people in the second half of life are frequently gripped by the youthful power of the hero myth, with which they are enabled to meet the next developmental challenge of their lives. Hence we had to postulate a cyclic character to each threshold crossing.

In analysis the archetype of initiation appears especially in the material of those who in youth were older and wiser than their years or who, during the second half of life, are striving to regain some of the youth which they originally lost. This fact supports my strong belief that a compensatory relation between youth and age is normal. Young people may understand temporarily the wisdom of age, while at significant times older people inwardly reexperience the enthusiasm of youth. Except when these tendencies are distorted or inappropriately acted out, the reciprocal qualities of youth and age are admired and encouraged in any cultivated society.

However, this complementarity of youth and age meets a definite limit for anyone who in full maturity is ready to find the way of individuation, and here we can see why Jung distinguished so carefully between an earlier and a later phase of life in this respect. For individuation to become an actuality, three conditions are necessary which cannot all be present in youth. Roughly, these are: (1) separation from the original family or clan; (2) commitment to a meaningful group over a long period of time; and (3) liberation from too close an identity with the group. Only when all these stages have been adequately realized, together with a partial resolution of the conflict necessarily felt to exist between the claims of the group and the needs of the individual, can one speak of individuation. As Jung explained, "on the one hand individuation is an internal subjective process of integration, and on the other hand an equally indispensable objective process of relationship."[2]

This is the ground plan for any genuine experience of individuation, but it does not help us to envision the completed structure. Clearly, from Jung's exploration and from our own continuation of this type of research, there is some final element which cannot be explicitly stated; being individual in each case, it defies any general classification. This is why it so frequently turns up first as a secret, often mystical, form of religious experience. Fortunately, it is possible to throw further light upon this phenomenon from a psychological point of view.

Examples of these ultimate steps in self-realization are not usually found in the material of patients during analysis; nor can analysis set up individuation as a goal.[3] Furthermore, we observe frequently that individuation must begin as a separation from the analytical situation itself, in so far as analysis has become too comfortable a resting place in which to avoid revaluing one's relation to the collective norm. Although analysis as an approach to individuation at first sets up an attitude of opposition to the collective norm, this provides no more than an impulse toward eccentric individualism. True individuality has an "*a priori* foundation in the psyche. The opposition to the collective norm, however, is only apparent, since on closer examination, the individual standpoint is found to be *differently* oriented, but not *antagonistic* to the collective norm."[4]

The individual feels himself essentially alone in respect to the collective norm in a new way and even his close relationship with the analyst is insufficient to protect him from the need to reconcile in his own way, after analysis, the ways of the ego and the ways of the Self. The analysand then resolves his transference to the analyst in the same way that, with his analyst's help, he withdrew his illusory expectations from those human figures who had most fully embodied his early ego-ideals.

The symbols of initiation which appear at the onset of this period to people for whom individuation really becomes a way of life, whether they have been analyzed or not, are all characterized by a compactness of image or a brevity of statement. Instead of the dramatic scenarios such as we saw in dreams illustrating the initiations of magical fraternities or the far-flung lonely journeys of the Hero Quests, the archetype of initiation at this level is expressed in images so simple, so natural, and occasionally so abstract that one may easily miss their real import.

In one such dream the image of initiation was represented by a drawing which a woman described to me as "resembling an ancient temple or maybe just seven great steps hewn out of stone. The lowermost step represented the mating of man and woman. Then there were ascending levels of 'yearning' and on the topmost level 'God's Image,' which represented the uppermost level." The importance of this dream in the symbolism of initiation lies in the paradoxical combination or union of the two basic conditions necessary for individuation, the temple as the symbol of commitment — or, as we may say, containment in the meaningful life of the socio-religious group — and the stairway with its seven steps, denoting the spirit of initiatory release for a religious experience of a transcendent nature. These two conditions, which could easily seem incompatible, are joined in one symbol, which mediates between the principle of human relatedness (union of man and woman) and the symbol of the Self (God's Image). The means by which these opposites are reconciled is expressed in a single comprehensive symbol of initiation, the temple that is also a stairway.[5]

Such a paradox is in fact literally represented in such architectural masterpieces as the ancient ziggurats of Mesopotamia and the step pyramids of Egypt, which combined in one place of worship a temple enclosure and a stairway leading from earth to heaven. The stairway or tower of the ziggurat "was not meant to storm and threaten heaven, but to provide a means by which the gods of heaven might descend to receive the worship of their slaves on earth."[6] A humbler but no less impressive version of this same symbol occurs in Navaho sand paintings representing the four underground worlds which the First People were supposed to traverse in the myth of Emergence. In the painting these worlds are placed one upon the other so that they represent one significant temple-like enclosure.[7]

In another sand painting the approach of the initiate is indicated by a "pollen path." He is imagined to enter this path by a lower entrance, traverse it — it is now indicated by a corn stalk — between the female (curved rainbow) and male (zigzag lightning) symbols, and exit at the top by the same "pollen path," now going in the opposite direction. At the lower entrance there are two "guardians of the threshold," and the upper exit is guarded by the "bird" (bluebird), which we may conjecture represents the spirit of transcendence by which the initiate is liberated from the passage rite itself.[8] This simple hieroglyph describes in a very condensed manner the highest form of initiatory transcendence and, at the same time, expresses its faith in preserving a basic attachment to life, represented by the corn stalk. This is a reaffirmation of the male-female polarity in the psychic experience of initiation such as we have seen in the youthful rites of passage.

While this symbolism can apply to both youth and age, in the end its comprehensive meaning undoubtedly relates to the symbolism of the Self and hence prepares the way for a process of individuation. I have spoken of three likely stages of initiation as a rite of *submission* followed by a period of *containment* and then a further rite of *liberation*.[9] Where it is is a question of individuation, these latter two may be combined in a single rite in which the opposite tendencies for containment or release are transformed, with the conflict generated between them serving as the medium of their transformation. If this construct is correct, the final stage cannot be called the stage of liberation.

In a mythological sense we may continue to equate this final stage with van Gennep's postliminal rite of incorporation, but this approach has some psychological drawbacks. *Incorporation* leads back to the symbolism of *containment* in the meaningful group, just as *liberation* leads back to the symbolism of *transcendence* from the group. Neither of these rites seems to define the true nature of individuation. Instead, this combined transformation, through the experience of death and rebirth, seems to lead to an as yet undefined final stage in which the individual may truly experience himself alone. At the same time he must, in accordance with Jung's definition, find his essential position in that form of reality which relates him to the people with whom he is most intimately involved. We must therefore look for an image of initiation which no longer needs to borrow its symbolism from the tribal rites of passage, no matter how differentiated or abridged they may become.[10]

This final stage of initiation, then, is represented by no rite of entrance or of exit; it is not a state of containment or incubation, nor is it a state of release or liberation. It is a unique state of being in a place which cannot even be symbolized except very tentatively and which, in ancient iconography, is most frequently represented by an empty circle or round object. The feeling of this type of experience was caught by Gerardus van der Leeuw in his paper "Immortality":

> The moment we begin to live, we begin to die. Every period of sleep is a half-death; Thanatos and Hypnos are brothers. Every transition from one phase of life to another is a kind of death. This is the truth of the primitive ritualistic dogmatism which looks upon each of life's transitions — accession to manhood, to the dignity of medicine man or chief, marriage, etc. — as a death and rebirth, a truth which is quite in harmony with biological insight into the periodicity of life. Life is an ocean with rising and falling tides. This means that death is always implicit in it. The ancient Egyptians

had a beautiful expression for this periodicity of life: *whm ankh,* "to repeat life." Life is something that repeats itself. But the same term means the life after death — immortality, as we call it. . . . This notion is not a paradox. Precisely because death not only transcends life but also forms a part of life, it is possible to consider death from an anthropological point of view; in this sense the "transcendent" becomes at least partially "immanent."[11]

The final stage of initiation, then, might best be called the state of *immanence* in the sense that individuation forces a man to obey the immanent law of his own nature in order to know himself as an individual. The inner activity by which this is made possible is an initiatory experience which, as van der Leeuw so beautifully states, is the theme of death and rebirth to be found on a purely individual level.

This may be illustrated by some fantasy material of a modern man.

Case XVIII (Male, age 50)

This man had completed a successful analysis several years previously but had returned from time to time to report his dreams or his experiences of active imagination.* He was a successful busi-

---

* As I observed in an early paper, "Resolution of the Transference in the Light of Jung's Psychology," patients who discover during analysis that their way lies toward individuation develop a method of association which allows them to conduct a form of self-analysis replacing the formal analysis, which was defined by their transference to the therapist. This method is arrived at by the analysand spontaneously during the formal period of analysis. It is characterized by his learning to interpret his own dreams or by his developing the capacity to evoke hypnogogic visions which can be partially directed by the conscious ego. What eventually occurs is the appearance of certain ego figures or self-figures which he has to confront and with which he has to converse. From this dialectic there emerge certain meaningful insights. These periods of active imagination are relatively short, and they occur only once or twice a month, or perhaps much less frequently. When they appear, the individual accepts them, records them, and only later, after much reflection, tries to integrate or act upon their meaning. Comparatively few people in my experience use active imagination with any regularity, although almost all analysands who are in the process of resolving the analytical transference have had some experience of this phenomenon. I personally do not urge or in any way influence my patients to develop such a method, but I encourage them to make the most of it when it happens to them spontane-

ness man, equally committed to his family and to helping maintain the welfare of his community. His initial problem had been felt as a split between his responsible working life, which had been sustained by an identification with his father's strong Christian ethical principles, and his wish to live a country life apart from the world. The underlying reason for this wish was a longing to secure for himself a sense of natural permissiveness which he had never been able to obtain in childhood from his mother. This mother had been essentially critical of him at the time he had needed her encouragement, and this had lamed his feeling for life. Yet it had also developed in him the strongest possible desire to find in the land, as a representation of Mother Nature, what he had missed in childhood. To this extent his desire sometimes followed a regressive trend and caused him to defend fanatically the superiority of his love of country over his urban adaptation. But his interest in the land was also quite genuine; in his mother's family and in the background of his father's family were a number of prosperous farmers, and he felt a legitimate sympathy with their mode of existence. It even seemed possible that he might appropriately leave his business and take up farming as a vocation.

The effect of his analysis, during his early forties, was to help him withdraw the projection of the elements of his own personal psyche, as conditioned by his upbringing, from these vocational alternatives. Then they appeared in quite a different light. No longer was it a question of making a willful personal choice. His work in the city seemed to correspond to the cultivated, ethical man who was also genuinely interested in his work, while his wish for life in the country corresponded to the natural, primordial man. In some obscure way both these men defined him as the man he had become. He could not arbitrarily deny the validity of one without also denying the validity of the other. He was forced to accept his life as a meaningful duality instead of an abstract, or ideal, unity.

He also came to understand that although his personality was

---

ously. My own role is less that of an interpreter than a friend sharing their experience or a commentator whose knowledge of mythology may help to provide some amplification of the archetypal background from which the visionary images arise.

primarily introverted, his adaptation to business and the urban life had always been predominantly extraverted. This fact seemed to provide another strong reason for his wishing to abandon the extraverted life and, in returning to the country, to develop more fully his native introverted side. But he saw gradually that both extraversion and introversion were necessary to him as a mature man and that if there is such a thing as unity, it lies in accepting the existence of these different modes of functioning and in learning to harmonize them inwardly. He saw that following an introverted direction at the expense of his extraversion probably would lead not to fulfillment but to isolation, and his experiments in active imagination confirmed this.

Other polarities in this man's life were also activated during analysis and to a large extent resolved. But there is no cure for the real problems of life, and the conflict of introversion and extraversion (and other pairs of opposites) went through many phases of partial reconciliation in the years following his formal analysis. A particularly important episode in this later process was reflected in the following sequence of imaginative events, abridged somewhat from his account.

FANTASY 1: I had begun to feel impatient with my life in the same old way I had often felt in the past, longing to retire from business and live exclusively in my country house. The first part of my fantasy again indicated that this solution would be wrong and I must find a deeper answer to this apparent problem. At length I imagined I had to travel down two tubes or tunnels in the earth at the same time, one of which was lined with greenery of nature, and the other lined with metal suggesting the mechanical, over-rational life of the city.

I felt uncomfortably split as I went down both tubes at once, but suddenly they came to an end before a moderately large pond. In the center of the pond there lay a monster, round in shape, covered with rounded bumps and hair, with no eyes or limbs. I felt this creature was both good and bad and had some special wisdom I wished to learn. I spoke to it and it returned my greeting. Then it said, "Do not ask me too much." I said, "What shall be my attitude, careful?" It said, "No." I then went through a series of adjectives such as "cautious," "humble," "patient" — but always it indicated that these were not quite right. Then I said, "Religious?" And it said, "Yes."

At this point the two tunnels I had traversed partially encircled the pond, one on each side. They were transparent in their inner aspects, so if I had been in one, I could have seen out toward the other. Before they met, however, they seemed to fade, as if they had each been cut tangentially and the interior exposed. I was near the one which was lined with natural greenery, and this now seemed to surround the whole pond.

Then I dove to the bottom of the pond and saw a dead creature which had lain in the water a long time. This was the remains of my mother. I touched this thing and it immediately dispersed. Then I walked into the monster, and I had the sensation of losing first my flesh, then my bones, and becoming only a single ego-center, like something one might attain at the moment of transcending physical awareness (at the moment of death?). I was suddenly shot out of the top of the monster and swam to the shore with my hair on fire. I heard the monster say, "You'd better be careful not to take on too much." I then drew a circle around the pond with a stick, and I gathered four logs and placed them in the water to form a square.

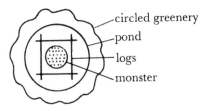

circled greenery
pond
logs
monster

FIGURE 5

I thought of putting four more logs to form a cross in the center, but this would have cut the monster in four sections when it arose to the surface, so I did not. I knelt upon one of the logs and prayed. Then I thought I was on fire, and this reminded me of the picture I saw of Buddhist monks who had set fire to themselves to protest the anti-religious activities in Southeast Asia. As they (or I) were consumed in the flames, a white dove was liberated from them and flew into the air. This in turn was suddenly multiplied into many doves. I felt the need to stop the fantasy. I was horrified at this idea of sacrificing the physical life.

Then the monster appeared and said, "How's your vegetable garden?" and "How's your work?" — and later said, "There's an answer to that. Don't wait too long. Don't live provisionally." Then it sank again out of sight, but I felt its ability, whether on the surface or submerged, to be its own center. During these encounters with the monster I maintained my own point of view and was ready to disagree with its judgments. But I realized that I could not deny their validity since they were in essence acceptable answers to questions I had in my own mind.

INTERPRETATION: The two tubes down which this man traveled simultaneously suggest that his conflict between city and country living could be reduced to two basic cultural modes originating from two basic archetypal images, Moira and Themis. Moira, representing a sanctity older than the gods, signifies social order as a Way of Nature, while Themis, representing behavior dictated by social conscience, signifies the Way of Civilized Man. We need not, however, return to ancient Greece to understand the necessity for reconciling the conflict between these two modes. In fact, we may reach a more contemporary understanding of the problem by studying this modern man's solution to it.

We should recall that another modern individual (Case XIII) whose dream material led us to discuss the approach to individuation had a similar problem. He had to accept initially the positive social meaning of the mechanistic, over-rational nature of modern life and only secondarily learn to reconcile it with the Way of Nature in the formation of his communal group identity. His new identity was not, however, a repetition of some original identity with the natural family group; it was a commitment arrived at by an initiatory dream experience which also emphasized the importance of maintaining within the symbol of communal containment (the clock) a symbol of individual freedom (the winged horse). This latter symbol pointed toward that future direction (the southwest) from which he might expect further insight to come concerning the individuation process.

The present analysand had accomplished the task of living his life in the communal sense with more than average self-assertion, and he was ready for this deeper type of insight. Accordingly, his need to live in two conflicting ways shows signs of coming to an end in his fantasy. The tubes become transparent, level out, and separate in such a way that he can turn his attention to the new symbol, a monster in its circular pond.

Here I suspect we can observe a form of the Primal God Image, which is older than Moira and older than the maternal order of nature. This monster embodies the opposites, good and bad (and probably also male and female); and though it lacks human senses and limbs, it is nevertheless inspired by a kind of benevolent wisdom which expects from its human inquisitor a religious, not just a mildly ethical, attitude. It is for this reason especially that we are entitled to assume that this monster is a form of the god image. Like all such images it cannot be approached intellectually; hence it warns its questioner not to ask too many questions. Yet it is not a form of the celestial or Ultimate God Image. It is closer to the Greek *nous,* or spirit, which permeates or embraces all spiritual life and yet is at the origin of spiritual life. The utterances of this being are not frighteningly numinous, however, or in any way portentous; they are humanly grounded, even personal, as if they came from a natural parent-figure or a humanistic philosopher. It is just this quality, presumably, which binds together the transcendental and the personal in such a way as to suggest the experience of individuation.

After the encounter with the monster, certain symbolic actions are performed by this man in active imagination. He dives to the bottom of the pond and disperses there some unresolved impression of his mother, as though a ritual act were necessary to dispel the effect of her actual death, which had occurred four years previously. His associations, however, did not indicate that what was, to be dispelled related only to death; they pointed rather to the early paralysis of his feeling, which he had associated with his original mother-complex. If he had been able to express these feelings naturally toward his mother, he could have expressed them toward others as well and, in doing so, have built up his self-esteem. Thus he dispels at this point in the fantasy the neurotic component of the original complex by means of his newly acquired religious attitude.

Such a liberating act might be expected to lead to a state of euphoria, which may easily end in the hubris of a psychological inflation. And here it does: he unwittingly walks into the monster, unconsciously identifying with an archetypal image, and experiences the inflation attendant upon such an identification. He loses the reality of his ego (flesh and bones), and his disembodied ego is literally shot out of the archetypal monster. He swims to shore with his hair on fire; this presumably means that, having become dis-identified with the archetype, he is again in possession of his physical ego — but ego-consciousness, here symbolized by the hair on fire, is still dangerously inflated by his mistake, and the monster benevolently warns him that such mistakes arise from a tendency "to take on too much." For a man who had always been both ambitious and successful, this advice points to the danger of continuing the youthful hero role at this time of life.

As if to repair this damage to his psychic integrity, he then creates a kind of central design similar to the Eastern mandala with its combination of circle and square, one inside the other, and with a central, circular center in which some powerful energic content is placed.[12] Here the pattern is made in an active, ritualized manner by the subject of the fantasy, encircling the pond by drawing a line around it and then cutting logs to make a sort of raft with its center empty where the round monster might appear or disappear in the water. He "thought of putting four more logs to form a cross in the center," but refrained because this would risk cutting the monster into four quarters.

It is quite clear from this action that the monster is itself to be the center of this man-made mandala, and the care with which the subject avoids placing a cross in the center emphasizes the importance of preserving some kind of primal wholeness.

Though he was not — and had not been since boyhood — a practicing Christian, he had long obeyed the strong Protestant ethic of his family without question. This ethic had been called into question during the period of analysis, especially in early periods of active imagination, by the appearance of strong representatives of this parental superego. He had learned gradually to loosen the power of this kind of social conscience (superego), but he also learned the danger of falling regressively into the irresponsible, pleasure-loving, opposite tendency (id). His newly found religious center, however, contains none of these dangers. It provides him with a self-regulating, religiously conscious awareness of what is right for him, as long as he does not try to force it to speak too often and minds his own business, keeping appropriately separated those two areas which we have learned to recognize as the ego and the Self. His temptation to place a cross in the center of his raft probably points to the tendency to follow a Christian pattern of behavior which has no further relevancy for him, and the space for it is left open for the Primal God Image to appear or disappear in accordance with some obscure but meaningful rhythm of a religious nature.

There is, however, one further question concerning the cross. Jung mentioned in his study of the mandala symbolism that in his experience the Western Christian does tend to place a cross in the center of the design, the implication being that that is the right symbol for Occidental man. But this patient in his fantasy produces a design more appropriate for the Oriental mandala, and we may therefore wonder if this represents a significant error in Jung's theory. In recent years the symbolism of these designs has been more fully studied, not only by Jungians but also by scholars from totally different fields,[13] and from this new work it appears that we must make a distinction between the original mandalas — as designs used for religious healing appropriate for individual use — and the designs of a similar character used in the formation of towns and temples, serving thus as outer forms providing a meaningful symbol for a whole community.

In the symbolism from an earlier dream (Case XIII, p. 125) we saw that man's memory of his home town stressed the cruciform nature of two intersecting streets oriented to the four quarters, north-south and east-west. His own direction proceeding downhill from west to east suddenly changed, and he was forced into the north-south axis directed south. This change in direction had the force of an initiatory ordeal which made him redefine his course in accordance with a four-fold cosmic pattern of development, in contrast to a simple and presumably personal duality. In the course of this change he became aware for the first time of his need for social commitment.

Joseph Rykwert, investigating this design from the point of view of architecture and town planning, points out that the earliest Etruscan towns (and to a large extent all Western town planning, which stems from the early Etruscan and early Roman era) were based upon an invariable tendency to combine a more or less circular peripheral wall with a central cross, arranged either as cross streets or with the cross at the center of the temple or of the most important civic building of the town. In larger towns or cities of the medieval or renaissance type, these crosses may be not in any geometric center but in several places, such as the cathedral, the town square, and the city hall. In our own state capitals and county seats in America, this ancient pattern was frequently reproduced exactly by placing the capitol building or the county courthouse at the actual center of the town; this building was almost always designed as a cross with a round dome over its intersection.

In describing Rykwert's study, Aldo von Eyck recognizes, quite independently of any psychological theorizing, that the design of towns in this sense is basically archetypal and that it even implies for us today a challenge of the kind we see in this analysand's response to his fantasy:

> The town, Joseph Rykwert reminds us, is an artifact — "an artifact of a curious kind, compounded of willed and random elements, imperfectly controlled. If it is like any piece of physiology at all," he adds, "it is more like a dream than anything else. . . ." If we today are unable to read the entire universe and its meaning off our civic institutions as the Romans did — loss or gain — we still need to be at home in it; to interiorize it; refashion it in our own image — each for himself this time. To discover that we are no longer Romans and yet Romans still is no small thing!
>
> Finally, as we read the closing paragraphs, the "ground of certainty" which our time can neither find nor face — call it shifting centre or lost home — momentarily reveals its whereabouts. "It is no longer likely that we shall find this ground in the world the cosmologists are continuously reshaping around us, and so we must look for it," Rykwert concludes, "inside ourselves in the constitution and structure of the human person!"[14]

In this part of the fantasy, our present subject seems to carry out his activities in accordance with the same archetypal pattern which impelled ancient man to plough the furrow which was to define his town. But the subject, having constructed the wooden square which was to define the actual center of his new watery temple, then ceases to be a town planner or a designer in the extraverted Roman or Christian sense. Instead of repeating the Roman or Christian formula, or the design for a town appropriate for it, he leaves his center free to accommodate this "shifting center or lost home," and his monster is no longer the recognizable god of the fathers but the inner religious nature of the individual human person. The occasional appearance of the monster will provide a round, living center for his square. Between appearances this place is left significantly empty.

Immediately following this decision, he kneels and prays, presumably repeating, as an act of humility, the willingness of the ego to submit to the superior power of the Self. Immediately he is seized by the image of what this would mean on a collective scale and is horrified by the vision of a suicidal act which, like a Buddhist or Christian saint, he might be capable of performing. In this case fire represents martyrdom, as in the first instance (when his hair was on fire) it represents a state of archetypal inflation. Fire is the expression of the overpowering emotion involved in such an ecstatic demolition of the ego. This reminds him of the Buddhist monks who set fire to themselves as a protest to anti-religious political activities. As he saw them in fantasy consumed in the fire, a white dove was liberated, flew into the air, and was multiplied into many doves, suggesting the compulsive repetition of a spiritual idea transcending an earthly one (Holy Ghost). He was horrified by this whole scene because, as he says, it meant a willingness to destroy the physical life in favor of the spiritual life.

Here we see the reaction of a modern Occidental man both to the religious mysticism of the extreme Eastern type and to the mysticism of traditional Catholicism in the West, which also applauds martyrdom and the glory of sacrifice for higher spiritual values. But this man is no more pleased by the multiplication of infinite spiritual possibilities (the doves) than he was by the idea of sacrifice in the first place. Perhaps this is not because he is modern or Western, but because this form of religious mysticism strikes him as inappropriate when he is trying to find an individual experience of religion, not a traditional one.

The last part of the fantasy seems to confirm this conclusion that he need not be concerned with traditional religious attitudes, whether of East or West, whether of the Buddhist or Christian methods of transcendence. The monster talks to him flatly of purely personal matters. "How's your vegetable garden?" and "How's your work?" it asks, in simple colloquial language, referring to his original conflict between his allegiences to the contrary and to the city life. Then it says, "There's an answer to that. Don't wait too long. Don't live provisionally," and from the monster we hear no more. We have then to derive what final meaning we can from these terse observations.

It is extremely difficult to convey in any literary form the peculiar immediacy and cogency of the images and conversations occurring in the course of active imagination. They have the peculiar effect of meaning everything or nothing: one thinks one grasps their sense at first, only to find a moment later that one is again floating in a sea of doubt. It almost seems better to abandon the attempt altogether and wait for further images which may confirm or disprove what one has already thought. Yet one is intrigued by the unexpected nature of the images or utterances, and in spite of the exasperation of futile efforts to understand, some suspicion of a deeper wisdom tends to keep one interested, even determined to persist in the quest. They may even come to have such a spellbinding effect that one cannot dismiss them without a definite sense of loss. This is certainly the effect of such unconscious products upon the person who has brought them into being, and if one is cast in the role of their psychological interpreter, one can do no less than attempt an interpretation, no matter how inadequate it may sound to anyone listening from outside the range of its magical effect.

In the interpretation of the final sequence of this fantasy, we begin with the impression, received from the previous sequence, that the subject has been in danger of some old-new form of self-sacrifice, a state in which he would come near to sacrificing his actual life in this world. Many men do actually die prematurely in our society from the effects of their ambition and their proved capacity for over-achievement. Such tendencies are usually rationalized: the men convince themselves of the nobility of their efforts and miss the fact that their work may be compulsively power-driven and their ambitions illusory.

When the monster asks the subject about his "vegetable garden" and his "work," is it not trying to minimize the conscious importance this man has placed upon his worldly attempt to solve a lifelong conflict, instead of learning to understand and adjust to its archetypal value? If so, the final statement, "Don't live provisionally," is a reminder that he is still in danger of making his psychological development (the vegetable garden) seem dependent upon his work (his business pursuits), and to this extent he is postponing his natural life and his creative task. Again we may compare this with the common problem of the successful man who postpones the life he means to enjoy until he may be too old, or tired, or ill, to enjoy it. He may know this danger with his head and may adopt all sorts of devices to avoid the catastrophe, but most of them — his travels, his collections, his sports, his sensuous pleasures, and his religious enthusiasms — merely require extra planning and effort of will superimposed on his regular work. The inner Self-image is not fooled by these acrobatics and reminds him that even such laudable solutions are all part of a provisional life, which prevents him from really living by the inner religious impulse which can dispense with false supports and the illusion of reaching some final harbor of bliss in heaven.

If we look for material in the records of religious history to illustrate this kind of religious need, we find very little, for the simple reason that most religious customs are devised to satisfy not individual but collective needs. Even the most esoteric rituals of the mystery religions suffer in reporting, since they lack the verisimilitude of an individual encounter with the unknown powers. Thus they tend to define too precisely the nature of the god image, whose iconography is so clearly represented that it brooks no individual variation. There are many people who rebel against the very word God because it evokes the image of a sour, white-bearded old man lacking any sense of gaiety or humor. The subject's "monster," by its very lack of differentiation and its living, changing quality, reflects the original nature of an individual's experience of God. The image of God as a monster may remind us also of the fact, so graphically represented in the fantasy with its inflationary danger, that it may be "a fearful thing to fall into the hands of the living God."[15]

There is, however, one sacred tradition which seems to encourage, even to render mandatory, this individual approach and which can certainly be included among the examples of initiatory experience. This is Zen Buddhism, in which the adept or novice learns to evoke the experience of enlightenment (satori). This special form of awareness is what analysts call (somewhat lamely, for want of a better term) "psychological consciousness" or just "becoming conscious." D. T. Suzuki, in a remarkably clear discussion of this phenomenon, shows himself fully aware of the parallelism between Zen and an experience of the Self.

> We ordinarily talk of self-consciousness as if we knew all about it, but in reality we have never come to a full knowledge of what self-consciousness is. Consciousness has always been conscious of something other than itself. As to "the Self" it has never even attempted to know, because the Self cannot be conscious of itself in so far as it remains dichotomous. The Self is known only when it remains itself and yet goes out of itself. This contradiction can never be understood on the level of the outward way. It is absolutely necessary to rise above this level if the meaning of self-consciousness is to be realized to its full depths.
>
> The awakening of a new consciousness so called, as far as the inward way of seeing into the nature of things is concerned, is no other than consciousness becoming acquainted with itself. Not that a new consciousness rises out of the Unconscious but consciousness itself turns inwardly into itself. This is the home-coming. This is the seeing of one's own "primal face" which one has even before one's birth. This is God's pronouncing his name to Moses. This is the birth of Christ in each of our souls. This is Christ rising from death. "The Unconscious," which has been lying quietly in consciousness itself, now raises its head and announces its presence through consciousness.

In this kind of experience the term *Unconscious* as we use it in depth psychology becomes so much a part of consciousness that it seems redundant. The attempt to keep "conscious" and "unconscious" phenomena separate may at this point give rise to a philosophic error and, as Suzuki goes on to say, leads to a confusion which "will upset our thought structure."

> This means that what is named "conscious" cannot be "unconscious," and vice versa. But in point of fact human psychology is a living fact and refuses to observe an arbitrary system of grouping. The conscious wants to be unconscious and the unconscious conscious.

And so we are led to a logical contradiction:

> But Zen's way of viewing or evaluating things differs from the outward way of intellection. Zen would not object to the possibility of an "unconscious conscious" or a "conscious unconscious" — therefore, not the awakening of a new consciousness but consciousness coming to its own unconscious.[16]

The Jungian analyst, in his understanding of the process of individuation, would certainly agree with this viewpoint. What he would miss, however, is the apparent absence of any reference to a religious cult object or a philosophic thought forming some sort of goal for the awakening conscious to aim for at its moment of enlightenment. But the reason for this omission is made good in Suzuki's description of the *kokoro*.

In typical Oriental fashion this apparent goal, which of course is not a goal at all but the "psychometaphysical aspect of the inward way," is originally identified with something devoid of any recognizable content.

> Buddhists call this the 'abyss of absolute nothingness.' [But the Japanese term] *kokoro* is originally a psychological term, meaning 'heart,' 'soul,' 'spirit,' 'mind,' 'thought'; it later came to denote the kernel or essence of a thing, becoming synonymous metaphysically with 'substance' and ethically with 'sincerity,' 'verity,' 'faithfulness,' etc. . . . Out of this *kokoro* all things are produced and all things ultimately go back to it. . . . [It remains] an abyss of absolute nothingness, [yet] there is something moving in the midst of the *kokoro* [and this is] "the mystery of being."

As if from the unfathomable depths of an abyss, the *kokoro* is stirred. The *kokoro* wants to know itself. . . . In Western terminology, the *kokoro* may be regarded as corresponding to God or Godhead. [Yet this God must not be understood in the purely Biblical sense where He is] always intensely personal and concretely intimate. . . . But His name, given to Moses at Mount Sinai as 'I AM THAT I AM,' . . . [if looked at from the inward way, no longer has the fiercely personal extraverted character and] is just as "spontaneous" as the fish swimming about in the mountain stream or the fowl of the air flying across the sky. God's isness is my isness and also the cat's isness sleeping on its mistress' lap. This is reflected in Christ's declaration that "I am before Abraham was." In this isness, which is not to be assumed under the category of metaphysical abstractions, I feel like recognizing the fundamental oneness of all the religious experiences.[17]

This type of religious experience leads to individuation:

The *kokoro's* wishing to know itself is, . . . humanly expressed, no other than our longing to transcend this world of particulars. While in the world, we find ourselves too engrossed in the business of "knowing" . . . with everything that follows from exercising what we call "freedom." [But true] freedom can be found in the inward way only and not in the outward way, [and by looking for it in the outward way] we are no more able to be in the "spontaneity of isness."

We can now see that "the awakening of a new consciousness" is not quite a happy expression. The longing for something we have lost and not for an unknown quantity of which we have not the remotest possible idea . . . is a shadow of the original *kokoro* cast in the track of the inward way.[18]

This harmonizes with the modern conception of individuation as a process of Self-restoration, since the Self is the archetypal matrix from which all original psychic being arose. But this does not mean a simple return or effortless homecoming, for it must include the continuity of ego-consciousness together with its awareness of its historical identity. Self-restoration only appears, as in this case, after a man has lived for many years fully engaged in shaping and being shaped by the material context of his life, and after he has resolved consciously, as far as he is able, the conflict between this material context and his need for developing the inward life. Then the return may awaken the qualities attributed to the *kokoro:* (heart, mind, soul, etc.) and the virtues to go with them (sincerity, verity, faithfulness, etc.). It is this second encounter, this confrontation of the ego with Self and the reconciliation of their conflicting natures, which constitutes the experience of initiation at this level.

The underlying pattern of this development, though highly charged with archetypal meaning, is not strictly religious but rather requires a kind of religious devotion to the task of Self-discovery, which is the essence of Zen. Naturally this does not imply that only Zen monks understand such individual experiments, which may be found in accounts of experiences throughout the literature of the perennial philosophy from all times and places.

Yet the appeal of Zen and its popularity in the West of recent years seem to reflect the same need we find in certain mature people coming for analysis — a need to live somehow more fully and deeply in the present and (to use Jung's favorite term) to learn to live as a "totality" in a way that is foreign to the precepts of organized religion, with its goal of spiritual perfection. Psychotherapists of other schools have responded to this need also in recent years, and this final stage of the initiatory experience — the discovery of man's immanent state of being — has become in one instance the leading idea of a whole new school of psychiatry, namely, existential psychiatry or, as it is known in Europe, *Daseinsanalyse.* The various members of this school derive their basic knowledge from Freud's psychoanalysis, Jung's analytical psychology, and other schools of psychology; but they seek to transcend these disciplines.

What all these existential analysts have in common (as far as I can make out) is the attitude, congenial to the Zen philosopher, that conceptualization of any kind is bad and that man's immanent awareness of his unique reality at any given moment is good. The existential analyst accordingly seeks to discredit evolutionary theories of development, and especially the archetypal patterns of mythology, since they imply that man is conditioned not merely by his immediate existence but by history, which in turn evolved from the collective unconscious. Although denying that he is identified with the philosophical ideas of Sartre and Heidegger, the existential analyst is nevertheless in spirit basically true to the original principles concerning the nature of Existential philosophy: Man must count on no one but himself; that he is alone without help, in the midst of an alien universe and responsible entirely for his own destiny.[19]

The whole of this present study — with its picture of each man's individual life with its ancient archetypal content, yet carrying within him the enormous formative influence of the wholesome patterns of initiation — argues the exact opposite of this statement. Yet if we limit our concern to the period of self-confrontation, we perhaps can feel its relevance. At the critical turning points of individual development, man is alone with himself and can fall back upon absolutely no preconceived, pre-learned patterns. Yet the psyche is not without content; far from being alone in his self-confrontation, he may feel more richly companioned than he has ever been in belonging to a religious group. This fact is well marked in the ensuing fantasy of our subject, after his encounter with the monster.

FANTASY 2:   I found myself in the presence of four personages who formed a closely related group, two men and two women. It was night and I did not see them clearly, but it seemed to me that they represented a special grouping of figures with a religious meaning. Then it occurred to me that they represented a revised Christian Trinity in which the Holy Ghost had been replaced by the Virgin Mary and to which there had been added another feminine figure, a kind of Earth Mother, making four altogether. As I approached them, one of the woman said, "Where are you going?" I realized she was asking me a test question, as one might do in children's games. I answered, "Nowhere." Then she asked, "When will you get there?" And I answered, "Never." Whereupon she cheerfully responded, "Right. You're in the club."

INTERPRETATION: Having experienced the Primal God Image in his own way, this man now returns to the Christian god image and finds that it has been transformed from a trinity to a quaternity in which the masculine and feminine elements are balanced. In this form it welcomes him when he has proved to himself that he expects from it nothing which would sharpen his ambition to achieve anything, to formulate a goal, or to promulgate a body of doctrine. This quaternity, outwardly, is unrecognizably Christian; yet it is still Christian on an inner level to this man, as if he had, in some strange meeting of East and West, harmonized Christian teaching with the spirit of Zen. He himself, in his associations, pointed out the likeness of the final paradox, throwing him back upon himself in a way that was reminiscent of existentialism. He also recognized the aptness of the comparison with Zen when the woman (probably the one he associated with the Virgin) asked him a question, for his answer is reminiscent of a Zen *koan.*

This trick question and answer, the *koan,* exchanged between a master and disciple, creates the impression of a meeting of opposites in such a way as to provide the shock to consciousness which forces the adept to become aware of the presence of the Self and of the need to subordinate the ego to the Self. Jung says of the *koan:*

> The koans are so various, so ambiguous, and above all so boundlessly paradoxical that even an expert must be completely in the dark as to what might be considered a suitable solution. In addition, the descriptions of the final result are so obscure that in no single case can one discover any rational connection between the koan and the experience of enlightenment. Since no logical sequence can be demonstrated, it remains to be supposed that the koan method puts not the smallest restraint upon the freedom of the psychic process and that the end-result therefore springs from nothing but the individual disposition of the pupil. The complete destruction of the rational intellect aimed at in the training creates an almost perfect lack of conscious assumptions. These are excluded as far as possible, but not unconscious assumptions — that is, the existing but unrecognized psychological disposition, which is anything but empty or unassuming. It is a nature-given factor, and when it answers — this being obviously the satori experience — it is an answer of Nature, who has succeeded in conveying her reaction direct to the conscious mind. What the unconscious nature of the pupil opposes to the teacher or to the koan by way of an answer is, manifestly, satori. . . . The answer which appears to come from the

void, the light which flares up from the blackest darkness, these have always been experienced as a wonderful and blessed illumination.[20]

A kind of redeemed tricksterism makes its appearance in such an interchange, and we recognize once again the mercurial power of the primitive master of initiation, half-concealed yet half-revealed, in such a witty gambit. This lightens the heavy sense of existential loneliness inherent in the act of self-confrontation.

The validity of active imagination demonstrated in this case may be questioned by the skeptical pragmatist on the grounds that the subject must have been influenced in his choice of symbolism by having read about it in books by Jung, or by existentialists, or by Zen Buddhists. The effects of such influence are undoubtedly present in this material, since the subject had read about the transformation of the trinity into the quaternity in Jung's later works and understood the principle underlying an experience of *satori*. He had, furthermore, learned in the course of his analysis a good deal about the meaning of the mandala symbol and it might well be inferred that in his fantasy he had at least semiconsciously sought to reproduce this symbolism. But while we should be mindful of this tendency and alert to the danger of encouraging such a person to dogmatize his experience, we can distinguish the true experience from a false one by making sure that the symbolism really speaks to his own individual problem and does not merely provide refuge in an obsessional flight from reality.

One frequently encounters the erroneous notion that whoever has dreamed or fantasied about the mandala symbol has hit a metaphysical target and thereafter need be concerned only with final things. But Jung's psychological description of the mandala symbol is totally outside any religious eschatology and is purely concerned with its therapeutic value. In perhaps his clearest account of its function he writes:

> *Mandalas* . . . usually appear in situations of psychic confusion and perplexity. The archetype thereby constellated represents a pattern of order which, like a psychological "view-finder" . . . is superimposed on the psychic chaos so that each content falls into place and the weltering confusion is held together by the protective

circle . . . . At the same time they are *yantras,* instruments with whose help order is brought into being.[21]

Jung also tells us that in his own personal discovery of the mandala symbolism he had to get over certain aesthetic and religious prejudices and in other ways had to analyze his own cultural resistance to allowing the mandala design to convey its own unique message.

The mandala symbol is not an end, but a beginning. It is nothing in itself. Anyone can draw magic circles or squares without significant effect. Only if it provides the initiatory approach to a valid symbol of the Self does the design truly come into its own. It becomes then the individual vehicle of initiation.

In this analysand's fantasy, the monster which constitutes the center of his mandala (i.e., the circle and the foursquare arrangement of floating logs) is itself the spontaneous living source of that wisdom which springs into being from the basic unit or togetherness of good and evil, of creation and destruction. Here there is no obsessional flight but the reverse, an experience of the immanent transforming power of the Self. His return to the Primal God Image in its mandaloid setting, which he himself had partly created, allowed him to leave behind forever the sense of being split by the two opposites represented by the two tubes. This allowed him to transform the image of Christian trinity into a quaternity with the male (father and son) and female (virgin and earth mother) elements balanced in accordance with a kind of phychic integration, compensating his type of patriarchal one-sidedness.

The dead mother, whose remains had to be disposed of before the mandala could be constructed, apparently represented the personal mother-complex. As a result of his encounter with the monster in an act of self-confrontation, the personal mother-complex was replaced by the archetypal Earth Mother, and his version of the Christian symbol was accordingly transformed by including her image within it. This means the inclusion of a healthy attitude derived from the totality of the archetype to cure (or remove) the effects of a personal neurosis.

This regrouping is identical with the analysand's new recognition of the Self; and his designation of a center that is not artificially constructed, but left empty for the appearance of the monster, is the true mandala symbol. Such transformations occur only when a religious attitude, such as he learned to adopt with the monster's help, enables the ego and the Self to be reconciled in a psychological sense. Whether they can ever find reconciliation in a metaphysical sense in this life is beyond the scope of this study. I shall be content to have demonstrated merely the initiatory approach to these ultimate secrets of human destiny.

We are ready at last to summarize the stages of initiation by which a person may approach the Self as a way of individuation. It is a much more complicated, and in some cases conflicting, picture than is given in the simple rite of transition, experienced as a puberty rite. It becomes a true experience of inner transformation in which symbols of containment and symbols of release alternate or conflict with one another. Thus van Gennep's initial rite of separation becomes on an individual level an experience of submission while the final rite of incorporation becomes an experience of immanence.

Initiation, then, in its final form becomes an approach to self-confrontation following this order of events:

(1) Submission
(2) Containment-Release (Transformation)
(3) Immanence

It is not to be imagined that one who experiences such an initiation is thereby set upon an exalted level apart from others. Like the Zen Buddhist adept in the ox-herding pictures, after his self-confrontation he returns to everyday life, "out into the market place . . . . There is no need for the miraculous power of the gods, For he touches, and lo! the dead trees are in full bloom."[22]

But even this return is not final. After a long period of time and in response to another inward pull, he may return once more upon the way of initiation. We cannot know, purely psychologically, why this is or how long it may take to complete the process. All deeply committed individual religious men maintain that it goes on periodically throughout life and into death, with no end in sight.

Appendix:
The Bear as Archetypal Image

THE IMAGINATIVE CHOICE of an animal image must first be studied as if it were derived from plain observation of the animal's appearance and habits; in fact, from the point of view of natural science. The analogy between man and animal, as reflected in a dream, is concretized by knowing what man has observed traditionally from this point of view. But natural science alone does not get us very far with the interpretation of a dream image. Until comparatively recent times, man's observation of nature has been colored by his traditional mythological thinking; this must be taken into account, since it provides the dream animal with allegorical characteristics. Only when the natural and allegorical features of the animal have been covered can we begin to determine its symbolic meaning.

The bear is a wild animal, but it frequently has a deceptively tame appearance, as though it would like to make friends with human beings. It is large — and even larger in imagination than in reality, so that it may seem threatening or even overwhelming. But it moves awkwardly and apparently slowly. It has a thick fur coat suggestive of personal protectiveness and warmth, and it maintains that warmth during a long period of hibernation in winter.

The mother bear is a fierce defender and careful nurse of her young, spending as long as two years in rearing each cub. Johann Bachofen remarks that in both Greek and Latin the word *bear* is of feminine gender, and it is in harmony with this that the old religion emphasized the bear's positive motherly qualities. Here motherliness does not emphasize the biological fertility of the animal (as in the symbol of the pig, representing the uterus). The bear represents the *ethical* side of maternity, the side of motherly concern and care. The bear cub is born a shapeless, unstructured mass, blind and white and the size of a rat; but the mother licks the cub incessantly and patiently until the beauty of its animal form emerges. The mother is extraordinarily meticulous with her cubs, more attentive and self-sacrificing than the human mother.

The bear mother's endeavor for her young ones is her main characteristic, and this infinite endeavor and loving care are symbolized in the bear, which becomes an expression of the *pietas materna*. This idea finds its parallel also in a Pythagorean symbol, for wise Pythagoras called the she-bears the hands of the goddess Rhea — an allusion to the formative skill of Mother Nature, who, like the mother bear, leads to beauty and perfection what was imperfect before. Clemens Alexandrinus amplifies the symbol of the bear still further in his reference to Isaiah 11:7; "And the cow and the bear shall feed; their young ones shall lie down together." For him the loving care of the bear mother becomes the symbol of the Christian teacher.[1]

The bear mother's method of weaning her cub and setting him free to fend for himself is remarkable. She trees him while she searches for food, and he learns to remain obediently in the tree until she returns. When, however, she deems it time for him to be on his own, she leaves him in the tree never to return. As the hours pass and still she does not come, the cub must eventually find his own courage to come down. By his own volition he must commit an initial act of disobedience, at the same time facing the dangers of the world, especially older male bears, who have been a threat to his life so far. How much of this knowledge of the bear's behavior was observed by prehistoric man and used to allegorize their own need for mother love and its corollary, separation from the mother, is impossible to say; but there are primitive ceremonies which suggest very strongly that the bear was an important symbol associated with the initiation archetype, with its central meaning as a special form of rebirth.

The Grizzly Bear Dance of the North American Indians begins as a mimetic rite of the bear's awakening from his winter's sleep. "The drummers assemble and chant 'I begin to grow restless in the Spring,' and they represent the bear making ready to come from his winter den. Then 'Lone Chief' drew his robe about him and arose to dance imitating the bear going from his den and chanting:

> I take my robe,
> My robe is sacred,
> I wander in the summer . . .[2]

This is clearly a rebirth symbolism such as we find in relation to many other creatures, notably the snake, whose yearly shedding of its skin symbolizes an initiatory process of death and rebirth.[3] More striking even than this is the recent discovery of evidence that our Neanderthal and Cro-Magnon ancestors chose the bear as a special, and perhaps the earliest, form of the master of initiation.[4]

Prehistoric rituals associated with the bear as a central, numinous figure to be placated, appeased and sacrificed are found in places associated with the earliest hunting cultures. Herbert Kühn reports that the same type of offering is still being made today among the hunting tribes of East Asia.*

> The bear skulls still are flayed and preserved in sacred places. . . . Such details . . . as the grinding down of the teeth of the bear and leaving of two vertebrae attached to the skull, just as in the European Interglacial period, proves that the continuity has actually remained unbroken for tens of thousands of years.[5]

A more detailed picture of this ancient bear sacrifice was found by Frobenius and his collaborators among modern African tribes. This modern sacrifice duplicates a paleolithic bear ritual, though it uses a panther or leopard instead of a bear. There is

> a circular enclosure of thorns, in the center of which the clay form of a beast of prey is set up, *without a head*. The pelt is then removed . . . together with the head, still containing its skull; the skin is arranged on the clay form; and then all the warriors surround the enclosure of thorns and the one who killed the beast goes dancing about the figure within, while the remains of the beast are buried.[6]

---

* Kühn is reported in Campbell, p. 345.

There is a magical gesture to avert the evil eye of the beast, suggesting the "long bones pushed through the eye-holes of the [ancient] cave-bear skulls," which probably had a similar meaning in prehistoric times as a magic ritual.[7] Ibid.

The sanctity of the bear in its role as tribal chieftain or animal master is emphasized in many tribal rites. The bear clan of the Ottawas "ascribe their origin to a bear's paw and call themselves Big Feet."[8]

> The well-born, well-bred little Athenian girls . . . danced as Bears to Artemis of Brauronia, the Bear-Goddess. . . . Among the Apaches . . . only ill-bred Americans, or Europeans . . . would think of speaking of the Bear . . . without employing the reverential prefix "Ostin," meaning "old man," and equivalent to the Roman title "Senator."[9]
>
> The strange and throughly mystical attitude towards the sacrificed food-animal comes out very beautifully in the Finnish *Kalevala,* where a whole canto is devoted to recounting the sacrificial feast to and of Otso the mountain bear. They chant the praises of the Holy Bear, they tell of his great strength and majesty, the splendour of his rich fur, the glory and the beauty of his "honey-soft" paws. They lead him in festal procession, slay and cook and eat him and then, as though he were not dead, they dismiss him with valedictions to go back and live forever, the glory of the forest.[10]

The bear's immortality and its identity with man point to a still higher function of the bear as a kind of primitive saviour figure. "In the bear sacrifice of the Ainu, the bear is thus addressed, 'We kill you, O bear! Come back soon into an Ainu.' "[11] Joseph Campbell tells us that this rationale derives from the primitive hunters' psychology, which demands a real facing of the mystery of death by man "both for the beasts killed in the hunt and for man. . . . The answer" from the shaman of the hunting tribes "was one that has been giving comfort to those who wish comfort ever since, namely: 'Nothing dies; death and birth are but a threshold crossing, back and forth, as it were, through a veil.' "[12] The individual hunter and the shaman must each face the great mystery of death alone (or together with the killed animal) and must therefore find an individual answer to allay his fear of being isolated and/or haunted by the ghost of the killed beast. Yet the totemic rites of the tribal group provide a similar picture of the animal's ritual death.

Alfred Howitt tells us of an animal sacrifice among the Kurnai, a tribe of southeast Australia.

> The "native bear" when slain is thus divided. The slayer has the left ribs: the father the right hind leg, the mother the left hind leg, the elder brother the right fore-arm, the younger brother the left forearm, the elder sister the backbone, the younger the liver, the father's brother the right ribs, the mother's brother of the hunter a piece of the flank. Most honorable of all, the head goes to the camp of the young men, the κουροι.[13]

This rite appears to represent a blending of two sorts of rite; the original bear sacrifice as the hunter's ritual placation of the animal ghost, and the ritual of a communal totemic meal. Did one grow out of the other? Which came first? When and how did they blend?

Instead of trying to answer these questions, let us ask another more immediate question: What function did the blending perform? The totemic communal meal is shared among the various members of the family; there is a pattern of group identity which brings all members of the family into an appropriate state of at-oneness, while respecting each one's individual rights to possess his own portion of the cosmic treasure symbolized by the animal's body. But the head goes to the young men's group. This head presumably represents the prestige and ultimate power of the animal master, his crown of consciousness and his burning inner soul made manifest through his eyes. The head, therefore, is emblematic of the Kouros, or leader of the band of initiated young men; it suggests the unique and independent character of the animal master, derived from the ancient rites of the hunting tribes. (The totemic rite probably derives from a later period during which the hunting tribes were influenced by the primitive planting cultures with their more close-knit social organization.)

The bear as animal master is ostensibly male and seems to embody in his presence, whether alive or dead, the image of godhead, which may also have been a sort of deity of head-hunting. We know that the ancestors of those men who were the first to kill bears ceremoniously had the unattractive habit of human head-hunting, perhaps to obtain food, more likely to obtain the prestige stored in the skull.[14] But we find a totally different tradition in those myths referring to the bear as female.

Jung points out that in the Algonquian Indian legends retold (from Henry Rowe Schoolcraft) by Longfellow in his poem *Hiawatha*, the hero's father, "the great warrior Mudjekeewis has overcome by stealth the great bear, 'the terror of the nations,' and stolen from him the magic 'belt of wampum,' a girdle of shells. . . . Mudjekeewis smites the bear on the head after robbing him of the treasure."[15] Again we have the familiar motifs of attacking the head and robbing the beast of its power. But here is no honoring of the beast to follow.

> With the heavy blow bewildered
> Rose the great Bear of the mountains;
> But his knees beneath him trembled,
> And he whimpered like a woman.

For this the hero's father pours scorn upon him.

Here the bear is no longer the animal master. What Mudjekeewis has slain is "his feminine component, whose first carrier is the mother. Like a true hero, he has snatched life from the jaws of death, from the all-devouring Terrible Mother." "Hiawatha's father first conquers the mother under the terrifying symbol of the bear; then, having become a god himself, he begets the hero."[16] Here we see an enormous change in man's relation to the animal — a transition from a primordial archetypal animal image to an image of culture-conscious, culture-ambitious man. From the earliest cultural level there is spread out before us a sequence of events which lead from the early experience of man as hunter to the comparatively recent grain-producing cultures. Hiawatha, as culture hero, encounters in his lonely journey not an animal but a human figure representing the spirit of the corn:

> From the Master of Life descending,
> I, the friend of man Mondamin,

Come to warn you and instruct you,
How by struggle and by labour
You shall gain what you have prayed for . . .

The hero wrestles with this corn god, overcomes him, and finds that he is really the "mother" as "divine creative power." He "buries him in the earth his mother, and soon afterwards, young and fresh, the corn sprouts from his grave for the nourishment of mankind."[17]

In *The Masks of God,* Joseph Campbell presents a graphic picture of some of the cultural differences between people of a hunting culture and those of a planting culture, and a difference between each of these and the cultures of the hieratic city-states.[18] It is quite possible that the Bear Goddess associated with so many ancient rites, especially those of Artemis, is transitional between the hunting peoples and the agricultural communities.

In discussing the many animals that can represent the Kouros in the settled communities of ancient Greece, Harrison states:

> Any young full-grown creature . . . can be sacrificed, sanctified, divinized, and become the *Agathos Daimon,* the "vegetation spirit," the luck of the year. . . . Best of all perhaps is a bear, because he is strongest; this the Athenian maidens remembered in their Bear-Service.

And she adds an unnecessary, but it seems to me very significant, comment:

> But bears, alas! retreat before advancing civilization.[19]

Just as we were about to make an easy transition from primitive head-hunting to the communal meal of the agricultural peoples, we are pushed back into the primeval forest world whence the bears have withdrawn, seeming to carry with them the timeless secret of this form of initiation. Jung traces them as beasts of Artemis, "the active one," in contrast to Persephone, who was "completely passive, . . . destined to a flower-like existence."[20]

Artemis is a sky goddess, in contrast to Persephone, who is

clearly an earth goddess. Jung cites two dreams of a modern person in illustration of this image of the great goddess.[21] In one of these, Artemis is the maternally protective form of the goddess, protective against fear of the bear's wildness. She is represented as goddess of wild life; as the Gallo-Roman Dea Artio she is protectress of the wild things and lives in a wild place herself, frequently a mountain. We can recognize her kinship with the Mountain Mother of Crete in whose service the Kouretes performed their function as guardians of the holy child, who would presumably grow up to become the beneficent father figure, or Kouros, whose primordial image is represented by the animal master of initiation of the hunting cultures.

But the goddess is not only a protectress; she is also a threatening mother who, in her temples, exacts the great animal sacrifices which still existed in Greece of Pausanias' time, Harrison tells us:

> Artemis was . . . Orthia . . . she is Kourotrophos, the Rearing Mother, nurse of the Kouroi to be. [But these were] the ministrants, the correlatives of the Great Mother, the "Lady of the Wild Things." To her the sacrifice of all living things is manifestly, if hideously, appropriate.[22]

Pausanias describes a typical ceremonial:

> They bring and cast upon the altar living things of all sorts, both edible birds and all manner of victims. . . . And they lay on the altar also the fruits of cultivated trees. Then they set fire to the wood. I saw indeed a bear and other beasts struggling to get out of the first force of the flames and escaping by sheer strength. But those who threw them in drag them up again on to the fire. I never heard of anyone being wounded by the wild beasts.[23]

"Such was the savage service of the Kouretes and of the Mother, and of that last survival of the Mother, the maiden 'sister' of Apollo, the Kouros."[24]

A second modern dream cited by Jung brings out this aspect of the goddess. This dream carries us further into the probable meaning of the rite by suggesting that the initiant felt himself transformed into an animal and so underwent a sacrifice, but also a process of regeneration. By submitting to the death-dealing power of the goddess, he experienced rebirth *as an animal*. For what a man can never experience fully on a purely human level, he can experience upon an animal level, and the quality which is thus acquired is expressed archetypally as *vis ut sis,* which may be roughly translated as *the power to be.*

Psychologically, this term designates the initiate's ability to achieve the ego-strength necessary to withstand the destructive onslaught of the collective unconscious on an infantile level. Separating himself from the wildness of the primitive mother by submitting to her rule, he nevertheless preserves some quality of his own wild nature, an autonomy which is inherent in man as a human animal man and which is always being eroded by the civilizing influence of the cultural mother. Unwittingly she therefore presents him with the fear of dismemberment via the unconscious. One may appropriately think of the use of a modern child makes of his teddy bear, through whose mediation he preserves contact with the mothering instinct, while separating himself from the real mother in a growing awareness of his instinctual, rather than his obedient, self.

Jung sees another symbolism in this dream which is of importance in amplifying the conception of the bear initiation. Several of the dream images suggest not merely ego-strength, but the delicate symbolism of the Self, as embodying a psychological non-ego. The sense of this is as follows: The initiate, who must of necessity "descend" to the level of his deepest animal nature, acquires an ego-strength which enables him to transcend the animal level and experience a form of transpersonal awareness, which effects a cure of the wounds he has suffered in the dismembered state of deep, matriarchal, preconscious life.

Practically speaking, the bear ritual points to integration of the new personality following such a period of dissociation.[25] On the level of the mother-son religions, of which Artemis and her half-animal Kouretes are an example, this reintegration is partially brought about by the Mother herself, who seems to have caused his death and dismemberment. But this mythologem is true only of masculine psychology, and the dual role of the Mother reflects man's ambivalence toward his own feminine nature projected onto the Mother. For women, the Great Goddess is Mother and

Maiden in one, and as such she is more adequately represented by the following schematic relationship:

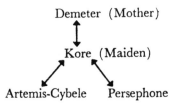

This points to an identity of girl and woman which speaks to woman's psychology in a special way — an awareness of female identity which it is the unconscious (if not conscious) desire of men to possess. Kerenyi stresses "the difference between 'knowing of' something and *knowing it and being it*. It is one thing to know about the 'seed and the sprout,' and quite another to have *recognized* in them the past and future of one's own being and continuation."[26] Jung emphasizes a sense of continuity with the ancestors "in such a way that these can prolong themselves via the bridge of the momentary individual into the generations of the future. A knowledge with this content, with the experience of *being in death,* is not to be despised."[27]

A capacity for *"knowing it and being it,"* transcends the natural animal state and is the central meaning of initiation to the Great Mother. But why need there be an initiation at all? Perhaps it is because men know it but can't experience it, whereas women experience it but do not know it. Each must learn to acquire the capacity for experience and for being conscious of that experience simultaneously. Only initiation as a rite of passage in some form can accomplish this. Besides unification, in which male and female versions of the Great Mother are joined, we find in the forms of initiation associated with an animal master a blend of weakness and strength — or submission combined with a spirit of independence — which represents the right kind of awareness of mankind's paradoxical identity with and separation from the animal world.

Bibliography of Major Sources

Adler, Gerhard. *The Living Symbol.* (Bollingen Ser. LXIII) New York: Pantheon Books, 1961
——— "The Logos of the Unconscious." In: *Studien zur Analytischen Psychologie; C. G. Jung's II Beiträge zur Kulturgeschichte; festschrift zum 80. geburtstag von C. G. Jung.* Zurich: Rascher, 1955
——— *Studies in Analytical Psychology.* New York: W. W. Norton, 1948

Aichhorn, August. *Wayward Youth.* New York: Viking Press, 1935

Angulo, Jaime de. "La Psychologie Religieuse des Achumawi," *Anthropos:* 23:141-66, 1928.

Angus, Samuel. *The Mystery-Religious and Christianity: a Study in the Religious Background of Early Christianity.* London: John Murray, 1925

Baynes, Helton Godwin. *Mythology of the Soul: a Research into the Unconscious from Schizophrenic Dreams and Drawings.* London: Kegan Paul, 1940

Bettelheim, Bruno. *Symbolic Wounds: Puberty Rites and the Envious Male.* Glencoe, Illinois: Free Press, 1954

Campbell, Joseph. *The Hero with a Thousand Faces.* (Bollingen Ser. XVII) New York: Pantheon Books, 1949
——— *The Masks of God: Occidental Mythology.* New York: Viking Press, 1964
——— *The Masks of God: Oriental Mythology.* New York: Viking Press, 1962
——— *The Masks of God: Primitive Mythology.* New York: Viking Press, 1959
——— *The Symbol Without Meaning.* Zurich: Rascher, 1958

Cornford, Francis Macdonald. *From Religion to Philosophy.* London: Edward Arnold, 1912

———— *The Origin of Attic Comedy*. Cambridge: University Press, 1934

———— "The Origin of the Olympic Games." In: Jane Ellen Harrison, *Themis*. Cambridge: University Press, 1912, pp. 212–59

Edinger, Edward F. "The Ego-Self Paradox." *J. Analyt. Psychol.* 5:3-18, January, 1960

Eliade, Mircea. *Birth and Rebirth: The Religious Meanings of Initiation in Human Culture*. Translated by Willard R. Trask. New York: Harper, 1958

———— *Mephistopheles and the Androgyne*. New York: Sheed and Ward, 1965

———— *The Myth of the Eternal Return*. Translated by Willard R. Trask. (Bollingen Ser. XLVI) New York: Pantheon Books, 1954

———— *Patterns in Comparative Religion*. Translated by Rosemary Sheed. New York: Sheed and Ward, 1958

———— *Shamanism: Archaic Techniques of Ecstasy*. Translated by Willard R. Trask. (Bollingen Ser. LXXVI) New York: Pantheon Books, 1964

———— *Yoga: Immortality and Freedom*. Translated by Willard R. Trask. (Bollingen Ser. LVI) New York: Pantheon Books, 1958

Erikson, Erik Homburger. *Childhood and Society*. New York: W. W. Norton, 1950

———— *Identity and the Life Cycle* ("Psychological Issues," Vol. 1, No. 1, Monograph 1) New York: International Universities Press, 1959

———— *Young Man Luther: A Study in Psychoanalysis and History*. New York: W. W. Norton, 1962

Euripides. "Bacchae." Translated by Gilbert Murray. In: Whitney Jennings Oakes and Eugene O'Neill, *Complete Greek Drama*. New York: Random House, 1938, Vol. 2, pp. 227–83

Evdokimov, Paul. *La Femme et le Salut du Monde: Étude d'Anthropologie Chrétienne sur les Charismes de la Femme*. Paris: Casterman, 1958

Fewkes, Jesse Walter. "The Snake Ceremonials at Walpi." *J. Am. Ethnol. and Archaeol.* 4:1-126, 1894.

Fordham, Michael. *Individuation in Childhood*. Paper delivered at Third International Congress for Analytical Psychology, Montreux, Switzerland, 1965. *Proceedings*. To be published

———— *New Developments in Analytical Psychology*. London: Routledge and Kegan Paul, 1957

———— *The Objective Psyche.* London: Routledge and Kegan Paul, 1958

———— *The Theory of Archetypes as Applied to Child Development with Particular Reference to the Self.* In: Second International Congress for Analytical Psychology, Zurich, Switzerland, 1962. *Proceedings.* Basle: S. Karger, 1964, pp. 48–60.

Franz, Marie-Louise von. "The Process of Individuation." In: Carl Gustav Jung, *Man and His Symbols.* New York: Doubleday, 1964, pp. 158–229

———— "Puer Aeternus." Unpublished lectures delivered in San Francisco, California, November, 1959–February, 1960

———— "Symbolism of Creation Myths." Unpublished seminar delivered at Jung Institute, Zurich, Switzerland, December 7, 1961

———— *Über Religiöse Hintergründe des Puer-Aeternus-Problems.* In: Second International Congress for Analytical Psychology, Zurich, Switzerland, 1962, *Proceedings.* Basle: S. Karger, 1964, pp. 141–154

Freud, Sigmund. *A General Introduction to Psychoanalysis.* Translated by Joan Riviere. New York: Liveright, 1935

———— "Leonardo da Vinci and a Memory of His Childhood." In: *The Standard Edition of the Complete Psychological Works of Sigmund Freud.* Translated under the general editorship of James Strachey, in collaboration with Anna Freud, assisted by Alix Strachey and Alan Tyson. London: Hogarth Press, 1957, Vol. 11

———— *Totem and Taboo: Some Points of Agreement Between the Mental Lives of Savages and Neurotics.* Translated by James Strachey. New York: W. W. Norton, 1950

Gaster, Theodor Herzel. *The Holy and the Profane.* New York: William Sloane, 1955

Gennep, Arnold van. *The Rites of Passage.* Translated by Monika B. Vizedom and Gabrielle L. Caffee. Chicago: University of Chicago Press, 1960

Gibb, Andrew Shirra. *In Search of Sanity.* New York: Farrar and Rhinehart, 1942

Guthrie, William Keith Chambers. *In the Beginning: Some Greek Views on the Origins of Life and the Early State of Man.* London: Methuen, 1957

Harding, M. Esther. *Psychic Energy: Its Source and Goal.* (Bollingen Ser. X) New York: Pantheon Books, 1947

———— *The Way of All Women: A Psychological Interpretation.* New York: Longmans, Green, 1933

———— *Women's Mysteries: Ancient and Modern.* Rev. ed. New York: Pantheon Books, 1955

Harrison, Jane Ellen. *Epilegomena to the Study of Greek Religion.* Cambridge: University Press, 1921

———— *Prolegomena to the Study of Greek Religion.* 2d ed. Cambridge: University Press, 1908

———— *Themis: A Study of the Social Origins of Greek Religion.* Cambridge: University Press, 1912

Head, Joseph and S. L. Cranston, comps. *Reincarnation: An East-West Anthology.* New York: Julian Press, 1961

Henderson, Joseph L. "Ancient Myths and Modern Man." In: Carl Gustav Jung, *Man and His Symbols.* New York: Doubleday, 1964, pp. 104–57

———— "Psychological Commentary." In: Margaret Schevill Link, *The Pollen Path.* Stanford University Press, 1956, pp. 125–40

———— "Resolution of the Transference in the Light of Jung's Psychology." *Acta Psychotherapeutica,* 2:267-83, 1954

———— and Maud Oakes. *The Wisdom of the Serpent: The Myths of Death, Rebirth and Resurrection.* New York: Braziller, 1963

Hobson, Robert F. "Psychological Aspects of Circumcision." *J. Analyt. Psychol.* 6:5-33, January, 1961

Hocart, Arthur Maurice. *Kingship.* London: Oxford University Press, 1927

Homerus. *The Odyssey of Homer.* Translated by T. E. Shaw. New York: Oxford University Press, 1922

The I Ching: or, Book of Changes. The Richard Wilhelm translation rendered into English by Cary F. Baynes. Foreword by Carl Gustav Jung (Bollingen Ser. XIX) New York: Pantheon Books, 1950

Jacobi, Jolande. *Complex/Archetype/Symbol in the Psychology of C. G. Jung.* Translated by Ralph Manheim. (Bollingen Ser. LVII) New York: Pantheon Books, 1959

———— *The Psychology of C. G. Jung.* 6th ed. rev. Translated by Ralph Manheim. New Haven: Yale University Press, 1962

Jung, Carl Gustav. *Aion: Researches into the Phenomenology of the Self.* Translated by R. F. C. Hull. (Collected Works, Vol. 9, Part II) (Bollingen Ser. XX) New York: Pantheon Books, 1959

———— *The Archetypes and the Collective Unconscious: A Study in the Process of Individuation.* Translated by R. F. C. Hull. (Collected Works, Vol. 9, Part I) (Bollingen Ser. XX) New York: Pantheon Books, 1959

———— *Basic Writings;* ed. with an introduction by Violet Staub de Laszlo. New York: Modern Library, 1959

———— *Civilization in Transition.* Translated by R. F. C. Hull. (Collected Works, Vol. 10) (Bollingen Ser. XX) New York: Pantheon Books, 1964

———— *Memories, Dreams, Reflections;* recorded and ed. by Aniela Jaffé. Translated by Richard and Clara Winston. New York: Pantheon Books, 1961

———— "On the Psychology of the Trickster," *Spring,* 1955, pp. 1–14

———— *Psyche and Symbol;* ed. by Violet Staub de Laszlo. Garden City, New York: Doubleday Anchor Books, 1958

———— *The Psychogenesis of Mental Disease.* Translated by R. F. C. Hull. (Collected Works, Vol. 3) (Bollingen Ser. XX) New York: Pantheon Books, 1960

———— *Psychological Types: Or the Psychology of Individuation.* Translated by H. Godwin Baynes. New York: Harcourt Brace, 1924

———— *Psychology and Alchemy.* Translated by R. F. C. Hull. (Collected Works, Vol. 12) (Bollingen Ser. XX) New York: Pantheon Books, 1953

———— *Psychology and Religion: West and East.* Translated by R. F. C. Hull. (Collected Works, Vol. 11) (Bollingen Ser. XX) New York: Pantheon Books, 1958

———— *The Structure and Dynamics of the Psyche.* Translated by R. F. C. Hull. (Collected Works, Vol. 8) (Bollingen Ser. XX) (New York: Pantheon Books, 1960

———— *Symbols of Transformation: An Analysis of the Prelude to a Case of Schizophrenia.* Translated by R. F. C. Hull. (Collected Works, Vol. 5) (Bollingen Ser. XX) New York: Pantheon Books, 1956

———— *Two Essays on Analytical Psychology.* Translated by R. F. C. Hull. (Collected Works, Vol. 7) (Bollingen Ser. XX) New York: Pantheon Books, 1953

———— and Karl Kerényi. *Essays on a Science of Mythology.* Translated by R. F. C. Hull. (Bollingen Ser. XXII) New York: Pantheon Books, 1949

Kerényi, Karl. "The Mysteries of the Kaberoi." Translated by Ralph Manheim. In: *The Mysteries.* Papers from the Eranos Yearbooks, Vol. 2 (Bollingen Ser. XXX) New York: Pantheon Books, 1955, pp. 32–63

Knight, W. F. Jackson. *Cumaean Gates: A Reference of the Sixth Aeneid to the Initiation Pattern*. Oxford: Basil Blackwell, 1936

Layard, John. "Homo-eroticism in Primitive Society as a Function of the Self." In: *Current Trends in Analytical Psychology*, ed. by Gerhard Adler. London: Tavistock Publications, 1961, pp. 241–60

———— "Note on the Autonomous Psyche and the Ambivalence of the Trickster Concept." *J. Analyt. Psychol.* 3:21-28, January, 1958

———— *Stone Men of Malekula*. London: Chatto and Windus, 1942

Leeuw, Gerardus van der. "Immortality." In: *Man and Transformation*. Papers from the Eranos Yearbooks, Vol. 5. (Bollingen Ser. XXX) New York: Pantheon Books, 1964, pp. 353–68

Levy, Gertrude Rachel. *The Gate of Horn: A Study of the Religious Conceptions of the Stone Age and Their Influence upon European Thought*. London: Faber and Faber, 1948

MacCulloch, J. A. "Baptism." In: *A Dictionary of Religion and Ethics*, ed. by Shailer Mathews and Gerald Birney Smith. New York: Macmillan, 1921, p. 374

Mead, George Robert Snow. *The Mysteries of Mithra* (Echoes from the Gnosis, Vol. 5) London: Theosophical Publishing Society, 1907

Metman, Philip. "The Trickster Figure in Schizophrenia." *J. Analyt. Psychol.* 3:5-20, January, 1958

Murray, Gilbert. "Excursus on the Ritual Forms Preserved in Greek Tragedy." In: Jane Ellen Harrison, *Themis*. Cambridge: University Press, 1912, pp. 341–63

Mylonas, George Emmanuel. *Eleusis and the Eleusinian Mysteries*. Princeton, New Jersey: Princeton University Press, 1961

Neumann, Erich. *Amor and Psyche: The Psychic Development of the Feminine*. (Bollingen Ser. LIV) New York: Pantheon Books, 1956

———— *The Great Mother: An Analysis of the Archetype*. Translated by Ralph Manheim (Bollingen Ser. XLVII) New York: Pantheon Books, 1955

———— "Leonardo da Vinci and the Mother Archetype." In: his *Art and the Creative Unconscious*. (Bollingen Ser. LXI) New York: Pantheon Books, 1959, pp. 3–80

———— *The Origins and History of Consciousness*. Translated by R. F. C. Hull. (Bollingen Ser. XLII) New York: Pantheon Books, 1954

———— "The Psyche and the Transformation of the Reality Planes." *Spring*, 1956, pp. 81–111

Northrop, Filmer Stuart Cockow. *The Meeting of East and West: an Inquiry Concerning World Understanding.* New York: Macmillan, 1947

Nourry, Émile Dominique. *Les Mystères Paiens et le Mystère Chrétien.* Paris: É. Nourry, 1919

Oakes, Maud. *Where the Two Came to Their Father;* a Navaho war ceremonial given by Jeff King. Commentary by Joseph Campbell. (Bollingen Ser. I) New York: Pantheon Books, 1943

Otto, Walter F. "The Meaning of the Eleusinian Mysteries." Translated by Ralph Manheim. In: *The Mysteries.* Papers from the Eranos Yearbooks, Vol. 2 (Bollingen Ser. XXX) New York: Pantheon Books, 1955, pp. 14–31

Perry, John Weir. *The Self in Psychotic Process: Its Symbolization in Schizophrenia.* Berkeley: University of California Press, 1953

Perry, William James. *Children of the Sun: A Study in the Early History of Civilization.* New York: E. P. Dutton, 1923

Plaut, A. "A Case of Tricksterism Illustrating Ego Defenses." *J. Analyt. Psychol.* 4:35–54, January, 1959

Portmann, Adolph, "Metamorphosis in Animals: The Transformations of the Individual and the Type." In: *Man and Transformation.* Papers from the Eranos Yearbooks, Vol. 5. (Bollingen Ser. XXX) New York: Pantheon Books, 1964, pp. 297–325

Progoff, Ira. *Jung's Psychology and Its Social Meaning.* New York: Julian Press, 1953

Radin, Paul. *Winnebago Hero Cycles: A Study in Aboriginal Literature.* (Indiana University Publications in Anthropology and Linguistics, Memo 1) (Supplement to *Internat. J. Am. Linguistics,* Vol. 14, No. 3, Jul, 1948) Baltimore: Waverly Press, 1948

Róheim, Géza. *Australian Totemism: A Psychoanalytic Study in Anthropology.* London: G. Allen and Unwin, Ltd., 1925

Rykwert, Joseph. *The Idea of a Town;* an extract from Forum. Hilversum, Netherlands: G. van Saane, n.d.

The Secret of the Golden Flower: A Chinese Book of Life. Translated and explained by Richard Wilhelm, with a European Commentary by Carl Gustav Jung. Translanted into English by Cary F. Baynes. New York: Wehman Brothers, 1955

Seligman, Paul. "Some Notes on the Collective Significance of Circumcision and Allied Practices." *J. Analyt. Psychol.* 10:5-21, January, 1965

Silberer, Herbert. *Problems of Mysticism and Its Symbolism.* Translated by Smith Ely Jelliffe. New York: Moffat, Yard, 1917

Smith, Grafton Eliot. *Human History*. Rev. ed. London: Jonathan Cape, 1934

Snow, Charles Percy. *The Two Cultures: and a Second Look*. 2d ed. Cambridge: University Press, 1964

Stekel, Wilhelm. *The Interpretation of Dreams: New Developments and Technique*. Translated by Cedar Paul. Arranged for American publication by Emil A. Gutheil. New York: Liveright, 1943

Stewart, Jessie G. *Jane Ellen Harrison: A Portrait from Letters*. London: Merlin Press, 1959

Suzuki, Daisetz Teitaro. "Awakening of a New Consciousness in Zen." In: *Man and Transformation*. Papers from the Eranos Yearbooks, Vol. 5. (Bollingen Ser. XXX) New York: Pantheon Books, 1964, pp. 179–202

Toynbee, Arnold. *A Study of History*. London: Oxford University Press, 1945. Vol. 3

Watts, Alan Wilson. *Myth and Ritual in Christianity*. (Myth and Man) New York: Vanguard Press, 1953

Webster, Hutton. *Primitive Secret Societies: A Study in Early Politics and Religion*. 2d ed. rev. New York: Macmillan, 1932

Weston, Jessie Laidlay. *From Ritual to Romance*. Garden City, New York: Doubleday, 1957

Wheelwright, Mary C. *Navajo Creation Myth: The Story of the Emergence*. (Navajo Religion Ser., Vol. 1) Santa Fe, New Mexico: Museum of Navajo Ceremonial Art, 1942

Whitehead, Alfred North. *Adventures of Ideas*. New York: Macmillan, 1933

Wickes, Frances. *The Inner World of Man*. New York: Farrar and Rhinehart, 1938

Wright, Dudley. *The Eleusinian Mysteries and Rites*. London: Theosophical Publishing House, 1919

References

Foreword

1. C. G. Jung, *The Psychogenesis of Mental Disease*, pp. 187–88.
2. Jung, *The Structure and Dynamics of the Psyche*, pp. 159–234.

CHAPTER I: The Rediscovery of Initiation

1. A. van Gennep, *The Rites of Passage*.
2. H. Webster, *Primitive Secret Societies*.
3. J. Stewart, *Jane Ellen Harrison*, p. 85.
4. *Ibid.*, p. 86.
5. J. E. Harrison, *Themis*, pp. 1–29.
6. *Ibid.*, p. 36.
7. Stewart, *op. cit.*, p. 97.
8. Jung, *Two Essays in Analytical Psychology*, p. 229.
9. J. L. Henderson, "The Archetype of Culture," in *The Archetype*. Proc. 2nd Internat. Cong. Analyt. Psychol., Zurich, 1962 (New York: S. Karger, 1964), pp. 3–15.
10. J. Campbell, *The Masks of God: Primitive Mythology*.
11. This transformation has been announced in different ways by A. N. Whitehead, *Adventures of Ideas;* C. P. Snow, *The Two Cultures;* and F. S. C. Northrup, *Meeting of East and West*.

CHAPTER II: The Uninitiated

1. See especially Karl Abraham, "Notes on the Psycho-Analytical Investigation and Treatment of Manic-Depressive Insanity and Allied Conditions," in *Selected Papers of Karl Abraham* (London: Hogarth Press, 1949), pp. 137–56.
2. H. G. Baynes, *Mythology of the Soul*, p. 99.
3. M. von Franz, *Puer Aeternus*. See also her *Über Religiöse Hintergründe des Puer-Aeternus-Problems*.
4. Jung, *Symbols of Transformation*, p. 340.

5. *Ibid.*

6. Harrison, *Prolegomena to the Study of Greek Religion*, p. 273.

7. Jung, *Two Essays in Analytical Psychology*, pp. 186–209 (the anima function described).

8. A. Aichhorn, *Wayward Youth*, p. 49–53.

9. Baynes, "The Provisional Life," *Zentrl. Psychother.* 8:83-85, 1936.

10. M. E. Harding, *The Way of All Women*, pp. 1–40.

11. Henderson, "Psychological Commentary," in Margaret S. Link, *The Pollen Path* (Stanford: Stanford University Press, 1956), pp. 125–40; Jung, "On the Psychology of the Trickster," *Spring*, pp. 1–14, 1955; J. Layard, "Note on the Autonomous Psyche and the Ambivalence of the Trickster Concept," *J. Analyt. Psychol.* 3:21-28, January, 1958; P. Metman, "The Trickster Figure in Schizophrenia," *J. Analyt. Psychol.* 3:5-20, January, 1958.

12. Johann W. von Goethe, *Faust*, translated by Bayard Taylor (London: John Slark, 1884), p. 54; Layard, *op. cit.*, p. 28. See Layard's discussion of the positive trickster, who "accepts every reverse and learns from it. He tricks the Trickster in himself by depriving it of its one-sidedness." For an illuminating discussion of the trickster archetype as Mephistopheles, see Eliade, *Mephistopheles and the Androgyne*, pp. 78–124.

13. Henderson, "Ancient Myths and Modern Man," in Jung, *Man and His Symbols*, p. 149.

14. P. Radin, *Winnebago Hero Cycles*, pp. 9, 25, 35–36.

15. In contrast to Jung's definition of the trickster as a shadow-figure, Metman rightly sees him also as an incipient ego (*op. cit.*, p. 5). A. Plaut even suggests that tricksterism may be preferred as a diagnosis for certain borderline conditions over the diagnosis of an irreducible pathology, i.e., psychosis. See Plaut, "A Case of Tricksterism Illustrating Ego Defenses," *J. Analyt. Psychol.* 4:35-54, January, 1959.

16. Radin, *op. cit.*, pp. 119–120. Cf. *The Book of Tobias. The Apocrypha.* We might, in this connection, recall how Tobias was accompanied by the Archangel Michael on his journey, which led to a successful quest.

17. *Ibid.*, p. 55.

CHAPTER III: Return to the Mother

1. Baynes, *Mythology of the Soul*, p. 186.

2. E. Neumann, *The Origins and History of Consciousness*, pp. 5–37.

3. W. Stekel, *The Interpretation of Dreams*, pp. 109–10.

4. Jung, *Two Essays in Analytical Psychology*, pp. 105–07.

5. Harrison, *Epilegomena to the Study of Greek Religion*, p. 17.

6. *Ibid.*, pp. 17–18.

7. M. Eliade, *Birth and Rebirth*, p. 30.

8. Harrison, *Prolegomena to the Study of Greek Religion*, pp. 442–43.

9. K. Kerényi, "The Mysteries of the Kaberoi," in *The Mysteries*, p. 39.

10. J. Campbell, *The Masks of God: Primitive Mythology*, p. 339.

11. Eliade, *op. cit.*, pp. 30–35.

12. M. S. Link, Personal communication.

13. M. Oakes, *Where the Two Came to Their Father.*

14. *Ibid.*, pp. 22–24.

15. *Ibid.*, pp. 28–33.

CHAPTER IV: Remaking a Man

1. Neumann, *The Great Mother*, p. 67.

2. F. M. Cornford, "The Origin of the Olympic Games," in Harrison, *Themis*, p. 247.

3. *Ibid.*, pp. 235–36.

4. Harrison, *Themis*, p. 190.

5. Cornford, *op. cit.*, pp. 236–37.

6. *Ibid.*, pp. 238, 240–42.

7. *Ibid.*, pp. 243, 248, 254.

8. Harrison, *op. cit.*, pp. 205–06.

9. Cornford, *op. cit.*, p. 255.

10. Cornford, *The Origin of Attic Comedy;* G. Murray, "Excursus on the Ritual Forms Preserved in Greek Tragedy," in Harrison, *Themis*, pp. 341–63.

11. For a critique of this tendency, see M. Fordham, *The Objective Psyche.*

12. Neuman, *op. cit.* pp. 82–83.

13. Quoted in D. Wright, *The Eleusinian Mysteries and Rites*, pp. 25–26.

14. G. R. S. Mead, *The Mysteries of Mithra*, p. 13.

15. É. D. Nourry, *Les Mystères Paiens et le Mystère Chrétien.*

16. Neumann, *The Origins and History of Consciousness*, pp. 364–65.

17. Cf. Neumann, "Leonardo da Vinci and the Mother Archetype," in his *Art and the Creative Unconscious*, pp. 3–80.

18. A. Watts, *Myth and Ritual in Christianity*, p. 181.

19. Jung, *Aion*, p. 89.

20. Jung, *Psychology and Alchemy*, p. 71.

21. von Franz, *Symbolism of Creation Myths*, Lecture 7, p. 7.

22. *Ibid.*

23. P. Evdokimov, *La Femme et le Salut du Monde*, Plate, p. 224 (L'Icone de la Deisis: Le Christ entre la Vierge et Saint Jean Baptiste, École de Moscou, XVᵉ siècle).

24. *Ibid.*, p. 239.

25. *Ibid.*

26. *Ibid.*

27. *Ibid.*, p. 240.

28. *Ibid.*, pp. 219–20.

29. *Ibid.*, p. 228.

30. Jung, *Two Essays in Analytical Psychology*, pp. 80–100. (In a brilliant analysis of this problem affecting a modern woman, Jung demonstrates the symbolism of the regressive pull of the Mother archetype, represented in a dream by a crab encountered at the crossing of a ford of a river. The parallel with our Case VI is apparent. Equally apparent is the striking difference: The woman is as yet unprepared to meet the danger of the regressive pull, while the man is able to protect himself in the knowledge that a rescuing Father image is making its appearance to counteract the danger. This difference, of course, was provided by the analytical transference to his analyst.)

31. Watts, *Myth and Ritual in Christianity*, pp. 181–82; Jung, *op. cit.*, pp. 100–07. (This case follows immediately the one mentioned above in Note 30. The symbolism of baptism as represented in modern dream sequence is provided in Jung's analysis of a young man's problem of freeing himself from his mother by transference to the Mother Church.)

32. Evdokimov, *op. cit.*, p. 103.

33. Watts, *op. cit.*, p. 201.

34. Baynes, *Mythology of the Soul*, p. 749.

35. For lack of space I cannot go into all the ramifications of this interesting subject and must refer the reader to the excellent articles in *The Encyclopaedia Britannica* and Hasting's *Encyclopedia of Religion and Ethics,* and the whole mythological background of the theology of Christianity in Campbell's *Masks of God: Occidental Mythology,* pp. 334–94.

36. von Franz, *Über Religiöse Hintergründe des Puer-Aeternus-Problems*, p. 142.

37. R. F. Hobson, "Psychological Aspects of Circumcision," *J. Analyt. Psychol.* 6:5-33, January, 1961.

38. P. Seligman, "Some Notes on the Collective Significance of Circumcision and Allied Practices," *J. Analyt. Psychol.* 10:17, January, 1965.

39. Hobson, *op. cit.,* p. 16.

40. Seligman, *op. cit.,* p. 18.

41. *Ibid.*

42. *Ibid.,* p. 19.

43. T. H. Gaster, *The Holy and the Profane,* p. 72–75.

44. *Ibid.,* p. 76.

45. Eliade, *Birth and Rebirth,* p. 15. Cf. Lindbergh's account of his transatlantic flight (Charles A. Lindbergh, *We.* New York: Putnam, 1927).

46. Eliade, *op. cit.,* p. 9.

47. *Ibid.,* pp. 9–10.

48. *Ibid.,* p. 11.

49. See, for example, Harrison, *Themis,* pp. 15–17.

50. Eliade, *op. cit.,* p. 12.

51. *Ibid.,* p. 13.

52. J. Layard, "Homo-Eroticism in Primitive Society as a Function of the Self," in G. Adler, ed., *Current Trends in Analytical Psychology,* pp. 251–54.

53. Eliade, *op. cit.,* p. 10.

54. *Ibid.,* p. 11.

55. *Ibid.,* p. 26.

CHAPTER V: The Trial of Strength

1. H. Webster, *Primitive Secret Societies,* p. 1.

2. J. W. Fewkes, "The Snake Ceremonials at Walpi," *J. Am. Ethnol. and Archaeol.* 4:106-19, 1894.

3. *Ibid.,* p. 63.

4. Jung, *Symbols of Transformation,* pp. 342–43.

5. Eliade, *Birth and Rebirth,* pp. 27–28.

6. Fewkes, *op. cit.,* pp. 67–95.

7. Eliade, *op. cit.,* p. 77.

8. *Ibid.,* pp. 77–78.

9. *Ibid.,* p. 78.

10. Cf. J. W. Perry, *The Self in Psychotic Process.*

11. Neumann, *The Origins and History of Consciousness,* pp. 286–87.

12. Eliade, *op. cit.,* pp. 70–71.

13. *Ibid.,* p. 71.

14. See Campbell, *The Symbol Without Meaning.*

15. Kerényi, "The Mysteries of the Kabeiroi," in *The Mysteries,* p. 45.

16. *Ibid.,* p.49.

17. *Ibid.,* p. 57.

18. *Ibid.*

19. *Ibid.,* p. 56.

20. *Ibid.*

21. Jean Doresse, *Les Livres Secrets des Gnostiques d'Égypte* (Paris: Plon, 1958), Vol. 2, p. 158, quoted in Eliade, *Mephistopheles and the Androgyne,* p. 121.

22. A. M. Hocart, *Kingship.* (Hocart, in fact, originally derived initiation from the coronation ritual of the king and tended to regard all tribal rites as degenerate forms of this ritual. Today we are able to see the reciprocal relationship between these two forms of initiation, a particularly striking example of which is found in the psychological studies of kingship and initiation in relation to the fantasy systems of schizophrenics in John Perry's *The Self in Psychotic Process* and his "Reflections on the Nature of the Kingship Archetype," *J. Analyt. Psychol.* 11:147-161, July, 1966.)

23. Eliade, *op. cit.,* p. 73.

24. *Ibid.,* pp. 79–80.

25. A. S. Gibb, *In Search of Sanity.*

26. Elizabeth Drew, *T. S. Eliot: the Design of His Poetry* (New York: Charles Scribner's Sons, 1949), p. 49.

27. Geoffrey Gorer, *Exploring English Character* (New York: Criterion Books, 1955).

28. Jung, *The Archetypes and the Collective Unconscious.*

CHAPTER VI: The Rite of Vision

1. Goethe, *Italian Journey, 1786–1788,* translated by W. H. Auden (New York: Pantheon, 1962), p. 17 Introduction.

2. Campbell, *The Hero with a Thousand Faces.* (See Diagram, p. 245. See explanation of the typical hero's journey, p. 246.)

3. See, for example, Carlo Levi, *Christ Stopped at Eboli: The Story of a Year,* translated by Frances Frenaye (New York: Strauss, 1963).

4. G. R. Levy, *The Gate of Horn,* p. 127.

5. *Ibid.*, p. 136.

6. E. H. Erikson, *Young Man Luther*, p. 43.

7. *Ibid.*, p. 42.

8. A. Toynbee, *A Study of History*, Vol. 3, pp. 248–377.

9. W. K. C. Guthrie, *In the Beginning*, pp. 26–27.

10. Levy, *op. cit.*, p. 156.

11. J. Layard, *Stone Men of Malekula*.

12. W. J. Perry, *Children of the Sun*, p. 255.

13. Eliade, *Patterns in Comparative Religion*, pp. 243–45.

14. *Ibid.*, p. 253.

15. Levy, *op. cit.*, p. 156.

16. *Ibid.*, p. 155

17. W. F. J. Knight, *Cumaean Gates*, p. 34.

18. *Ibid.*

19. *Ibid.*, pp. 35–36. For the reference to "stone demonology," cf. "the account of the Idaean Sibyl" (Knight's footnote).

20. *Ibid.*, p. 36.

21. See G. Adler, "The Logos of the Unconscious," in *Studien zur Analytischen Psychologie.*

22. Knight, *op. cit.*, pp. 2–3.

23. Levy, *op. cit.*, p. 155.

24. Knight, *op. cit.*, p. 27.

25. Cf. Eliade's discussion of sliding as a symbol of rebirth in *Patterns in Comparative Religion*, p. 222.

26. Harrison, *Themis*, pp. 60–61.

27. Campbell, *The Masks of God: Primitive Mythology*, p. 393.

28. Levy, *op. cit.*, pp. 156–57.

29. Eliade, *Birth and Rebirth*, pp. 67–68.

30. J. de Angulo, "La Psychologie Religieuse des Achumavi," *Anthropos*, 23:154-56, 1928.

31. Harrison, *op. cit.*, p. 138.

32. *Ibid.*

33. This series of events again illustrates van Gennep's schema for a typical rite of passage: a preliminal rite of *separation* or *purification*, followed by a rite of *transition* and then by a post-liminal rite of *incorporation.*

34. Levy, *op. cit.*, p. 221.

35. G. Adler, *Studies in Analytical Psychology*; E. Harding, *Psychic Energy*; F. Wickes, *The Inner World of Man.*

36. Jung, *The Archetypes and the Collective Unconscious*, pp. 292–319. A similar case is described by Adler, with another "vine

mandala" reproduced in the section of illustrations, in color (*The Living Symbol*), p. 27, pp. 242–43.

37. All references in this paragraph are drawn from Harrison's *Prolegomena to the Study of Greek Religion*, pp. 407–410.

38. From Euripides' *Bacchae*, translated by Gilbert Murray. Quoted in *ibid.*, p. 436.

39. Picture 23 in Jung, *op. cit.*, pp. 292–93.

40. Harrison, *op. cit.*, p. 439.

41. [Translation], quoted in *ibid.*, p. 412.

42. W. F. Otto, "The Meaning of the Eleusinian Mysteries," in *The Mysteries*, pp. 14–31.

43. Henderson, "Ancient Myths and Modern Man," in Jung, *Man and His Symbols*, pp. 104–57.

44. Eliade, *Shamanism*, pp. 388–89.

45. *Ibid.*, p. 391.

46. *Ibid.*, pp. 391–92, 488–89.

47. *Ibid.*, p. 504–05.

CHAPTER VII: Thresholds of Initiation

1. Jung, *Memories, Dreams, Reflections*, p. 382.

2. J. Head and S. L. Cranston, comps., *Reincarnation*, p. 187.

3. *Ibid.*, p. 210

4. *Ibid.*, p. 289.

5. Campbell, *The Masks of God: Occidental Mythology*, p. 160.

6. *Ibid.*, p. 164.

7. Homerus, *The Odyssey of Homer*, p. 437.

8. *The I Ching*, Vol. 1, p. 166.

CHAPTER VIII: Initiation and the Psychology of Ego-Development in Adolescence

1. E. H. Erikson, *Identity and the Life Cycle*, p. 123.

2. *Ibid.*, pp. 125–26.

3. *Ibid.*, p. 55–65.

4. *Ibid.*, p. 166.

5. *Ibid.*, pp. 64–65.

6. *Ibid.*, p. 144.

7. *Ibid.*, p. 102. Cf. Case XI (p. 173).

8. M. Fordham, *The Theory of Archetypes as Applied to Child Development with Particular Reference to the Self*, pp. 50, 52.

9. A. Portmann, "Metamorphosis in Animals," in *Man and Transformation*, p. 321.

10. E. F. Edinger, "The Ego-Self Paradox," *J. Analyt. Psychol.* 5:3-18, January, 1960.

11. See pictures in Rhoda Kellogg, *What Children Scribble and Why* (Author's edition, n.d.). (R. Kellogg is at Golden Gate Nursery Schools, 570 Union Street, San Francisco, California.)

12. Eliade, *The Myth of the Eternal Return.*

13. May Sarton, *Mrs. Stevens Hears the Mermaids Singing* (New York: Norton, 1965), p. 31.

14. *Ibid.,* p. 215.

15. *Ibid.,* p. 220.

CHAPTER IX: Initiation in the Process of Individuation

1. See the "Case of Henry" by Jolande Jacobi in Jung's *Man and His Symbols*. (Fordham says the idea that the roots of individuation originate in childhood has been expounded by Baynes, Harding, and Perry. He refers to this as "the extended thesis" begun by Jung, and, as I have indicated, he has extended this thesis back to the origins of childhood itself.)

2. Jung, *Psychological Types,* p. 562.

3. Cf. Jung, *ibid.*: "Under no circumstances can individuation be the unique goal of psychological education."

4. *Ibid.,* pp. 562–63.

5. This whole dream is interpreted in Henderson and Oakes, *The Wisdom of the Serpent,* pp. 69–73.

6. Campbell. *The Masks of God: Occidental Mythology,* p. 113.

7. See photograph in Mary Wheelwright, *Navajo Creation Myth,* Set 1, First Sandpainting.

8. See Frontispiece to Margaret S. Link, *The Pollen Path* (Stanford: Stanford University Press, 1956).

9. Henderson, "Ancient Myths and Modern Man," in Jung, *Man and His Symbols,* p. 157.

10. Henderson and Oakes. *The Wisdom of the Serpent,* p. 59.

11. G. van der Leeuw, "Immortality," in *Man and Transformation,* pp. 353–54.

12. Concerning *mandala* symbolism, see *The Secret of the Golden Flower;* Jung, *The Archetypes and the Collective Unconscious;* von Franz, "The Process of Individuation" in Jung, *Man and His Symbols,* pp. 158–229. Western examples of this type of symbolism have been found chiefly in the tradition of alchemy, but they appear spontane-

ously in some ecclesiastical designs, such as stained glass windows or illuminated manuscripts.

13. W. F. J. Knight, *Cumaean Gates;* J. W. Perry, *The Self in Psychotic Process;* J. Rykwert, *The Idea of a Town.*

14. Aldo van Eyck, "Introduction" to J. Rykwert, *The Idea of a Town,* unpaged.

15. *The Bible,* Hebrews, 10:31.

16. D. T. Suzuki, "Awakening of a New Consciousness in Zen," in *Man and Transformation,* pp. 196–97.

17. *Ibid.,* pp. 182–85.

18. *Ibid.,* p. 185.

19. Beside the works of Sartre and Heidegger and Jaspers, the existentialist tradition goes back to Pascal in whose *Pensées* are clearly stated the existential loneliness and fear of modern man unsupported by religion.

20. Jung, "Foreword" to Suzuki's *Introduction to Zen Buddhism,* in Jung, *Psychology and Religion: West and East,* pp. 549–50.

21. Jung, *Civilization in Transition,* pp. 423–24.

22. Suzuki, "Awakening of a New Consciousness in Zen," Plate X and legend, p. 202.

APPENDIX: The Bear as Archetypal Symbol

1. Johann J. Bachofen, *Der Bär in der Antike* (monograph). Translation made for me by Max Zeller.

2. Harrison, *Themis,* pp. 112–13.

3. See Henderson and Oakes, *The Wisdom of the Serpent,* p. 36.

4. Campbell, *The Masks of God: Primitive Mythology,* pp. 339–47.

5. Herbert Kühn, "Das Problem des Urmonotheismus," pp. 1646–47, quoted in Campbell, *op. cit.,* p. 345.

6. Leo Frobenius, *Kulturgeschichte Afrikas,* p. 81, quoted in Campbell, *op. cit.,* pp. 346–47.

7. Campbell, *op. cit.,* p. 347.

8. Harrison, *op. cit.,* p. 140

9. *Ibid.,* p. 450.

10. *Ibid.,* pp. 140–41.

11. James G. Frazer, *The Golden Bough; a Study in Magic and Realism,* 3d ed. (London: Macmillan, 1912), Vol. 8, p. 189, quoted in Harrison, *Themis,* p. 141.

12. Campbell, *op. cit.,* p. 342.

13. A. W. Howitt, *Native Tribes of South-East Australia* (New York: Macmillan, 1904), p. 759, quoted in Harrison, *Themis*, p. 141.

14. Campbell, *op. cit.*, pp. 321–23.

15. Jung, *Symbols of Transformation*, p. 316.

16. *Ibid.*, p. 322.

17. *Ibid.*, pp. 336–37.

18. Campbell, *op. cit.*, pp. 357–418.

19. Harrison, *op. cit.*, p. 206

20 Jung and Kerényi, *Essays on a Science of Mythology*, pp. 150–51. See p. 239 for an interpretation of the goddess as maid and mother.

21. For the discussion of these two dreams, see *ibid.*, pp. 229–45.

22. Harrison, *op. cit.*, p. 504.

23. *Ibid.*, p. 505.

24. *Ibid.*

25. See Chapter V, Section I, "The Centering Process."

26. Jung and Kerényi, *op. cit.*, 254.

27. *Ibid.*

Index

About the Author

JOSEPH L. HENDERSON is an analytic psychologist. He has contributed chapters and commentaries to books by C. G. Jung and Margaret Schevill Link, and was co-author, with Maud Oakes, of *The Wisdom of the Serpent*. His *Collected Papers* were published in 1988. He is also the author of *Cultural Attitudes in Psychological Perspectives*. A festschrift, *The Shaman from Elko*, was presented to Henderson on his seventy-fifth birthday by the C. G. Jung Institute of San Francisco. He lives in Ross, California.